# JOHN SHEA
## an experience named

Spirit

ThomasMore®
A DIVISION OF TABOR PUBLISHING

Allen, Texas

Grateful acknowledgment is made for permission to reprint the following copyrighted material:

John Hick, from "Mystical Experience as Cognition," in *Mystics and Scholars*, Coward and Penelhum (eds.). Wilfrid Laurier University Press, Waterloon, Ont. Can. Copyright the Canadian Corporation for Studies in Religion.

James P. Mackey, multiple citations from *Jesus: The Man and the Myth* by James P. Mackey. Copyright ©1979 by James P. Mackey. Used by permission of the Paulist Press.

Henri Nouwen, from *Gracias!* by Henri Nouwen. Copyright © Henri Nouwen, 1983. Used by permission of Harper & Row, San Francisco.

Anne Sexton, from *The Awful Rowing Toward God* by Anne Sexton. Copyright © by Anne Sexton, 1975. Used by permission of Houghton-Mifflin Co., Boston.

Edward Robinson, from *The Original Vision,* used by permission of and copyright © by The Religious Experience Research Unit, Manchester College, Oxford, England 1977.

Cover design by Karen Malzeke-McDonald

Send all inquiries to:
Thomas More® Publishing
200 East Bethany Drive
Allen, Texas 75002–3804

Printed in the United States of America

ISBN 0–88347–209–0

8 9 10 11 12     00 99 98 97 96

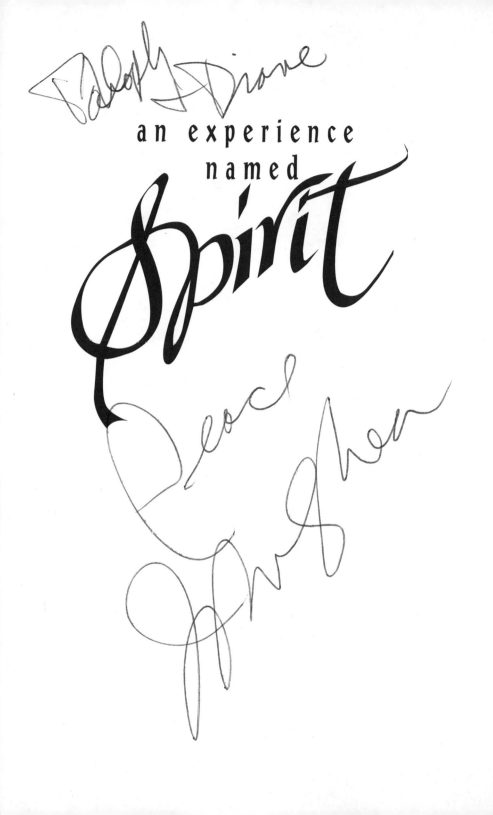

an experience
named

# Spirit

# CONTENTS

# PREFACE

*R*ay Hart has remarked about prefaces: "What-It's-All-About in a few words in advance of the many is out of the question—is, that is, if language is not to be denied its indissoluble link with apprehension."

That is undoubtedly true. But browsing prefaces is more fun than reading books. A preface cannot "give the book away" but it can "let the reader in" on the style and themes of the pages to follow. A story from the Rabbis is always a good place to begin.

Two brothers shared a farm. One brother was married and had seven children. The other brother was single. They worked hard and the land was good. Each year the harvest was abundant, and each year they split the wealth of the land evenly. They gathered the perfectly divided grain into their separate barns and thanked God for his goodness.

One night the single brother thought to himself: "It is not right that we should divide the grain evenly. My brother has many mouths to feed and he needs more. I have only myself to look after. I can certainly get by with less." So each night the single brother would take grain from his barn and secretly transfer it to the barn of his married brother.

That same night the married brother thought to himself: "It is not right that we should divide the grain evenly. I have many children who will look after me in my old age. My brother has only himself. Surely he will need to save more for the future." So each night the married brother would take grain from his barn and secretly transfer it to the barn of his single brother.

Each night the brothers gave away their grain. Yet each morning they found their supply mysteriously replenished. They never told each other about this miracle.

Then one night they met each other half way between the barns. They realized at once what had been happening. They embraced one another with laughter and tears.

On that spot they built the Temple.

This is a book about divine and human love. It explores how the two are interwoven, how the human mediates the divine and how the divine suffuses the human.

The Ganges was calm. Peace was upon the waters as the young girl walked the banks of the river. Her thoughts were the thoughts of youth. Who would she marry? What would she do? How many children would she have? Would she be rich and have servants? Ahead of her she noticed an old woman. She was dressed in a beautiful sari, and her face was radiant. Next to her the Ganges appeared a troubled river.

As the young woman approached her, the old woman suddenly bent over some branches that had washed into shore. Her hand moved among the branches, then she quickly pulled it out. When the young woman was close enough, she saw what was happening. A spider had impaled itself on a thorn, and the woman was trying to free it. But every time she attempted to lift the spider off, he bit her. She would remove her hand, suck the poisonous blood from her finger, and try again.

The young woman watched her for a while and spoke. "Old woman, what foolishness is this? Leave the spider to its fate. Every time you try to help it, it repays you with a bite."

The old woman smiled. "The spider's nature is to bite. Mine is to save. Will I lose myself on the banks of this sacred river?"

The younger woman said nothing, but her face showed that she was puzzled. In her heart the old woman hoped that her smile was not lost on the young one.

This is a book about divine and human love. It explores the resistance of the human and the persistence of the divine. Both are not what they seem. They are more.

The priest was locking up the church at three o'clock on a Sunday afternoon. The baptisms were over, and he was heading for a vodka martini and a roast-beef dinner. When he saw the woman kneeling in front of the Blessed Virgin's altar, he let out an audible sigh, followed by a more audible, "Oh, no!" He couldn't lock her in the church, but liquor and beef called. He walked up behind her and stood there. Finally, an "ahem" got her to turn around.

She was twenty-five, 125 percent Italian, and crying. The priest pronounced the three worst words of ministry, "What's the matter?"

She launched into a terrible tale about the loss of her job and discrimination. When she stopped, the priest reached back into his seminary training, into his pastoral ministry courses, into his clinical pastoral training, into one hundred hours of supervised counseling, into the most sophisticated of his Rogerian techniques and said, "You feel bad, eh?"

She cried more. And somewhere only five blocks away the ice melted in a martini and the roast beef got cold.

Finally the priest said, "What generation are you?"

"My parents came over," she sniffed.

"Look it!" The priest was hitting his self-righteous stride. "If your parents could come over on the boat, learn the language, get jobs, and have you, then you can find another job."

She instantly dried up and looked at the priest with 2,000 years of feminine anger. But, more importantly, as far as the priest was concerned, she left. And step by step the man of God made his way toward the vodka and beef.

A week later she appeared at the door. The priest answered it. "Remember me," she said.

"Remember you?" said the priest, "I'm Irish. You appear in my dreams, but not the way you should. I'm filled with guilt. I threw you out of the Church for vodka and beef."

"Huh?"

"Forget it."

"I found a job. You know, I always heard my parents talk about coming over on the boat and all the troubles, but I never knew that was my story."

This is a book about stories. It explores how contemporary life stories interact with inherited stories, and how the hearing of inherited stories uncovers the depth of present experience and funds the future. Most of all, it is about the story of Jesus and the experience of life that it communicates.

Many years ago, a woman called a priest. Could he meet her and her daughter at the cemetery? Her husband had died a week ago. He was non-Catholic, and he was buried in a non-denominational cemetery. Could Father come and say a few prayers at the graveside? It would make her feel better. The priest said, "Sure."

When the day arrived, it was a freezing December Sunday afternoon with six inches of snow on the ground. The cemetery was a field of monuments. No simple plaques pushed into the ground but angels, small houses, large, imposing slabs—a series of poor man's pyramids. The wife and daughter met the priest at the gate. "He's right over here," said the wife. All three trudged through the snow. It topped their boots and began to freeze their feet.

But he wasn't there.

"Maybe, it's the next row," the wife said.

It wasn't.

"It's this way, Mother," said the daughter. "Father, it's over here," she repeated.

It wasn't. So all three stood silently in the snow. Suddenly, the wife's gloved hands were on her hips. Her face had turned stern. She was mad at him once again.

"George, where the hell are you?" she shouted.

The priest began to laugh. Next the daughter broke up. Finally, the wife laughed. They all laughed. When they stopped, the mother and daughter cried. They put their arms around each other. The priest hid his face in the ritual book.

Then all three of them breathed an icicle prayer into the December air for George—wherever he was.

This is a book about mortal victory. It comes down to a simple, unvarnished truth: love is more than life and death.

These are some of the themes that are played out in story and theology over five chapters. They need to be elaborated more precisely.

Jesus was the catalyst of a salvific experience. This is the experience named Spirit and Jesus eventually became the man named Spirit, the bearer of divine salvation. Jesus now lives in the far reaches of God, but the experience named Spirit which he inaugurated did not "ascend heavenward" with him It continued among his followers who called themselves the Body of Christ, the ongoing possibility of salvation.

The transmission of Christian faith is incurably people-centered, dependent upon the press of flesh from generation to generation. But no matter how many years distance us from Jesus, we will not forget him. His life, death, and resurrection are the authentic revelation of the living relationship to God. The upshot of all this, Chapter One suggests, is that we are a People of Spirit and Memory.

The soul of the People of Spirit and Memory is their living relationship with God which is activated by the experience named Spirit. This foundational experience is explosive. It inspires the human mind and heart to myriad creations. The People of Spirit and Memory have produced myths and rituals, elaborated beliefs and theologies, espoused values and behaviors. As generation succeeds generation, these diverse creations stockpile. They are in constant need of reform in order to be faithful to the living God they reflect.

The principle is that the Church is always reforming but never fully reformed. The creations of the People of Spirit and Memory have many different and very important functions, but only one ultimate purpose. They are expressions of the experience named Spirit and are meant to facilitate that experience for all who come in contact with them. At least that is what Chapter Two seems to think.

A preeminent creation of the People of Spirit and Memory is narrative. Story is one of the primal expressions of the experience named Spirit, and Christian faith regularly retells its sacred stories. The great hope of every retelling is that the tale will powerfully intersect the life of the hearers and they will experience, however dimly, the reality of Spirit.

The second half of Chapter Three explores the dynamic of hearing the sacred stories of the tradition. But those stories are old, and these are secular times (so the propaganda runs). People are interested in their own personal stories. We must begin with contemporary stories and bring forward the story of Jesus, the premier sacred story of Christianity, to interpret the depth of what is happening. So the first half of Chapter Three starts with personal narrative and merges it with the sacred stories of the tradition. The great hope remains the same—that in the merger of the two stories the experience named Spirit will emerge.

Chapter Four probes the abiding concerns of the experience named Spirit. If this experience and the living relationship to God it activates is the connection between Christ and Church, the source and goal of the creations of the Christian tradition, and the ambition of Christian storytelling, what does this experience entail?

The first moment of the experience named Spirit is an inrush of divine love mediated by human love. This love seeks and finds the heart of each person. More often than not, our hearts are living in either rejection or envy. For the rejected, this love sets a table; for the envious, this love holds up a mirror. For both it offers the opportunity for another way of being human.

The mystery of iniquity is that our hearts kill the love that seeks to save us. But this divine love does not give up. The crucifixion of love becomes the everlasting offer of new life. Of course, Jesus, the Son of God, is the one who revealed all this to us.

The first moment of the experience named Spirit is the swift inrush of divine love. The second moment is the stumble of human response. What will we do with the Love that loves us more than we love ourselves? Chapter Five struggles with a few suggestions. The surrender to divine love liberates human love.

This love moves in two directions at once—toward God and toward neighbor. Both these directions are intimately bound together. Love for God means praying and plotting and holding on. (Unless, of course, letting go is what is called for.) Loving God is the ultimate adventure. Loving our neighbor in God is the proximate passion. To love the neighbor is to see their well deserved injuries as our own undeserved wounds. It also entails a reversal of personal power. It is no longer ingeniously employed for personal gain, but lavishly spent for human reconciliation. The experience named Spirit results in joyous struggle. Of course Jesus, brother to us all, is the revelation of this struggle.

Even in minor moments of honesty, anyone writing a book admits that he or she is talking to himself or herself. The primary audience is the writer's soul. But hopefully there are soul mates. They are envisioned as people who are trying to think and live faith to the full; who know that genuine religious living is the key to what Kazantzakis called the "luminous interval between birth and death"; who have a heritage they honor, but wish they understood more deeply; who want to say something to the next generation, but want to make sure it comes from their heart; who believe in more than they have experienced, but want to experience most of what they believe; who want to allow religious truth to illumine interpersonal and social life, but reject simplicism and fanaticism; and who know that complexity and struggle are the name of the game, but who party like five-year-olds whenever hope arrives. If these feelings shape your soul, welcome.

A few thank-yous are not enough, but that is all there will be. To Rita, as always, who typed in the beginning, but, more importantly, corrected and edited. To Wayne who never said he liked it when he didn't, but when he liked it, said it. To Andy, for endless encouragement. To all my family and friends—to whom *An Experience Named Spirit* is dedicated—who, on finding me smiling, had the courtesy to ask me how it was going and, on finding me frowning, had the compassion to say nothing and to pass the potatoes.

## CHAPTER ONE

# A PEOPLE OF SPIRIT AND MEMORY

OLD MAN:   *You get old and you can't do anybody any*
          *good any more.*
BOY: *You do me some good, Grandpa. You tell*
     *me things.*[1]

                                    Robert Penn Warren

*The matter of the fact is that we can contact*
*Jesus only through the Church. The decision of faith*
*can take place within her alone, because she alone*
*supplies us with the situation basic to faith, contem*
*poraneity.*[2]

                                      Romano Guardini

*N*ine Catholic Christians were gathered in a
home on the northwest side of Chicago. They were discussing
the condition of their parish and the changes they hoped
would come about. One of the more zealous members of the
group opened a Bible which throughout the conversation sat
on her lap like an obedient cat. She began, "Jesus says here
that . . . " But she got no further. The man sitting next to her
reached over and with a flick of his hand flipped the Bible shut.

"Why are you reading in the presence of Christ?" he
asked angrily.

Our initial exploration concerns the inner energy of this
brief confrontation. We might approach the situation in terms

of its social dynamics. It would be predictable to convict the man of rudeness and the woman of a certain pious obtuseness. It might be noted that hurtful exchanges that take only an instant to happen can take over a year to heal. The strain between these two might jeopardize the well-being of the entire group. There is some need for reconciliation. No doubt the polar solutions for making up will be proposed—either talk it out and smooth it over or have a drink and forget it.

Another approach, almost irresistible in small, liberal church groups, is to psychologize the situation. The woman is insecure and needs the Bible to do her thinking for her. The man is upset at the parish leaders or his wife or his kids or his job or all of these and more and has found a convenient "dumping ground" in the woman sitting next to him. But as much fun as this pop psychology is, it will not get us where we want to go. Our perspective is theological. We want to examine the ecclesiological and christological issues that are at work in the conversation.

Christians love bold statements. The good news seems most at home in immodest claims ("Know that I am with you always, until the end of the world!"—Mt. 28:20) and unreasonable expectations ("If you trust and do not falter . . . say to this mountain, 'Be lifted up and thrown into the sea,' even that will happen."—Mt. 21:21).

This tendency for audacity can be traced all the way back to Jesus who, as a recent convert understated it, "had a way of putting things." The problem, of course, with our grand moments of boldness is the weeks and months of timid explanation that follow.

The man who so unceremoniously closed the Holy Book in favor of the Holy Company spoke one of Christianity's most daring claims: "Christ is present." Jesus Christ is not only the past founder of our relationship to God but also its present mediator. He not only overcame the law of time by not being forgotten, he overcame the law of death by not being lost. He lives among us! And our rhetoric for his presence ranges from the lyrical Hopkins' verse "Christ plays in ten thousand places" to the sudden, shocking revelation of Zooey Glass: "And don't you know—listen to me now—don't you know who that fat lady really is? . . . Ah, buddy. Ah, buddy. It's Christ himself. Christ himself, buddy."

What are we to make of this? How are we to understand the contemporary presence of Jesus Christ? How do we have access to Jesus Christ today? And how is that access related to the long ago historical personage of Jesus of Nazareth and the witness to him that we have in the Second or New Testament? What is the next moment in the conversation between the woman who opened the Bible to find Jesus and the man who flipped it shut in the name of Christ?

**People, Always People**
At Christmas time throughout the Christian world, an ordinary event takes place. It is a truly remarkable happening.

Parents and children stand before crib scenes and take note of what is represented. Three-year-old fingers point to the center of the scene and ask, "Who's that?" "Baby Jesus," is the time-honored reply. "And who's that?" No three-year-old settles for one question or one answer. "His mother Mary. And that's his foster father Joseph. And those are the shepherds and those are the Wise Men." By this time the three-year-old is experiencing information glut and wanders away in search of something new.

So it goes. The latest generation is beginning to hear about Jesus.

Charles Peguy highlighted this same experience of passing on the meaning and message of Christ:

17

Just as at the church door, on Sundays and feastdays,
When we go to Mass,
Or at funerals,
We pass holy water to each other from hand to hand,
One to another, one after the other,
To make the sign of the cross, upon ourselves, the
　　living, or on the coffins of the dead,
So that step by step the same sign of the cross is, as
　　it were, carried by the same water . . .
In the same way, from hand to hand, from fingers to
　　fingers,
From finger-tip to finger-tip, the everlasting
　　generations
Who go to Mass age after age,
One generation succeeding another,
Pass on the word of God, in the same hope,
In the same breasts, in the same hearts, until the
　　world itself is buried . . . [3]

So it goes. From the fingers of one to the fingers of another the word of God makes its way through history.

In Robert Browning's poem "A Death in the Desert," the apostle John is dying. He reflects on his life until the end comes and he "lies as he lay once, breast to breast with God." One of his musings concerns his role as the last living witness to Jesus Christ:

If I live yet, it is for good, more love
Through me to men: be nought but ashes here
That keep awhile my semblance, who was John.
Still, when they scatter, there is left on earth
No one alive who knew (consider this!)
—Saw with his eyes and handled with his hands

> That which was from the first, the Word of Life.
> How will it be when none more saith "I saw"?[4]

The entire Christian tradition is an answer to that final question: "How will it be when none more saith 'I saw'?" This is how it will be—people will tell others what those who saw told them. They will remember and tell the next generation.

This fact dictates the beginning of any contemporary retelling of the story of Jesus. It must start with "I never saw him. I never heard him. I never touched him. But there were those who did. And they told others, who told others, who told others still, who eventually told me. And now, in my turn, I tell you. And you, then, can tell others. And so, you see, there will never be an end to it."

This is the thrust of the interchange from the poem of Robert Penn Warren quoted at the beginning of the chapter. The young boy knows the old man is worthwhile because he can tell him things. The old connect the young with the past that is important. In the language of the "life-stages," the generativity needs of the older generation meet the identity needs of the younger generation.

Catholic Christianity stresses that access to the original long-ago event of Jesus Christ is mediated through people. It cultivates a romantic vision of hands clasping hands, linking backward through time until they touch the hand of Jesus Christ who holds the hand of God. The conversational flow of this long, historical line is largely one-sided. The older generation confides to the younger generation the sufferings and glories of Jesus Christ, the Son of God and Savior of the World.

What is important is not the bare fact that the conversation takes place, but what happens between the people who tell and listen to the story of Jesus Christ. Therefore, present-day contact with Jesus Christ occurs through a chain of people stretching over 1,900 years, and of course, people being people, the pervading fear is that with each added link the chain grows weaker.

Some contemporary thinkers have complemented this "line" image with the ambiguous metaphor of "contagion." The reality that Jesus unleashed into the world spreads like a disease. Each person who is exposed becomes, in turn, a carrier to other people. The revelation of Jesus Christ is catching. But this epidemic does not take place on the unthinking, bacteriological level. It is the result of human purpose and planning. Each generation of Christians, since the first, has preserved the memory of Jesus and, as best they could, lived within, acted out of, and passed on his Spirit. Tradition is a premeditated act of fragile people not wanting to lose what they love.

This insistence that people are the ultimate carriers and communicators of the Christ event is hinted at by Paul in the second letter to the Corinthians. When some require of him a letter of recommendation, he points to the community itself as a "letter from Christ . . . written not with ink but with the Spirit of the living God, not on tablets of stone but on the tablets of human hearts" (2 Cor. 3:3).

Human hearts that have been written on by the Spirit of the living God become a communication from Christ to other people. This is why Walter Kasper insists that the starting point of Christology is "faith as it is actually believed, lived, and proclaimed and practiced in the Christian churches. Faith in Jesus Christ can arise only from encounter with believing Christians."[5]

It may seem banal to stress that it is people, always people, who bring us into contact with Jesus Christ. But it is a fact that is easily forgotten. We tend toward "false objectivisms" which give the impression that Christ arrives independent of his flawed followers. We say we reach Christ through the Scriptures. But what is the New Testament but the witnessing words of people who had to speak of what they found through Jesus of Nazareth?

We say Christ is present in the sacraments. But what are the sacraments but the creations and recreations of people bent on continuing the salvific experience Jesus inaugurated?

We say Christ is present in the Church. But what is the Church but the collectivity of us all, the master and the slave, the Jew and the Gentile, this man and that woman who are mysteriously united, beyond the differences that divide them? The messy truth is that Christ comes to us fingerprinted by every generation that ever embraced him.

To stress the people grounding of Scripture, Sacraments, and Church is not meant to slight the presence of God in Christ in these realities. This is not a reductive humanism which overlooks the divine or a revisiting of the Donatist controversy which makes the presence of God in Christ dependent on human virtue. Rather, it attempts to recognize and underline the fact that Scripture, Sacraments, and Church are ventures of divine-human cooperation. They are the divinely inspired creations of people which have become the privileged locale of contact with God.

Christ is present in Word, Sacrament, and Church. But to say that Christ is present we do not have to say that we are not present. The history of Scripture, Sacraments, and Church show that they have been created, participated in, reinterpreted, and reformed by people. A nonnegotiable of the human condition is the co-presence of the divine and the human. If we would hear the thunderous voice of God, we must attend to human mumblings.

This people-base of Christian faith is more than an unfortunate but unavoidable fact. This way of passing on the faith is intimately related to the "essence" of what is to be passed on. The essence of Christian faith is not a message, so it is not enough to hear and understand what Jesus said and did. Neither is the essence a series of ethical mandates, so it is not enough to strive for the perfection the Gospels outline.

The essence of Christian faith is a living relationship with God, a relationship which was inaugurated by Jesus of Nazareth and which is presently available through his Spirit as it suffuses and transforms the lives of his followers. From this relationship, there emerged and continues to emerge, as surface waters of a lake are refreshed by hidden springs, a message and an ethic. But without the experience of the lived relationship to God, the message becomes gibberish and the ethic becomes folly.

If the content of Christian faith is ultimately the relationship to God which originated in the divine-human event of Jesus Christ, then what better way to pass it on than in the divine-human events that are our encounters with one another. Perhaps our language about faith is too "treasure" oriented. We call it an inheritance and tend to envision it as a sack of gold handed down from generation to generation.

Much truth about Christian faith can be wrung from this metaphor, but it can also give the false impression that faith is a "thing" to be protected and prized. This "crown jewels" approach tends to engender an attitude of vigilant defense. We become defenders of the faith and beat off people who approach it with new ideas. We caricature them as motivated by plunder and desecration. Most often, they have merely come to talk.

If there is a time for every season under heaven, there is certainly a time for defense. But is not the deeper Christian instinct toward faith and its transmission an attitude of invitation and hosting? Those who enjoy a relationship with the God of Jesus invite others into a relationship with themselves. In and through these relationships, which are resourced and critiqued by the Spirit, the possibility of entering into a relationship with the God of Jesus emerges. The present company of believers hosts new people, both searching adults and growing children, into their life together, and through this life into the abundant life which flows from God. In this way faith is passed on.

This "people focus" is the perspective behind John Coventry's answer to the question "What in fact is handed on by the Church?"

> The radical answer to this question—which is then seen also to answer the question, HOW is it handed on?—may seem at first sight very inward-looking. The radical answer can only be, THE CHURCH. The living Church hands on, perpetuates in history, the living Church. The Church, one might say, is history; it is living and believing men and women, perpetuating their faith in succeeding generations, and expressing it in manifold ways.[6]

"The living Church hands on the living Church" is a dense statement. Some might take it to be classic Catholic arrogance suggesting that the Church has no larger reality it must be faithful to. It is its own reward. But purged of this distortion, it does touch upon the interpersonal truth of Christian religion. Men and women of today in their extravagance and timidity, their cowardice and courage, their sacrificial love and self-serving schemes somehow continue what Jesus began. They make Christ present anew in every age.

The best way to understand this incorrigible and corruptible "peopleness" of Christian faith and its transmission is to return to the beginning. We must explore the experiential and relational reality that is at the heart of that faith. This reality is summed up in the phrase "Jesus Christ."

## Jesus Christ

"Jesus Christ" refers to an interpersonal event initiated by Jesus of Nazareth and received by the people he encountered. In relationship to Jesus, people contacted the transformative power of divine reality. One response to this mediated encounter with God was to call Jesus the Christ, the Anointed One.

It is interesting to note that Jesus did not call himself the Christ. Although Jesus had a definite consciousness of himself and his mission, it is difficult to tell if he ever used any titles for himself. But where he was reluctant, others were eager. It was the people who were saved through Jesus who bestowed the titles. "Jesus Christ" designates the relational flow between Jesus of Nazareth and his followers. It is a Christian code, a compressed way of talking about an experience which the Gospel of John suggests could not be compressed into all the books ever written.

This interpersonal focus on the core Christian reality is important to maintain. In the first place, it reflects the fullness of the scriptural accounts. The New Testament writings are deeply relational documents, creations of transformed witnesses rather than neutral observers of the Jesus scene. Although it is important at times to distinguish the historical Jesus from the Christ of faith, it is even more important to hold them together as the full expression of the saving encounter.[7] Willie Marxsen, in examining the structure of the Gospels, states this point strongly:

> The primal datum of the church is therefore not a person, but rather a relationship starting from this person . . . To put it more exactly, we would have

to say that Jesus and the one who believes belong together . . . This means . . . that the beginnings of Christology cannot be defined in such a way that a decision must be made either for the primitive Christian community or for the historical Jesus. Rather, the beginnings lie at the point where the relationship between Jesus and the believer becomes visible for the first time.[8]

The Gospels, as they stand, give us neither an isolated Jesus nor an isolated believer but the fire and ice between them.

A second perspective on the interpersonal origins of Christian faith concerns the way our interest moves "from presence to person." In the presence of some people we feel enhanced. Life is richer when we are with them; life is poorer when we are away from them. If this is the case, we want to know more about them. We try to uncover the mystery of their impact on us. We pursue the uniqueness of their person because of the uniqueness of their presence. Our interest in who they are is piqued because of what they are able to generate in us when we are with them. The blunt fact of relational life is that we do not seek out the "person" of those people who, as the wag puts it, "when they enter a room, it is like someone has left." When Jesus entered the room, something happened.

In regard to Jesus, this simple process is captured in the story of the tempest at sea (Mk. 4:35–41). Jesus and his disciples are in the boat. Jesus is asleep. A storm comes up. The disciples are terrified. They wake Jesus and ask him to help. He rebukes them for their lack of faith, calms the winds and sea, and goes back to sleep.

In this situation the disciples ask, "Who is this that even the winds and sea obey him?" The suggestion is that if Jesus had been washed overboard, they would never have asked. The question of inner, religious identity (the individual's ultimate relationship to God) becomes important when the relational reality between people becomes salvific.

The theological rendition of this "interest dynamic" is that soteriology is temporally prior to Christology.[9] The salvific impact that Jesus had on people precedes the question of his identity. Who he is becomes important because of what he is doing.

> Let me put this in exaggerated form. It was not Jesus who was important but what he DID, what he BROUGHT, what EVENT OCCURRED through him, what he SET IN MOTION. Nevertheless, what HE did, what HE brought, what HE effected was also important but HE was not important apart from his DEEDS. In short, the conviction of the first witnesses was: Jesus actualizes God.[10]

This emphasis does not lessen the importance of Christology nor relegate it to the realm of afterthought. It merely stresses a developmental rather than a logical pattern. The logical approach of much classical thinking about Jesus established his personal identity in relationship to the Father and then proceeded to a consideration of his saving work. The contemporary developmental approach begins with his saving power and moves to the God-grounded source of that power. In both approaches, soteriology and Christology must be tightly held together.

When we consider the relational reality that Jesus generated, it is especially necessary to move to the mystery of his person. This is more than just a "next step," a logical unfolding of a fascinating presence. It comes as an imperative from the experience itself. The level on which Jesus interacted with people forced them to focus on his deepest identity and on their own.

Given the central witness that the encounter with Jesus was salvific, the question is often asked "What was it about Jesus that mediated the divine? Did he speak the words of God?" Yes, but more. "Did he do the deeds of God?" Yes, but more.

It was the very person of Jesus, his core self, a self constituted by his intimate relationship to God whom he called "Abba," that made the divine accessible. In the images of the New Testament, Jesus is not only the Word of God and the Servant of God, he is also the Son of God. The metaphor of Son points to the centered self, the inner, foundational constitution of the person. Meeting Jesus meant more than exchanging words or sharing actions. The encounter moved through words and actions to their secret source, two people personally present to one another. In this situation, divine reality, whom Schillebeeckx once called the transcendent third in every relationship, also appears.[11]

The most profound appreciation of the event of Jesus Christ is that it is an "I–thou" encounter. Jesus interacted with people in such a way that their core self came in contact with his own, and this contact was an invitation to participate in his salvific structure of selfhood. That is why Christians call themselves "sons and daughters in the Son." Who they are is indebted to the One who reached them at the level of sonship and daughtership and reconstructed their identity to conform to his own.

In the history of Church reflection, Jesus will eventually be confessed as the Second Person of the Trinity. This confession acknowledges the true revelatory center of the event of Jesus Christ. It occurs on the deepest level of the self, the level where personhood is constructed. The event of Jesus Christ is preeminently an occurrence of "person calling out to person."

**The Real Absence and the New Presence**
From this relational perspective, the crucial events of the origins of Christianity concern the presence and absence of the person of Jesus. John Bowker suggests that the core religious problem of Jesus' day was the question of theistic effect, discerning "God's effect in the world." For this problem there were many proposed solutions. Jesus' solution was "literally idiocentric."

> For what is clearly suggested by the surviving evidence is that Jesus offered his own self as the solution to the problem; or perhaps more accurately one should say that Jesus seems to have located the solution to the problem first and foremost in his own person, and that it was in and through his own person that he claimed to be mediating God's effect in the world.[12]

If this is true, the loss of Jesus is of immeasurable consequence. When he is present, God is saving the people. When he is absent, God has drawn back into the sky. The near God is the far God once again. And the people are abandoned.

The ascension narrative in the Book of Acts is the clearest expression we have of the loss of Jesus. What must be remembered is that this is the second time the disciples have lost him. They knew him in the "days of his flesh" and lost him to death. Then they knew him, at least some of them, in the "days of his glory"—the resurrection appearances—and lost him to the transcendent realm of God.

In different language, the disciples knew Jesus as both a physical and a spiritual body and were not able to hold on to him in either form. In the total picture of Luke–Acts the ascension narratives function to close one era and to open another. In the Gospel of Luke the ascension ends the story of Jesus; in the Book of Acts it begins the story of the Church. But this transition is not without apprehension.

The two men in white who interpret the meaning of the ascension say:

> Men of Galilee, why do you stand looking into heaven? This Jesus, who was taken up from you into heaven, will come in the same way as you saw him go into heaven.
>
> Acts 1:10

Much is implied in these words. The disciples are not to worry about the destiny of Jesus. He is with God, and at the appointed time, he will come from God. They should be about the mission that has been entrusted to them.

This is certainly sound advice. But it may be that it is precisely the mission that they are worrying about as they watch Jesus disappear into the clouds. If the mission is more than just telling people about Jesus, if it entails initiating people into the relationship with God which Jesus made possible, then how is this going to be done if Jesus is not here to do it?

To extend the image of ascension, one can fantasize that it was not curiosity that made them stare but panic. If they could have, they would have reached up and pulled Jesus back to earth by his heels. What they were watching move ever farther away from them was the One who made it possible for them to love one another. What will happen now that he is gone?

"As he departs, so will he come" proves to be scant consolation. The parousia is delayed, and many scholars think its failure to arrive is the overriding dilemma of early Christianity. But viewed from a Lukan perspective, it is the tail end of the situation created by the ascension. The hope for a second coming springs, in part, from the heartbreak of a second leaving. The proclamation of Jesus' exaltation to the right hand of the Father pointed to the bittersweet experience of his not being in the company of his friends.

With the loss of the person of Jesus, both in his earthly and risen state, came the fear that the salvific experience he mediated would also go away. As Boniface Willems states it: "Christ died, and 'a cloud took him out of [our] sight' (cf. Acts 1:9). During the twenty centuries which have passed since then a huge mass of clouds has built up."[13] He is gone.

Of course the fullness of Christian faith has more to say. The resurrection-ascension-exaltation experience is both a statement about Jesus' personal destiny with God and his continued companionship with his followers. But this more should not be quickly rushed into. It is easy to slip into a "Christ is present" rhetoric which does not give sufficient attention to the radically different forms of presence.

> The significance of this central tenet of the faith of the apostolic Church (Jesus is Lord) lies in her confident and optimistic conviction that Jesus Christ through His exaltation to the Father's right hand has not been removed to some mythical existence beyond the furthest galaxy, but is actually more dynamically present in the world than ever He was when He walked the hills of Galilee. . . . This unshakable belief of the apostolic Church explains a noteworthy feature of the entire New Testament, an outlook particularly prominent in the theological attitudes of the four Evangelists. Search as you

will, you will discover in their books no nostalgia
for "the good old days."[14]

The optimism and confidence of statements like this bolster our trust in the first witnesses to Christ. But they leave little room for tears.

Yet there must have been, if not tears, the ache that
accompanies waiting for the one they love to return. The disciples may not have longed for the "good old days," but they
did long for the "good new days" when he would be with them
again. When this second coming did not occur, his presence
through the Spirit received more attention. Although there is
real continuity between presence of Jesus in his physical body,
in his resurrected body, and in the Spirit, there is also differ-
cnce—vast difference, painful difference.

Real loss must be acknowledged. The man who made
mud for the eyes of the blind and inserted his fingers into the
ears of the deaf, who ate and drank, wept and shouted, argued
and prayed, told stories and kept strangely silent, died and
rose—that man is gone. Gone in glory, according to believers,
but gone nonetheless.

The Jesus whose feet could be anointed by perfume and
whose hands could be pierced by nails is no longer among us
the way he once was. His Spirit continues his presence, but it
is manifestly not the same. Those first friends he left behind
cried, "Maranatha!" Come, Lord Jesus! It may have been a plea
for the victor to come back and vanquish their foes. But it
may also have been the heartfelt cry that love lets out for
reunion. In fact, it may be the Spirit itself, the presence of Jesus
in one way, calling to the Risen Lord, the presence of Jesus in
another way.

There is always a poignancy about Christian faith, a
yearning for the Missing One. The way to understand the

perennial presence of Christ is to recognize the absence of Jesus. The real absence must precede the new presence. This new and distinctive presence is captured most powerfully in the images of "bequeathing the Spirit" and "Body of Christ." To explore these images is to penetrate the paradox: the One who is gone is with us all days, even until the end of time.

**The Spirit of Christ**

Chapters 13–17 of the Gospel of John is a reading by the soon-to-be-deceased Jesus of his last will and testament.[15] To over-hear this final conversation between Jesus and his friends, even with its heavy theological accents, is to sense its emotional power:

> My little children
> I shall not be with you much longer.
> You will look for me
> And where I am going
> You cannot come.

His friends will search for Jesus (once again this hints at the depth and poignancy of their loss), but they will not find him. He must journey to a far place, and they cannot accompany him. Yet in the vision of the Johannine Christ, even this loss turns to gain:

> I will not leave you orphans . . .
> You are sad at heart.
> Still I must tell you the truth:
> It is for your own good that I am going
> Because unless I go
> The advocate will not come to you; but if I do go,
> I will send him to you.

Jesus must leave, but the Spirit, sent from both Jesus and the Father, will arrive. So the heartbreak of departure gives way, not only to the hope of reunion—"In a short time you will no longer see me/ And then a short time later you will see me again"—but also to a new form of presence:

> The Spirit will glorify me
> Since all he tells you
> Will be taken from what is mine.
> Everything the Father has is mine;
> That is why I said:
> All he tells you
> Will be taken from what is mine.

The initial resolution to the absence of Jesus is the giving of the Spirit. Since this Spirit is the Spirit of Jesus, it becomes a guarantor of his presence in a new way and, through his presence, the salvific experience he initiated. As Ray Brown succinctly puts it: "John presents the Paraclete as the Holy Spirit in a special role, namely, as the personal presence of Jesus in the Christian while Jesus is with the Father."[16]

James Dunn spells out this function of the Spirit in the Gospel of John in illuminating detail:

> The lengthening time gap between John and the historical Jesus, and the continuing delay of the parousia do not mean a steadily increasing distance between each generation of Christians and the Christ. On the contrary, each generation is as close to Jesus as the last—and the first—because the Paraclete is the immediate link between Jesus and his disciples in every generation. That is to say, the link and the continuity is provided not by sacraments or offices or human figures, but by the

33

Spirit. The vitality of Christian experience does not cease because the historical Jesus has faded into the past and the coming of Jesus has faded into the future; it retains its vitality because the Spirit is at work here and now as the other Paraclete. (Jesus is the first Paraclete.)[17]

We are now in the land of bold assertions. Peter looked into the eyes of Jesus; we have never seen his face. Yet we have as intimate an access to him as Peter. The disciples sat at the feet of Jesus and listened to his words; we have never heard his voice. Yet he is present to us as authentically as he was present to them. The truth of this audacious faith hangs on the reality of Spirit.

But what is this Spirit that Jesus passes on and how is it experienced? The word *Spirit* is extremely elusive. Although it cannot be completely pinned down, its implications can be explored. Geoffrey Lampe says that

[Spirit is] one of those "bridge" words which express the idea of God's outreach towards, and contact with, the created world . . . (It speaks) of God directing his thought towards his creation, purposing, willing, bringing into being, sustaining, guiding the cosmos and everything within it.[18]

Edmund Dobbin sums it up in a sentence: "As a symbol (Spirit of God) evokes the sense of divine power experienced in creation by a people with a strong sense of divine transcendence."[19]

In general, then, Spirit signifies the immanent presence of God to creation. But Spirit is more concretely grounded than that. It is an image taken from the experiences of breathing and wind. In Genesis, the passionate God breathes his breath into the clay human shape. The result is life, and the implication is that every inhalation of the human is the exhalation of the divine. God is not a distant reality but as near and intimate as breath. In passing on the Spirit, Jesus performs the same act (Jn. 20:22). He breathes on his disciples and tells them they are receiving the Holy Spirit. To talk about the Spirit of God is to indicate a presence as necessary, as subtle, and as sustaining as breath.

Spirit as breath suggests God's ubiquitous, permanent, life-supporting presence to creation. But God's involvement with creation is not confined to mere maintenance. Spirit as a steady divine influence is complemented by Spirit as an explosive divine outbreak of love, judgment, and transformation. Quiet breathing becomes a driving wind. Spirit not only upholds at all times; it especially inspires at crucial times.

It is best to talk about these special times as "break-outs" rather than "break-ins" because they are specifications of a presence that is already there and not intrusions of an absent power. It is these special times that we most often interpret as advents of the Spirit. We take breathing for granted; wind catches our attention.

Spirit, therefore, signifies the sustaining and transforming presence of God. This dynamic presence suffuses all creation. But it is not a reality that is directly known. It is known only by the effects it is producing in human life. The divine is not nakedly apprehended but intuited by what it is making happen. Said in another way, God is co-known as the ultimate source and catalyst of certain experiences which have many other causal factors.

In any concatenation of events, there are many proximate players. These players are easily observed, and most of what goes on can be attributed to their agency. But in some events, the proximate players become responsive to an ultimate author. What happens is not only the result of the energies of the proximate players but of a larger creative energy which is working through them. When the ultimate Author of the event is discerned amid the fury of the proximate players, we say, "The Spirit is present." To say this entails an act of discernment. Discernment is a difficult business, but there is no other way to uncover and acknowledge the divine that is intimately involved in the human.

The necessity of discernment to proclaim the presence of the Spirit is seen from an episode in the Gospel of Matthew. Jesus cures a blind and dumb demoniac (Mt. 12:22–37). Everyone is amazed but no one is quite sure what to make of it. The people have questions: "Can this be the Son of David?" The Pharisees offer an interpretation: "It is only by Beelzebub, the Prince of Demons, that he casts out demons." Jesus offers an alternate understanding: "If it is by the Spirit of God that I cast out demons, then the Kingdom of God has come among you."

No one disputes that a healing has occurred. The quarrel is over the interpretation. Is the ultimate source and catalyst of the healing God or Satan? If the experience is discerned as permeated by divine influence, then Spirit is the image used to express and convey that conviction. Spirit is introduced into the conversation as the truest and fullest appraisal of what happened in the experience.

During the life of Jesus, he interpreted his own activity and people interpreted their experiences of him as Spirit-created. They did this because through him the peace and power of God entered human life. The Spirit Jesus leaves his friends is this same Spirit of God precisely as he specified it.

As James Dunn puts it, Jesus is the personality of the Spirit.[20] In another image, Jesus is the signature of the Spirit. The invisible, immanent presence of God gains visibility and definition in Jesus. It is no longer merely the Spirit of God. That is too vague a designation. Neither is it the Spirit of the God who "delivered Israel out of the house of bondage," the Spirit of God as specified by the Exodus-covenant experience. It is the Spirit that burst forth in the life, death, and resurrection of Jesus. In Trinitarian language, it is the Spirit of the Father and the Son.

The presence of the Spirit of Jesus among his followers is known in precisely the same way as the presence of the Spirit of God was known in Jesus, with one major change: the physical mediation of Jesus of Nazareth is replaced by his followers. Spirit is no longer an interpretive image for the depth of encounters with Jesus of Nazareth, but an image to interpret the depth of encounters among Christians.

As once Jesus mediated the Spirit to his followers, now they mediate the Spirit to one another and to all who come in contact with them. In and through experiences with the followers of Jesus, life is sustained and transformed not only by human ingenuity and creativity but by the ultimate Mystery of life itself. The precise way of sustaining and transforming is indebted to Jesus who sustained and transformed life in a particular way. This is the experience named Spirit, and when it happens, Christians often express its reality by saying, "Christ is present!"

This new mediation is captured in the "great condition" that the Johannine Christ places on his continuing presence. He promises his friends another Paraclete "to be with you forever" (Jn. 14:15); that the Father will love them and that he will love them and reveal himself to them (Jn. 14:21); that he and the Father will make their dwelling place with them (Jn. 14:23–24). But all these promises of continued presence are on the condition that they keep Jesus' commandments. In the

Johannine literature, Jesus' words and commandments are summarized as " love one another as I have loved you."

But this condition should not be looked on as an automatic codicil: if they love one another, then Christ magically appears as a bonus. Rather, their love for one another activates his presence. But it is a presence that is doubly mediated. First, it is mediated through the disciples and their effort to love one another. This effort at love discerns a divine encouragement, a greater Mystery that initiated the effort and accompanies it as it proceeds. This divine lure and assistance is named Spirit.

But it is not just *any* Spirit of *any* God. It is the Spirit of the God of Jesus and therefore carries the divine gift and demand that came to expression in the life, death, and resurrection of Jesus of Nazareth. This forms the second mediation. Through the disciples and through the Spirit, Jesus Christ is present. This is the complex, but not forced, logic that structures the image of "bequeathing the Spirit." This image is an interpretation of the crucial experience of the early Church—the simultaneous loss and presence of Jesus Christ.

We are now close to the heart of our reflections. With the miracle of birth, we enter into inescapable relationships with other people and God. The relationship with God is mediated through the other people and, once it is articulated and inhabited, it redounds back on them. But this living relationship with God can be neglected. Consciousness can be narrowed to the immediately observable.[21] The proximate players can overshadow the ultimate Author.

This was not the case with Jesus. Jesus was a proximate player completely in accord with the ultimate Author. When he was with people, he was the catalyst of an experience named Spirit. This experience brought the living relationship to God into the minds and hearts of people with both passion and precision. It is this experience named Spirit, this conscious activation of the living relationship with God, that is the center of Christian reality.

## The Body of Christ

The Johannine image of bequeathing the Spirit is a natural companion of the Pauline image of the Church as the Body of Christ. In fact, in chapter 12 of 1 Corinthians, Paul smoothly connects Jesus, the Spirit, and the Church as the Body of Christ. The Spirit is discerned in believers because it urges them to cry, "Jesus is Lord!" and never "Cursed be Jesus!" It is also this Spirit which is the source of their many gifts and binds them into one body. "It was in one Spirit that all of us, whether Jew or Greek, slave or free, were baptized into one body" (1 Cor. 12:13). Therefore, Spirit looks both to the One who gave it and to the effects on the ones who received it.

"Body of Christ" is a phrase that is found often in the letters of Paul. D. E. H. Whiteley points out four different designations—the body of Christ in his earthly life, the Resurrected Body of Christ, the Church, and the Eucharistic body.[22] These four realities are closely connected but should not be collapsed into one another. Spelling out the relationships between them is part of the Christian enterprise. An initial suggestion is that "Body of Christ" refers literally and really to the earthly and resurrected body of Jesus. It refers metaphorically and really to the Church and the Eucharist. Our concern is with one of the meanings it conveys when it is metaphorically applied to the people who are the Church.[23]

As an image for the deepest identity of the Church, "Body of Christ" is rich in meanings. These multiple meanings are brought out in interaction with different social situations. In Corinth, the problem was that the diverse gifts of the community were creating disunity. Jealousy, rivalry, and factionalism

were resulting from the fact that one had the gift of
prophecy, another the gift of tongues, another the gift of healing, and so on. The gifts were competing with one another,
not cooperating.

In this situation, the Body of Christ becomes a call to har-
mony, to allow the diversity to become contribution and not
division. The basic metaphor is spelled out in terms of eyes,
feet, head, hands, and ears all working together. None of them
can claim to be autonomous. Each needs the other to be
whole. The meaning pulled from the Body of Christ in interaction with the conflicts at Corinth is that our unique gifts must
unite us and not pull us apart.

But at Colossae, the situation was different. The people
were worshipping elemental cosmic spirits that ruled the
world. Between God and humankind there were a galaxy of
mediators—"thrones, dominions, principalities, authorities"
(Col. 1:16). These powers had to be appeased if life was to be
secure and productive. Jesus Christ was imaged as one of these
powers, one who would give protection if properly placated.

In response to this situation, the Body of Christ image is
developed in a different direction. At Corinth, the head was
just one more member. At Colossae, Christ becomes the Head
and the people are the Body. As Head, Christ has the fullness
of authority and can guarantee the Body freedom from the
cosmic spirits. There is no need to grovel before them, for as
Church we are members of the Body whose Head is Christ.
This Head has won a victory over the powers and principalities of the world. In the conflictual world of Colossae, the
image is played out differently than in the conflictual world
of Corinth.

Different meanings are elicited from the same image as it
relates to different conflicts. The conflict we are considering is
the loss of the physical presence of Jesus of Nazareth. It is a

conflict because his physical presence is the precondition for triggering the salvific experience of God. Without this presence, the salvific experience may disappear.

In this situation, to call the people the Body of Christ is to say that the physical presence to one another functions as Jesus' physical presence did when he walked the earth. Although he is gone, the salvific experience he precipitated is still possible. The people who are the Church now mediate to one another what Jesus once mediated to them. When this happens, they become the Body of Christ, the visible offer of God's salvific love.

This is what Guardini meant in the second quote that opened this chapter about the Church making Christ contemporary. We live after Jesus Christ but not without him. He is present wherever and whenever the God he revealed is sustaining and transforming human life. This God of Jesus needs but, paradoxically, never forces flesh. The divine seeks free people to freely give themselves. No hirelings, only daughters and sons.

The preeminent son, Jesus, opened himself to this divine reality, and it flowed through him. His followers attempt the same openness and the same mediation. That is their ultimate identity, and when they are faithful to it, they are living in his Spirit and functioning as his Body. In Christian shorthand, they are making the event of Jesus Christ contemporaneous to each generation.

Schillebeeckx opens *Christ: The Experience of Jesus as Lord* with "It began with an encounter."[24] Our insistence is that what began as an encounter continues as an encounter. The original event of Jesus Christ was an interpersonal meeting of Jesus of Nazareth with other people. This encounter penetrated to their core person, their relationship to ultimate reality, and restructured it salvifically. Through his human love, divine love entered and transformed the lives of people. In this experience people recognized the presence of God, and they named the experience Spirit.

Although this Jesus of Nazareth now lives in the far reaches of God as the Risen Lord, the salvific experience that he made possible continues.[25] When this experience happens, we acknowledge that its ultimate author is his Spirit and that we are functioning as his Body. We are in a relationship to one another like the revelatory relationship he had with some of his contemporaries. Through our human love for one another, inspired and supported by the Spirit of Jesus, we initiate each other into a relationship with that Ultimate Love which Jesus revealed.

When this happens, the event of Jesus Christ occurs, not in the original way, but in a way dependent upon, yet different from, those long-ago encounters. Therefore, access to the event of Jesus Christ is through our Spirit-suffused love for one another which transforms us into the Body of Christ.

### The Memory of Jesus

No Christian pondering can go on for long without the sobering subject of sin. Things go wrong. The Spirit may blow where it will and unpredictability may be part of God's gracious surprise. But there is also a question of which Spirit is blowing. The perennial concern of Christian faith is how to test the Spirit. How can we be sure it is the Spirit of Jesus which prompts us? How do we know we are handing on the authentic revelation? As Karl Barth pointed out, the New Testament uses the same word for Judas "handing over" Jesus and for Christians "handing over" their tradition to one another.[26]

This problem of discerning the authentic Spirit was central to the early Church. Paul mentions it in one of his earliest letters:

# An Experience Named Spirit

Do not stifle inspiration, and do not despise prophetic utterances, but bring them all to the test and then keep what is good in them and avoid the bad of whatever kind.

1 Thessalonians 5:19–22

The test of the Spirit which Paul developed had three main features.[27] Was the present activity attributed to the inspiration of the Spirit in continuity with the founding gospel traditions, did it manifest love, and was it for the benefit of others? These criteria are indebted to the memory of the event of Jesus Christ. It was this event that revealed the love of God and made possible an other-centered life. "The most profound safeguard which Paul offers against enthusiasm is the touchstone of Christ—the character of his ministry as testified in the gospel."[28] If there is to be contemporary access to the event of Jesus Christ, it is not enough to encounter people vivified by his Spirit. These people must also be in dialogue with his Memory.

The classic role for the Memory of Jesus has been as a critical corrective for Spirit. It has been called in to check the excesses of spiritual experiences. From a Christian viewpoint, spiritual experience is always in danger of breaking our life-giving bonds with the interpersonal world and setting us free to soar into private, ecstatic states. The Spirit lifts us out of the human circle, and we begin to prefer this "disengaged" feeling.

We wait and pray for these "escape moments" and tend to disdain the earth that holds us down. Before we know it, these peak experiences begin to consume us. We relish the emotional highs and have little energy or interest in the ordinary. Any belief that does not bring with it the "thrill and feel of the Spirit" we suspect or discard. And in the inner chamber of

# JOHN SHEA

the soul, a new dizziness, which prides itself as beyond the struggles of earth, reigns.

In spiritual excess "Praise the Lord!" is on our lips but forgotten is "Not everyone who says, 'Lord! Lord!' enters the Kingdom of God." As Paul seemed to suggest, these experiences may take us to the seventh heaven, but they seldom seem to visit the cross of Christ. Their connection with other-centered love is weak. The ongoing, concrete demands of charitable living are drudgery compared to this spiritual excitement and are soon neglected. Rational analysis is shunned as "killing the Spirit" and practical planning avoided because it shows a "lack of trust in God." Martin Luther mocked it well: "These people have swallowed the Holy Spirit, feathers and all."

But the question is "Just what have they swallowed?" The experience does not seem to arise from the bonding of the human and the divine and does not seem to lead to a new bonding. It arrives unaided by human love and often departs without inspiring human love.

It is doubtful whether this type of experience should be called Spirit-created. The reason for this hesitancy is the Memory of Jesus. When we recall his life, death, and resurrection, we begin to question whether we should attribute to the inspiration of God any experience so isolated in its origins and so confined in its effects. Are these experiences authored by the Spirit of Jesus? If they are, how do we cultivate them and respond? Or are these experiences alien to the Spirit of Jesus? If they are, how do we criticize and control them? The only way these crucial questions can be answered is to consult the Memory of the Spirit-Giver.

But the Memory of Jesus does more than confront the excesses of spiritual experience. It also questions the arrogance of spiritual possession. "We have the Spirit," we say, as if it were a bird in a cage of our making. "Jesus promised it would be with us forever," we say, like a greedy nephew at the reading of a rich uncle's will. We complacently assume the Spirit is ours. We do not point to a life of love grounded in God to support this belief. We prefer to take it "on faith" which is comfortably defined as "beyond experience." The danger of spiritual enthusiasm often appears on the periphery of the people who are the Church. The danger of spirit possession is a temptation at the center. It is the seduction of those in authority.

Now there is a great deal of truth in holding tightly to Jesus' promise that the Spirit would accompany us. We must trust in the presence of the Spirit even when the experiences that validate that presence are not there. But this truth turns treacherous when we smugly use it to claim possession of the Spirit even though the love, justice, and peace which are signs of that presence are nowhere to be found.

It is one thing to trust in the Spirit when the Spirit appears absent. This attitude understands the Spirit as the free gift of God and is receptive to its comings and goings. But it is another thing to claim the Spirit without openness to the experiences the Spirit generates, to lightly boast of its presence in the face of lovelessness, apathy, and envy. This attitude has taken the Spirit hostage.

Spirit possession is a theology of election gone sour. A Church which claims the Spirit as a prerogative begins to glory in itself, emphasize its privileged status, and blur the distinction between itself and Jesus Christ. The rhetoric ranges unnuanced: "The Church is the continuation of the Incarnation." No distinctions are forthcoming. In this situation, it is time for the Memory of Jesus. Yves Congar, who strongly emphasized the Spirit as the animating life force of the Church, subtly pointed to this aberration: "The Church's fidelity to her Lord demands not only that she listen to him within herself, in her own

# JOHN SHEA

conscience, but also as the voice of Another, her Master."[29] Without the memory of the Master we make ourselves the master and put the Spirit at the service of our self-aggrandizement. An important task of the Memory of Jesus is to keep his followers from an infatuation with spiritual highs and from a self-righteous posturing which will not brook criticism.

It has often been charged that Memory has done this job too well. If there can be an excess of Spirit, there can also be an excess of Memory. The dominance of Memory begins with praising the past as a time of extraordinary events. There was a time, the days and nights of Jesus of Nazareth, when the presence of God was immediate and tangible. These past events of which Jesus was the center were recorded, and we must be rigorously faithful to them. We must preserve these traditions intact and jealously guard them from error. Northrop Frye has slyly remarked: "In the post biblical period both Christianity and Judaism seem to have accepted the principle that the age of prophesy had ceased, and to have accepted it with a good deal of relief."[30] The wild ways of the Spirit give way to trustworthy truths taken from the age of revelation, rationally defended and authoritatively passed on.

With Memory so enshrined, present religious experience is ignored or, at best, highly suspect. This opens the way for authoritarian religion at its worst. Since we cannot trust any intimation of God garnered from our experience, we must blindly believe the witnesses of the past. More particularly, we must submit to the authoritative interpretations of what those witnesses had to say.

There is no possibility of dissent for we have no other access to the divine except through their witness. We believe on the word of another, and we construct edifices of argument to convince ourselves that these others are trustworthy. We console ourselves with the words of the Johannine Christ to the doubting Thomas. Thomas was granted every believer's fantasy. He fingered the wounds of the Risen Christ and physically bolstered his sagging faith. But he is not blessed. It is we who are blessed, the ones who believe and do not see.

But this will not get us through the winters of our doubt and discontent. The day arrives when the past is not solid certainty we can base our lives on but just someone else's truth. Franz Kafka caught the tone of that day in a brief parable:

> They were offered the choice between becoming kings or the couriers of kings. The way children would, they all wanted to be couriers. Therefore there are only couriers who hurry about the world, shouting to each other—since there are no kings— messages that have become meaningless. They would like to put an end to this miserable life of theirs but they dare not because of their oaths of service.[31]

When we retain the message of the King but lose the feel for his presence, the passion of religious mission turns to dull obligation

Christian faith points to certain events of the past as extraordinary and special. No one living today was present at them. And if the reports are to be believed, the majority of people who were fortunate enough (Christian nostalgia) to be present at these events missed their revelatory impact. But the specialness of the past should not usurp the specialness of the present. The life and times of Jesus and the early Church may have been bursting with Spirit but we are not bereft of it. The same Spirit that suffused the life of Jesus in a preeminent way, and through him the disciples, prophets, and mystics of the Christian tradition, is also at work in the life of the ordinary believer of today. John Hick, in discussing the rationality of belief, tries to work out this connection:

> Suppose, for the sake of argument, we accept the right of the great theistic mystics to believe in the reality of God on the basis of their own religious experience. We shall then be prepared to acknowledge that such a person as Jesus or St. Paul or St. Francis or Martin Luther, or again Mohammed, or Ramanuja, or Guru Nanak, have been entitled, as rational persons, to claim on the basis of their own experiences to know that God exists. But what about ordinary religious believers, who do not enjoy the same overwhelmingly powerful forms of theistic experience? Does our line of thought point to any justification for belief in the existence of God . . . on the part of the ordinary people? Not, I would say, if they do not experience religiously in any degree whatever. For the absolutely unmystical—if such there are—there can be no good grounds for religious belief. However, the ordinary believer does, I would think, have some at least remote echo within his own experience of the much more momentous experience of the great religious figures. And it is this that makes him take their reports seriously. If he experiences his own life religiously at least to some slight extent, this makes it possible, and I would suggest reasonable, for him to be so impressed by the reports of the great souls that he comes to share their belief in the reality of the Transcendent. His belief is not as well-grounded as theirs. But I would suggest that it is well enough grounded for it to be reasonable for

him to proceed in faith in the footsteps of a religious leaders, anticipating the full confirmation
which his faith will ultimately receive if it does
indeed correspond with reality.[32]

The memory of Jesus records a time of the intensification
of the Spirit. But this does not overshadow or discount less
intense experiences of the same Spirit. In fact, it is the present
experience of the Spirit, however weak or powerful, which
makes it possible for the contemporary believer to recognize
the fullness of Spirit in the Memory of Jesus.

In the excesses and pretensions of the Spirit, we look to
the Memory of Jesus for direction and perspective. But when
Memory threatens to alienate us from the depth of the present,
we look to the Spirit to bring us life. Spirit and Memory are
critical correctives.[33] The enduring adventure of Christian faith
is to keep them in creative tension with one another. Which
brings us by a tortuous and circuitous route back to that living
room in a home on the northwest side of Chicago.

The woman holds the witness to the original event of
Jesus Christ and wants to insert it into the discussion. The man
is "into" the conversation among the people and wants no
interference from the Bible. As might be expected, both have
a piece of the action.

The most positive interpretation of the man's closing the
Bible is that he is sensitive to the sustaining and transforming
of life that is happening in the group and through the group in
the parish. He sees the introduction of the biblical witness as
shifting attention from the present to the past. Christ is present
now. The experience named Spirit which is Jesus' legacy is
happening among his latest band of followers. With this perspective, the dilemma he will eventually run into is how to

discern the Spirit's impulse. When this happens, he might turn to the woman with the Bible with less irritation.

The most positive interpretation of the Bible-quoting woman is that she is consulting the Memory of Jesus in order to better discern the dynamics of the present. She is not trying to distract from the group processes and the necessary decisions that have to be made; she is trying to focus those processes and clarify the real terms of the decision. She might be afraid that the group will go "off on its own" and analyze and plan without the illumination that comes from the Jesus story. If it does that, the group might not hear the ultimate Author in the noise of the proximate players. She is trying to give the group "ears" or, in another metaphor, "eyes."

With this perspective the dilemma she will eventually run into is what do these words from the past have to do with the dynamics of the present situation. When this happens, she might turn to the man who just turned to her and ask, "What were you saying about the presence of Christ?"

### Conclusion

It is people, always people, interacting with the world and other people. But it is never only people. There is always More, a crucial but often overlooked More. This More is the ultimate Mystery of life which is the permeating context of the interacting people. This ultimate Mystery both sustains the human adventure and enters into the fray. It is the source of both being and becoming. When we discern this sustaining and transforming activity, we name it Spirit.

Spirit is the ultimate author of life itself and of certain specific events within life. But ultimate authorship never excludes the proximate players. In fact, it is the proximate players, the people themselves, who speak of the Spirit's influence or neglect to mention it. A religious appreciation of the human condition locks the divine and human spirit, the ultimate Author and proximate players, in a living relationship.

Jesus was a proximate player of immense vitality. When people were with him, life was sustained with such a love and transformed with such a passion that the only adequate interpretation was that the "Spirit of God was upon him." This Spirit that worked through him during his life sustained him through the terrors of death and transformed him into a new existence.

Jesus now lives in the unimaginable transcendence of God which John had the nerve to imagine as a mansion with many rooms and Jesus as a housekeeper, gone on ahead, to ready the place for our arrival. This homey metaphor does not tame Mystery, nor even strip it of its terror, but it does suggest that its otherness from us lies in the infinite graciousness of its welcome. The Jesus who once drank wine with his friends now drinks wine with his Father.

For the early Church, the resurrection of Jesus meant that he had taken on a new role. The imagery for this new role was that he "sat at the right hand of the Father." The implication is that everything that the Father does is now channeled through Jesus, the Son. The preeminent activity of the Father is the sending of Spirit. Jesus is now part of that commissioning. As Moltmann has observed, a switch has taken place.[34] During Jesus' earthly life the order was Father-Spirit-Son. The Father sends the Spirit which descends upon Jesus and empowers him to be the Son.

But with the resurrection, the order becomes Father-Son-Spirit. The Father and the Son send the Spirit upon the Church. The resurrection links Jesus so closely to God that he moves from being the recipient of the Spirit to being the co-sender of the Spirit.

The experience named Spirit now happens among the ones whom Jesus left behind but did not leave orphans. The inheritance that Jesus left his brothers and sisters was the Spirit. This Spirit is the animating energy of their interaction with one another, and it effects what Jesus' earthly presence once brought about. In this sense, the people become the Body of Christ, the current mediation of the event that happened in and through Jesus of Nazareth.

The contemporary people who are the Body of Christ do not replace Jesus, the first Body of Christ. Rather, they mediate his presence to one another and to the world in which they live. The Spirit which is sent by the Risen Lord and which empowers the people to be the Body of Christ is bringing about what it brought about in the earthly life of Jesus. Therefore, the Memory of Jesus is necessary to discern the present activity of the Spirit. This exploration suggests that the deepest identity of the Christian Church is that they are a People of Spirit and Memory.

The heart of Christian faith is this salvific experience which we have named Spirit. There is an experiential continuity between what Jesus made happen and what happens among his followers. The vitality of this experience has generated immense creative activity. This central animating experience is the source of the many creations of the People of Spirit and Memory. Their rich and varied traditions flow from this experience and lead back to it. We have identified an experience named Spirit. We must now explore its manifold expressions.

# THE CREATIONS OF THE PEOPLE OF SPIRIT AND MEMORY

*The classic event for the Christian is the religious event of God's self-manifestation in the person Jesus the Christ: an event that happened, happens, and will happen.*[1]

David Tracy

*Christ only wrote once, and then it was in the sand.*[2]

Maurice Blondel

*T*he time is 1954. The place is Chicago. The boy is thirteen. He belongs to the People of Spirit and Memory. But the People of Spirit and Memory have journeyed far—spatially, temporally, and developmentally—since the inaugural events of first-century Palestine.

The boy is wearing a cassock, sash, surplice, and cape. He is kneeling in a Gothic church before a monstrance. At the center of the monstrance is a consecrated host. The boy has been told since childhood that Christ lives in this host. He is not especially pious, but he believes it. Whatever doubts he had were allayed by a heavy classroom discussion on transubstantiation. The idea was just far enough beyond his intellectual abilities to convince him.

This kneeling boy contemplating the host as a sacred object seems a far cry from the original eucharistic setting of eating and drinking with Jesus. The People of Spirit and

Memory have been journeying through time and space and living off the land. Many things have changed; fewer things have remained the same.

Within the Christian tradition many have deplored this process of development and adaptation. For them, every change has smacked of betrayal. Others have welcomed development. For them change is a sign of vitality. Both groups, from time to time, have misgivings about their strong stances, but they seldom share these qualms with each other.

This faded photo from 1954 is itself a lesson in historical development. The clothes the boy is wearing were fashionable centuries earlier in Western Europe. The architecture that surrounds him was inspired by the towering spirituality of the Middle Ages. The particular form of piety he is practicing— exposition of the Blessed Sacrament and praying before it— started around the thirteenth century. Scholars trace the reasons for its emergence and the furious debates it has generated.[3] Eucharistic worship outside mass was always seen as prone to abuses. But it has "hung on" for many centuries. Countless Christians have knelt in countless churches and said secret things to their eucharistic Lord.

The boy is one of a long series of altar boys who will kneel before the Blessed Sacrament on this day. They work in half-hour shifts, two at a time. It is part of the Forty Hours Devotion. The boy has been assigned adoration time since he was ten. He knows the routine—kneel fifteen minutes, sit fifteen minutes. He has a prayer book which he reads and ponders; then his mind wanders. Although he tries hard, he has always had trouble with "paying attention."

His knees were hurting and he was checking his watch to see if it was time to sit when the host, without saying a word, spoke to him.

"I'm not just a host, you know."

The boy sat immediately. To put it mildly, he was discombobulated. But every time he looked at the monstrance the same wordless words came to him.

"I'm not just a host, you know."

He looked over at his fellow server. This boy, also thirteen, was famous for his ears. They were enormous jug handles, and with immense concentration and teeth grinding, he was able to slide them noticeably back and forth on the side of his head. As Nelson Algren was fond of saying "Talent can spring up anywhere."

The fellow server looked back at the boy with one of those "only fifteen minutes left" looks. But also a wordless communication flowed from him.

"I'm not just a stupid kid who can wiggle his ears, you know."

The boy's world got "mysteriouser and mysteriouser." On the way home, everything talked to him. Two old ladies on the street addressed him without saying a word: "We're not just two old ladies, you know." The trees felt compelled to repeat the message; so did the sky. The boy was dizzy with all this unsolicited companionship.

It was the "you know" at the end of all these unexpected outbursts of communication from all these normally silent realities that most shocked the boy. The fact is he had not known. Until that day everything was what it was and nothing more. Never again was this to be the case. Something had happened to the structure of his awareness. It had been broken and recast to include more of what was. Everything was more than it seemed; everything opened onto something greater.

And it was the something greater that whispered the message. It was as if the boy had been let in on a great secret. So, in the secrecy of his soul, he gave the day a name. He called it the Day of the Haloes. For now he knew the radiance of each person.

Of course, the boy grew up and in a rage of sophistication rejected the happenings of that day. From the liberated vantage point of young adulthood it seemed to him to be ghetto Catholicism at its narrowest. How could he trust voiceless communications from a host and then from the entire world? Was not this the wish fulfillment of a mind seduced by magic? He must have been a lonely boy and his own loneliness spoke to him from the host.

In his heart, he knew this was not true but at least it was understandable. Also, with the latest revamping of tradition known as Vatican II, he knew that exposition of the Blessed Sacrament was suspect. It was mocked as "staring at your food." The eucharistic bread was to be eaten and not played with. How could so questionable a development as Hours of Adoration result in anything genuine? The answer was obvious: it could not. The questioning adult disallowed what the wide-eyed boy delighted in.

The boy-turned-man moved from piety to people. Did not Jesus switch the locale of the sacred from the Temple to the person? He abandoned the church buildings, both physically and spiritually. He traded the dimly lit spaces where hosts spoke in solitude for the world of "I-Thou" encounters and social conflicts.

A theology accompanied him on his journey. God was present in people, not things; in the events of history, not in buildings. What counted was bread in people's mouths, not hosts in monstrances. He felt like a spaceship that had jettisoned its bulky exterior and was finally free to explore and soar. In actual fact, the soaring included a lot of crashing. But it was a move toward life and love, and he still travels, as best he can, that road.

It was in his early thirties that the boy-turned-man read a passage from Teilhard de Chardin about a man kneeling before the Eucharist.

> Thus in the midst of a great sigh suggestive both of an awakening and of a plaint the flow of whiteness enveloped me, passed beyond me, overran everything. At the same time everything, though drowned in this whiteness, preserved its own proper shape, its own autonomous movement; for the whiteness did not efface the features or change the nature of anything, but penetrated objects at the core of their being, at a level more profound even than their own life. It was as though a milky brightness were illuminating the universe from within, and everything were fashioned of the same kind of translucent flesh.[4]

The boy-turned-man knew what the writer was talking about. It was not the same as his experience of long ago. There was no paradoxical communication without words. The experience was expressed in visual terms. But the result was very much the same—the sense of an inner radiance which etched everything in its unmistakable uniqueness. Nothing was just anything. Everything was more than it seemed. The opaque world became translucent.

The boy-turned-man was still unsure about the day the host, without speaking, spoke. He could not wrap his critical mind around it. But even though he could not comprehend what happened, he was more ready to accept it. The experience had left a mark on him and he might as well acknowledge it.

Every time he tried to reduce the reality of another person (and he tried it often) something happened, and the communication inevitably came through: "I'm more than just a person who wriggles their ears, you know. " Whenever this happened, the boy-turned-man was startled by the "you know." He knew but yet he did not know. He kept forgetting, and each time he was reminded, the new experience connected with the old ones to deepen his awareness. He was tempted to speak of a conspiracy, but he was afraid someone would reinterpret it as providence.

**The Boy in Context**

The last chapter stressed that the People of Spirit and Memory were constituted by a living relationship with God. The experience of this relationship was inaugurated and definitively enacted in the event of Jesus Christ. But it is not a relationship or an experience that is lost in the onward rush of time and history.

Even though Jesus is not with us the way he once was, the experience of this relationship with his Father continues in the Church. Jesus remains the permanent and indispensable mediator of this relationship because, in mythological language, he sits at the right hand of the Father and sends the Spirit.

But the people who are the Church are the new earthly catalysts of the experience of this relationship. As such, they take as their identity the image Body of Christ, because they continue the incarnational mediation of divine salvation that Jesus Christ began. This living relationship with divine reality and the experience of it named Spirit is the "energy center" of Christian faith.

This energy center releases the creative powers of people. Whenever the experience named Spirit, as David Tracy suggests, "happened, happens, and will happen," there is a rich and diversified human response. The inrush of divine reality sets people rushing off in many directions. In the throes and wake of this experience, people create, and the sum of their creations form the Christian tradition. All the creations, or in a more majestic phrase "the monuments," of the tradition flow from this experienced relationship to God and are meant to continually refer back to it. The divine which originates the creativity ultimately claims it.

But this dynamic, emerging from and returning to the experience of God, is not always easy to trace. Many liturgical, doctrinal, ecclesiastical, and political developments of Christian history seem to have little to do with the living relationship to God. Yet when the historical spadework is done, what often turns up is a theological rationale for the development, an attempt to connect it to the foundational revelation.

Our suspicious natures surmise that the theological reasoning is window dressing. The development was generated by personal or political self-interest and later made presentable with theology. But even if in a given instance this was the case, the instinct that guides all creations of the People of Spirit and Memory was at work. Every development must be related—somehow—to the experience named Spirit.

The creations of the People of Spirit and Memory defy neat categories. Christian history is not a model of progressive and orderly development. It is a sprawling chronicle of a people who are energized by their living relationship to God and who are creating multiple responses to their diverse environments. They were, in a current phrase, "productively perverse."

Their efforts range from the Gospels of Jesus Christ to the legends of the saints; from the eucharistic meal to a long forgotten burial custom of fourth century Italy; from the theological synthesis of Thomas Aquinas to the countless sermons that died in mid sentence; from the music of Palestrina and the art of Michelangelo to the tavern ditties spruced up for church services and the rosy-cheeked Christs of weepy piety; from Pope John XII to Pope John XXIII. Any tradition as old as Christianity is a motley mix of motley people parading the motley work of their hands.

Our opening scene of a Catholic boy kneeling before the Blessed Sacrament in 1954 is a snapshot of one moment in the life of this pilgrim people. What happens to him and how he processes it is a cameo of socialization and dissent. To be born into or to convert into a religious tradition is to encounter its myriad creations.

There is no direct access to the experience named Spirit. What a person initially "bumps up against" are the structures, ethics, beliefs, theology, spiritual practices, myth, and ritual of the religious people he or she belongs to. The Church is not just a People of Spirit and Memory, but a historical people who have undergone the struggles of time and space and have a storehouse of created traditions. When these created traditions are functioning properly, they seduce believers into a living relationship with God.

The boy cannot escape time. He cannot leapfrog back to Christ to find a more palatable mediation of God. Initially we all take what we get, and in time we change what we have received in ways we think are more appropriate. In doing so, we insist that the generation after us initially take what they get. Such seems to be the inescapable dynamics of life caught in time and bound to other people.

In Chapter One we focused on the People of Spirit and Memory. In this chapter we focus on the traditions the people have generated. It is impossible to survey the panorama that is Christian tradition. We will squint our eyes considerably and view only a few of the types of traditions that have developed and how they relate to the experience named Spirit. We will use the ambiguous experience of the boy and the ambiguous reflections of the boy-turned-man as a touchstone.

### Embodying the Experience: Myth and Ritual

Although there may be no method to the madness of how the Christian tradition developed, there are priorities. The most prized creations of the Christian tradition are its core myth and ritual. The core myth is the life, death, and resurrection of Jesus Christ which is embodied in the four Gospels; the core ritual is the eucharistic eating and drinking together that he initiated.

In the course of Christian history, this myth and ritual was elaborated into six other rituals with readings from the core myth and the other books of Scripture. This became known as Word and Sacrament and formed the center of the Christian tradition. The Protestant reformation is often analyzed, in hindsight, as the "effective but not total" separation of Word and Sacrament. Generally speaking, the Protestants took the Book and the Catholics took the Sacraments. The result is that both groups were impoverished.

The core myth and ritual of Christianity is prized because it is the primary expression of the salvific experience triggered by Jesus, the experience known as Spirit.[5] Myth and ritual are not secondary reflections upon the experience; they are the very embodiment of the experience. They are the privileged creations that carry the experience through time and history and make it available to each new generation.

This is what is meant by saying that the core myth and ritual is symbolic. When people participate in them with receptivity and openness, they can move through the words, gestures, and objects into the reality of God. This myth and ritual was generated by the experience of God and so is capable of communicating that experience. This capacity to put the participant into the living relationship to God that was revealed in Jesus Christ is signified by calling the myth the Word of God and the ritual elements the body and blood of Christ.

The Catholic boy in the story that opened our reflections is participating in a historical offshoot of the core ritual. He has been baptized, and so, in one understanding of baptism, he has been formally initiated into the living relationship to God. He has also been socialized into the Catholic, Christian tradition. He has been exposed to the theological understanding of the real presence of Christ in the Eucharist and has found it persuasive. So he is an open, if somewhat distracted, adorer of Christ.

What happens to this boy is that through no effort of his own (at least as far as he knows) this living relationship to God enters his mind and heart. He becomes conscious of the transparency of all things to their divine grounding. The mediation of this awareness came through one of the historical developments—Hours of Adoration—connected with the core ritual of Eucharist.

This is not a "squeaky clean" example of how participation in the core myth and ritual of Christian religion puts one in contact with the founding salvific experience. First, the myth dimension is missing during the experience. The boy knows the story of Jesus, but that knowledge is not an active component of the experience.

Second, it is not really the core ritual but a development which is significantly different from original intentionality of the ritual. The original table fellowship was a meal which involved active engagement with actual others and symbolized the advent of God's reign. In this paraliturgical activity, the interaction is between the individual and the holy object. It begins with pondering and wondering and ends in encounter. It would seem that the only hope of continuity through the labyrinth of historical development is the dynamics of the underlying experience.

But just what does the boy experience? He becomes aware of the host, his fellow server, the old women, and everything else in a new way. He perceives them in relationship to a fullness of reality which they are capable of revealing.

In his reflections on the experience later in life, he is leery of what "actually went on." Although paradoxical language like "talking without words" is fully at home in his religious tradition and he feels this expresses what happened, his adult, secular self is skeptical.

What he is not skeptical about is the truth he has taken from the experience. He is convinced people are more than they seem. He struggles with this truth and tries to be faithful to its implications. When he is not, something happens which reminds him of the uniqueness of each person in relationship to the fullness of reality, and he learns again this easily forgotten truth and reforms his response.

What can be said about this experience in relationship to the salvific experience which is expressed in the New Testament witness? It is partial and fragmentary but important. It seems that one of the effects of Jesus' table fellowship with people was the growing conviction of their uniqueness. The ending of the Zacchaeus story states that he knows what it means to be a son of Abraham (Lk. 19:9).

This signals the emergence of an identity to which he must be responsible. The boy's experience parallels this. He has a growing awareness of the unique reality that each person is, a uniqueness grounded in a transcendent otherness, a uniqueness that cannot be collapsed into the obvious and the observable. He senses a call to respond to this uniqueness and not just the functional dimension of relationships. What he experienced is in continuity with the experience named Spirit.

But this is only an inch of inroad into the territory the New Testament charts. It says little of sin and nothing of love, sacrifice, struggle, and hope. As far as communicating anything like the fullness of the experience named Spirit, this was only the merest whisper. But it seems that for most people, life is composed of whispers that gradually become a distinct voice. The rhetoric that the core myth and ritual of Christianity "re-presents" the reality and produces "repetitive"[6] and "dependent"[7] revelations assures us of the possibility, but it neglects the tentative and piecemeal actuality.

Receiving the salvific experience at the center of Christian faith is usually a gradual, diverse, and cumulative process of many contacts with its core myth and ritual. Appropriating this experience as the center of one's thinking and action is equally gradual, diverse, and cumulative. T. S. Eliot was correct in his observation that a tradition is made one's own only with great labor.

The core myth and ritual of Christianity reflects the artistic dimension of the human person. For our purposes, the artist in each person appropriates reality by feeling its fullness. Feeling includes both cognitive appreciation and affective resonance and unites both in the deeper center of the responding person.[8] Feeling responses to divine-human interaction are usually initially expressed in imaginative forms. Imaginative forms—poetry, story, art, music—are capable of a fullness of expression, of bringing the totality of what was experienced to light. They are also capable of triggering feeling-responses in others.[9] They have powerful interactive potential.

This potential includes the feeling-responses to reality that the people who created the imaginative form intended and the feeling-responses to reality which they were not aware of. Myth and ritual, as artistic forms, are multivalent and plurisignificant. They can evoke many feelings and many meanings.

Once, through myth and ritual, the living relationship to God has been experienced, other human processes take over. We "chew over" what has been experienced and tease out its implications for cognitive beliefs, ethical actions, and structural possibilities. But logically, previous to this process is the experience.

A story is told about a teacher who taught by poem, story, and art. He never explained the poems, stories, or art; he merely solicited responses of the students as they heard or viewed the art. This infuriated the students who were continually asking him what these works meant. One day the teacher put an apple on the desk. He asked the students what they saw. "An apple, " was the wary response, sure they were being tricked. "Is anyone hungry?" said the teacher. One young man was. "Do you want the apple?" "It looks delicious," said the young man. "Good," replied the teacher, "but first let me chew it up for you." Experience precedes reflection.

The artist's response to art is often more art. When we hear the passion of Jesus Christ, the thinker in us may puzzle over God's seeming passivity in the face of evil. The artist in us may compose a poem on suffering, tell a story of courage, sing a song of sorrow, paint a picture of death. Both responses, and many more, are within all of us, and both responses are appropriate. But the qualities and possibilities of the responses differ.

When the mind answers the experience mediated through the core myth and ritual, we move toward theology. When the imagination answers the experience mediated through the core myth and ritual, we move toward a new and contemporary embodiment of the experience. This new embodiment attempts to express what was found in the experience and evoke that in all others who come in contact with the imaginative work. Art and theology are complementary, but they have different ambitions.

The importance within a tradition of new, imaginative recastings of the foundational salvific experience can hardly be exaggerated. First, it is a sign that the core myth and ritual is working. In participating in the core myth and ritual, something is being experienced with enough depth and power to generate an imaginative response.

Word and Sacrament are the sun of Christian faith. When their inner energy is exploding outward, they produce the planets of Christian culture. When the art of a religious tradition becomes mundane or is gradually disappearing, it is a sign that the vital center is not communicating. On the other hand, when Christian-inspired art is flourishing, it is a sign that the core myth and ritual is functioning symbolically and initiating people into the experience known as Spirit. A Christian culture of poems, plays, novels, music, sculpture, and painting is not merely the take-it or leave-it periphery of the indispensable center of Bible and Liturgy. It is a sign that Bible and Liturgy are vibrant realities.

Second, the artistic creations of a tradition provide fresh access to the founding salvific experience. Since they are inspired by the living relationship to God expressed in the core myth and ritual, they have the possibility of evoking the felt-experience of that relationship. They are indebted to the privileged Scripture and Liturgy and continue its communicative mission in new ways. Their role within the totality of the Christian tradition is to make the experience known as Spirit contemporary.

The sense of sin may not come through in reading Genesis 3, but it is overwhelming in Mauriac's novels. We may become inured to the constant call for conversion in the Gospels, but it is immediate, real, and costly in the short stories of Flannery O'Connor. The emotional power of Jesus' presence might escape notice as we parse Matthew, but it will sweep us away in Zeffirelli's *Jesus of Nazareth.* Myth and ritual, Word and Sacrament, Bible and Liturgy remain the central mediations of the experience. But the artistic endeavors of the tradition reflect those mediations and create new, and often more compelling, mediations for each generation.

Our boy is not much of an artist. But like most people, given the right circumstances, a poetic streak shows up. He calls his revelatory experience the Day of the Haloes. He borrows what is all around him in the Church—statues of saints with haloes—and suffuses it with personal meaning. This image then carries the experience in compressed form, and whenever he sees a halo (they are hard to come by these days), he will be reminded of the experience.

The boy also articulates the experience in more expository language, but this language will not function in the same way. The image is evocative code for the total impact of the experience. "Day of the Haloes" is not a metaphor for the ages. But it does exemplify the quiet imaginative way all of us who are not Shakespeare express and communicate our depth experiences.

## Thinking the Experience:
## Belief and Theology

The experience named Spirit expressed and communicated in Christian myth and ritual affects the total person. It is not geared merely to the mind or to the affections or to the will or to behavior. It addresses the centered self, the person as ultimately constituted.

Jesus called this centered self "heart" and made it the primary target of his ministry. As the Church entered the

Hellenistic world, new terminology developed. "Soul" replaced "heart" and became the classic term for the primary arena of divine activity. If we could divest the term "soul" of its dualistic overtones and false competition with "body," its more powerful meaning might emerge. Soul is the ultimate source of all human activity. It is the hidden, unifying center of the person.

When God stirs the soul and the soul responds, the soul speaks the experience. Mary's prayer in the Gospel of Luke says it explicitly: "My soul magnifies the Lord." This initial language of religious experience has the qualities of immediacy, passion, abundance, and imagination. The language is rushing out of the experience, tumbling over itself in the effort to express what has happened.

But what has happened has been the immanent touch of a transcendent God. The experience is essentially ineffable. The soul cheerfully admits this, and then continues to bubble forth image after image. What happened is more than words can say, but we cannot stop saying words. Theologians often categorize this immediate, expressive activity as the first-order language of religion.

The mind, in a cooler moment, takes note of the soul's exuberance. The soul spoke out of abundance and produced a language of "prayerful explosion," a language designed to express and evoke. This language is rich in insight and feeling but not precise.

The mind wants a clearer cognitive grasp of what happened in the experience. So it inhabits anew the first-order language and through it explores the living relationship to God. Through this activity it comes to some touchstone truths and states them in a first-order language of its own.

It is not always easy to distinguish the first-order language of religious experience and the first-order language of cognitive appropriation. Some biblical candidates might be: "God was in Christ reconciling the world to himself" (2 Cor. 5:19) or "It is precisely in this that God proves his love for us: that while we were still sinners, Christ died for us" (Rm. 5:8). Expressions like these try to deliver the cognitive content of the experience. They might be called the basic beliefs of faith.

Our Catholic boy has cognitively grasped his experience as "people are more than they seem" or "everything opens onto something larger." There was more in the experience than these phrases capture. But the nature of this type of activity is to articulate the experience in a summary phrase in order to clarify its meaning. This crystallizing of the experience makes it permanently available. The experience ends for the boy, but he carries with him the distilled truth. His phrasing of the experience is typically secular. God is intimated in the language but not boldly present. The boy reflects the timidity of the modern mind concerning matters metaphysical.

Once the touchstone truths are in place, the mind begins to investigate these truths. This is the second-order language of theology. The religious experience is crystallized into basic beliefs and the basic beliefs are explored. Faith seeks understanding. Schillebeeckx tries to work out this distinction with regard to Christology:

> If we should affirm our belief that in Jesus God saves human beings ('first-order assertion'), how then are we to understand Jesus himself, in whom God's definitive saving action has become a reality ('second-order' assertion)? One is already a Christian in entertaining the former conviction, even though at the level of 'second-order' affirmations a whole range of nicer distinctions and definitions may exist . . . In a second phase of reflection the quest must be for a fitting answer to the

question of how it is possible that whoever is brought in contact with Jesus is confronted with God's definitive saving activity. In answer to this reflection on our part has a major role to play.[10]

The first type of mental activity called theology investigates the meaning and truth of the basic affirmations of faith.

From this perspective, the history of theology within a religious tradition is the continual activity of conceptually penetrating and interrelating the distilled affirmations of religious experience. This activity is fueled by the development of human knowledge. The findings of science, psychology, sociology, biology, and philosophy dialogue with belief.

The basic affirmation that "God is at work in the world" finds different conceptualities in Aristotelian and White-headean metaphysics. Petitionary prayer takes on new meaning in a Chardinian universe. The doctrine of creation unfolds slowly when it confronts the "big bang." Belief in life after death finds some unlikely allies in the mind-body debates of contemporary biology. The enigma of sin can receive a depth interpretation from psychoanalytic theory. The history of theology is an account of basic beliefs in dialogue with cultural knowledge.[11]

This mental activity is a drive toward intelligibility and coherence. It is running with the suggestion of 1 Peter to give an account for the hope that is in you. This theological effort is extremely important. Without intelligibility, basic beliefs languish. It is not that they disappear. The Christian religious tradition is enormously retentive. Everything gets stored in the attic; very little is thrown out.

But the beliefs that are not accompanied by intelligent understanding cease to be influential in the decisions that make or break individual and social life. It is not that they are actively refuted; they are just passively not considered. Without a clue to their truth and meaning, they are often maddeningly relegated to the "mystery" of faith. But this is merely polite dismissal. The real word is not *mystery* but *mystification.* Mystery occurs when the mind reaches its furthest exploration and lives in wonder. Mystification happens when the mind is paralyzed and lives in confusion. Theology which seeks intelligibility is not optional; it is essential to vital faith.

But the mind is infinitely agile. It does more than explore its kernelized affirmations. A second mental move attempts to extend the influence of the basic beliefs to all areas of human life. Most first-order faith statements have to do with the God-World relationship. They try to construe the flow of the ultimate relationship people experience. But this God-relationship cannot be isolated from all the other relationships which constitute the fabric of human existence. The religious relationship is the depth of personal, interpersonal, social, and ecological relationships.[12] As such, it attempts to influence how we perceive these realities. The theological activity that flows from ultimate affirmations instinctively moves to gather all realities "under its wings."

This is the integrating activity that is natural to all deeply religious people. If divine reality is the most important relationship of human life, should not all of life be apprehended from that perspective? So the mind works to construct an appreciation of everything within life from its foundational convictions about the Mystery of Life.

What does our relationship to God have to say about joining the military, sexual love, the distribution of wealth, fame, relationships with non-Christians, enemies, the exercise of authority, dietary laws, the way we worship, membership requirements, slavery, political systems, medical procedures, mental illness. This theological activity constructs a world from which to see properly the dynamics of every area of life. It results in endless "theologies of"—marriage, body, world, politics, and so on. At its best, this activity is the prelude to action.

This mental activity which is generated by the foundational religious experience is constantly interplaying with contemporary events. Time and history "throw up" new situations which faith immediately tries to comprehend from its unique perspective. How does faith see the problem of world hunger? What is the faith response to both capitalism and socialism? What is the place of technology when it is viewed from a faith perspective? What does faith have to say about the use of nuclear weapons? The Christian people at their best do not try to escape the conflicts and developments of each historical epoch. They attempt to create perspectives and responses out of their most foundational convictions.

The mind both explores the basic beliefs of faith and constructively extends their influence into the diversified concerns of human living. In a third move, the mind turns self-critical. It looks sympathetically but unflinchingly at its own religious formation. One of its faith affirmations concerns the depth of sin, and it knows that it is no exception to this contamination.

Theology attempts to raise consciousness about the processes of religion. How does religious experience and belief function in the life of the individual and society? The manifest objective of basic beliefs is to disclose the ultimate nature of the divine-human mystery. But the latent functioning of any given belief may be something completely different. Belief in life after death may state the truth about human destiny, but it can function to sap energies from the tasks of this life. That the Son of God died on the cross may be the supreme revelation of God, but it may also encourage a sick fascination with pain. The mind's passion for a "fullness of truth" demands that it becomes critical of the functioning of its own cherished beliefs.

This third type of mental activity focuses on the personal and social ecology of belief and theology. It is deeply suspicious and attempts to unmask false processes that may be operative in the espousal of belief and the construction of theology. An example from individual life might be a man who makes the cornerstone of his faith the belief that "the poor shall inherit the earth."

Suspicious minds ask why this statement has become so prominent. They may spy beneath this belief a convoluted process. These people may deeply desires wealth but are impotent to achieve it So they mask this impotence by espousing the opposite, and in this way secretly takes revenge on those who have the riches they want. Their belief does not flow from the fullness of religious experience but from distorted psychic processes.[13] The long-term effect of falsely grounded religious beliefs is the corrosion of the human spirit.

On the social level, this mental activity detects the ideological mechanisms in belief and theology. What is explicitly held because it is revelation may be implicitly reinforcing the prestige, power, and position of the group. After belief is stated and theology elaborated, the critical question is "Who wins?" If after a theology of salvation has been elaborated the Catholic Church is more gloriously reigning than ever before, the critical mind becomes suspicious. If the end result of a theology of ministry is that everyone is the bishop's helper, the critical mind becomes suspicious. If when the Gospel is proclaimed the chests of people puff with pride at how good they are, the critical mind becomes suspicious. The question "Who wins?" tries to keep belief and theology honest and make them true servants of the experience named Spirit.

The multiple moves of the mind energized by religious experience are beyond charting. We have merely mentioned three. Our Catholic boy has tentatively engaged in these processes. At the time of the experience, he had a belief that "Christ is present in the Eucharist" and some theological understanding of that conviction. Given the time and place—1954 in Chicago—the theology was transubstantiation by the power of the priest. For our limited purposes, it is enough to say that at that time that particular theology was intelligible and persuasive for him. It opened him up, made him receptive, to whatever might come his way. Intelligible theology paves the way for religious experience.

This illuminates a crucial principle of religious sensibility—persuade the mind; alert the spirit. If the mind is persuaded by reasonable theology that God is present to all creation, the spirit becomes alert to this presence and can consciously experience it. If the mind is persuaded by reasonable theology that all people need forgiveness, the spirit becomes alert to its own sinfulness and opens itself to grace. If the mind has a working and coherent understanding of Word and Sacrament, the spirit becomes alert to their possibilities. The ultimate purpose of persuasive conceptualizations of core beliefs is to sensitize the person to the religious experience which the beliefs reflect. Theology not only flows from the experience, but it returns to it.

The boy-turned-man has lost the theology of his youth. The belief that "Christ is present" remains, but the lack of a reasonable conceptuality for this belief makes him doubt. The theology that was intelligible in 1954 is not persuasive in 1983. When the mind cannot account for its convictions, the convictions lose their power to direct spirit.

Without a persuasive theology the boy-turned-man will not open himself to Eucharist as he did in the past. His new theology points him in the direction of interpersonal and social situations, and so it can be expected that his religiously significant experiences will be in those areas of life. People mediate the divine, and so it will be in relationship to people that he will await God.

He is comfortable with this perspective, and when he talks faith and theology, this is what he talks. But "deep down inside" he knows his sensitivity to the divine presence is indebted to the host that talked without words. He cannot yet make all the connections he senses are there. Like most Catholics today, his theology is incomplete and shifting.

He has also made, in a minimal way, the other two mental moves of theology. He tries to appropriate everything he comes in contact with from the perspective of the fullness of reality it lives within. He wants his conviction of "inner radiance" to be the permanent way he sees reality. He is not quite sure how to do this. More creative and constructive thinking is required.

What he needs is someone to help him. And like most moderns, he is hypercritical of religious experience and its communications. He does not talk about the experience. He is tempted to reduce it to interior psychological processes. He wants to know whether it has diminished or enriched him. Is he living out of an illusion, or is he tuned into the depth of reality? Modern critical consciousness has bequeathed an atmosphere of suspicion. This man has inherited it.

The formulation of beliefs and their theological exploration, extension, and criticism is the natural overflow of religious experience. A religious experience that did not find embodiment in myth and ritual would disappear, and a religious experience that did not move toward belief and theology would remain idiosyncratic and unpersuasive.

Once beliefs are established and theologies constructed, they function as legitimations of the experience and guide others to that locale of the sacred. When belief and theology are divorced from experience, the result is rationalism—the masturbating mind. Belief and theology that arise from the religious experience of one generation have the ambition to aid the religious searches of succeeding generations.

## Enacting the Experience:
## Imperative and Behavior

Jesus told a story, recorded in Chapter 18 of Matthew, about a servant who was forgiven a "huge sum" by a king, but who, in turn, refused to forgive a fellow servant "the merest fraction of what he himself owed." Although the story does not tell us, we can be assured that the first servant profusely thanked the king for his generosity. There was no lack of gratitude toward the magnanimous master. But when he hears his own recently spoken plea for mercy in another's mouth ("Be patient with me and I will pay you back in full"), he does not recognize it.

The forgiven servant jails his fellow servant. When the king hears of this, he calls the forgiven servant before him and speaks these angry words: "You worthless wretch! I canceled your entire debt when you pleaded with me. Should you not have dealt mercifully with your fellow servant, as I dealt with you? " Sin, among other things, is having a short memory.

One message that flows from this parable is to "imitate the reality you have known." From our perspective, the core religious experience contains a core imperative. The dynamics of the living relationship to God which comes to mind and heart in the experience named Spirit includes a drive to action. This drive to action is immediate to the experience and might be more basic than the need to express the relationship in myth and ritual and to cognitively claim it in belief and theology.

The ethical impulse is to pass along what has been experienced. The religious grounding of behavior is enshrined in the imperative: "You must be made perfect as your heavenly Father is perfect" (Mt. 5:48). It is also reflected in how people should view the behavior of Christians: "Your light must shine before people so that they may see goodness in your acts and give praise to your heavenly Father" (Mt. 5:16). The experience of God catapults the person into the human world with the divine agenda.

But the core imperative which flows from the religious experience is an overall orientation. "Be merciful. Be loving. Be just" are broad-based leanings. They are pervasive attitudes which qualify every experience from burping a baby to firing an inept cashier.[14] As basic stances, they direct our energies and ingenuity in a certain direction. We will exercise our creativity along merciful, loving, and just lines. But as religious imperatives they do not tell us exactly how to act in any given situation. They provide a dominant direction but do not immediately entail a specific project.[15] They need to be concretely mediated.

These mediations will always be imperfect translations of the core imperative. The imperative is a transcendent command which can never be completely embodied in any situation. Therefore, there is always the need to rethink and redo, to search for a more faithful mediation. The Christian ethical life is a process of action, evaluation, and new action. This is why many claim that conversion is not only the initial act of Christian identity but the continual atmosphere of Christian life.

The most familiar instance of how a foundational orientation needs to adapt and readapt itself in order to remain faithful is parenting. The parent's basic stance toward the child is love. For our purposes we will assume this pervasive attitude is generated not only from the fact that it is the parent's own child but from a living relationship to God which came to mind and heart with the birth of the child.

At one moment love plays itself out as protection; at another moment, discipline; at still another, the setting of boundaries; at yet another, the relaxing of boundaries. The living relationship to God sets the tone of the living relationship with others. The core impulse of the religious experience is diversified into many different actions. An apt analogy is that the core imperative is like a single ray of light which is refracted through the prism of "events and encounters" into a spectrum of responses. Guidelines for parental love can be established, but they must always be adapted to the demands of new situations.

As individuals age, they collect a history of what they consider to be the right thing to do in certain situations. This is the development of personal ethical wisdom and, when consulted, often comes under the heading of "sage advice." With collectivities, the process is similar but the results are often more enduring, resulting in the establishment of community standards.

A people living in the ongoing conflicts of history develop a tradition of ethical guidelines. In the confrontation between the core imperative and the concrete situation, specific responses are worked out. If this concrete situation is repeatable, these responses over a period of time become either law or custom or just the expectations of the group.

It is important for corporate identity to be able to say not only "This is what we believe" but also "This is how we act." To be part of the creation of an ethical tradition is different than to be the recipient of an ethical tradition. The creators are building the bridges between religious imperatives and concrete situations. The religious experience is alive and well and pushing to be recognized.

Many of the letters of the New Testament reflect this activity of fashioning new responses out of the experience named Spirit. What are the implications of this experience and its core imperative for offering food to idols, participating in prostitution, marrying an in-law, paying taxes, owning slaves, being married to a non-Christian? Forging ethical positions which are owned by a community is a process of conflict, argument, agreement, and disagreement.

Receivers of a tradition are initially in a more passive posture. To be born or to enter into a community of venerable age is to inherit its history of ethical responses. In effect, the communication to the newcomer is "We have seen this situation before. We are Christians who live out of love. The best loving thing to do in this situation is (fill in the blank)."

Often, religious and social sanctions reinforce these more-than-suggested behaviors. If the community standards are trespassed, the community's authorities may excommunicate the offender. And since this is a tradition of behaviors based on religious imperatives, the community, depending on how it sees its relationship to God, may declare the offender out of favor with God and predict future, divine punishment. Initially, ethical responses flow from the fullness of religious experience. But they soon become tangled with social systems of reward and punishment.

The enduring problem of receiving a religiously grounded ethical tradition is externalism. The behaviors are encouraged by the social and religious sanctions that have grown up around them. When these sanctions are no longer feared, the behaviors no longer appear desirable. Many commentators see contemporary Christianity suffering this fate. Ecclesiastical excommunication and eternal hell are not the motivators they once were.

There are undoubtedly many contributing factors to the collapse of this particular "sacred canopy." The most cited undermining force is the infamous "secular spirit of the age." But perhaps the more powerful influence is the contemporary religious sensibility. This sensibility tends to make a clear distinction, and at times a complete separation, between Church affiliation and true faith. Not to belong is not automatic disgrace. It may be the only path personal conscience can travel.

Also, for many people, the love of God has swallowed any thought of punishment. Afterlife, if and when it is considered, is seen as redress for the indignities of this life, not further indignity. But no matter what the reasons, the question arises: "With this external context of ethics collapsing, will the actual behaviors be abandoned?"

There has been a massive rational and pragmatic response to this situation. On one hand, the connection between basic beliefs and various behaviors has been spelled out. The dynamic reads: "If this is who we are and this is what we believe, this is what we must do." This is an attempt to move from external sanctions to internal reasoning.

On the other hand, there has been sustained argumentation that ethical living means good living. If we act toward each other in a certain way, our own lives and the lives of others will be enriched. Sinful behavior may appear to be pleasurable and have personal payoffs, but this is an illusion. The ethical behavior prescribed by the tradition is the path of fulfillment. Ethics is searching for a new grounding in belief and authentic living.

These efforts are certainly in the right direction and have had a tremendous impact on some people. Most importantly, they have brought together two of the major responses to the living relationship to God awakened by the experience named Spirit. The mental activity which flows from the experience seeks, in part, to view all of life from the perspective of the encountered God. The behavioral activity which flows from the experience seeks to act toward all of life as God acts.

These two activities come together in the unity of the person. What we see determines to a large extent what we are capable of doing, and when we do something in a particular way, we see the "object" of our action in a new way. But there is a real question whether Christian action can be promoted by spelling out the logic of belief and behavior. The underlying energy of both is the religious experience. Unless this experience "happened, happens, and will happen" the formulated beliefs and proscribed behaviors will remain groundless.

There is an indication that Christian ethical behavior springs from the activation of the core imperative in the concrete situation. A previous religious experience which grounds the imperative is assumed. Then something in the situation triggers the imperative anew.

In the parable of the unmerciful servant, the master "has compassion" on the servant the moment before he forgives the debt. It is this compassion that moves him to a new and unprecedented act. Conversely, even though the fellow servant uses the same pleading words, the forgiven servant "feels" nothing toward him. He does not experience the life of his fellow servant as his own, and so his actions are predictably callous. The hope for new action in an old world comes when the actual concrete situation triggers the core imperative of the religious experience.

This triggering of the core imperative is not a controlled rational process. Although it deals in the immediacy of insight, it does not deal in the torture of logic and obligation. The actual dynamics of the Christian ethical experience are powerfully revealed in the Lucan account of Jesus' confrontation with the lawyer (Lk. 10:25–37). At the center of this confrontation is the parable of the Good Samaritan. This parable could be isolated from its context and its tremendous influence in the history of Christian ethics discussed. But for our purpose, the contrast between what might possibly impel the lawyer to act and what actually impels the Samaritan to act is important. The distinction is between an argument from belief and a drive from religious experience.

The initial interchange between Jesus and the lawyer is a head trip. The lawyer wants to know what he must do to gain eternal life. In a Christian context, the inquiry is already misplaced. Salvation is the free gift of God, not something to be gained by human effort. The Pauline slogan—we are saved by faith not by works—refutes the question. But things are not that simple. The Epistle of James is an angry reply:

> What good is it to profess faith without practicing it? Such faith has no power to save one, has it? If a brother or sister has nothing to wear and no food for the day, and you say to them, "Good-bye and good luck! Keep warm and well fed," but do not meet their bodily needs, what good is that?
>
> James 2:14–16

The Lucan Jesus will negotiate this tension and bring faith and works together in the dynamics of religious experience and core imperative.

Jesus is typically evasive: "What does the law say?" The lawyer answers his own question with the double commandment to love. And Jesus, the master game player, closes the conversation with a compliment: "You have answered correctly. Do this and you shall live. " But the account tells us that the lawyer was not satisfied because he had not yet justified himself. And so another question: "Who is my neighbor?" With this, the trap is set. The one who came to test is about to be tested.

The mind of the lawyer is a maze. "What must I do to be saved" really means "What am I obliged to do in order to get what is ultimately good for me?" Deducing actions from obligations in light of ultimate punishments is an egocentric labyrinth. A loving response to concrete situations will never survive so torturous a process. The temptation to rationalize rather than truly reason is too great. It is often mentioned that as the lawyer hears the story, he easily excuses his fellow religious elite from helping the man in the ditch. There is the question of ritual impurity and exactly what is the higher value in a situation like this. There are many good reasons for the priest and the Levite to pass by. But the man with the best reason to pass by has yet to arrive.

If we assume the man in the ditch is a Jew, the expected Samaritan response would be "Good! One less Jew." But the Samaritan does not ask the question "Am I obliged?" At the sight of the man in the ditch, he is moved with compassion. A new dynamic is happening. He is first of all responding to a reality which is moving him in a compassionate way.

In later theological language, this is the movement of grace. The concrete situation has activated the core imperative which flows from the core experience. But as we have noted, core imperatives are not specific suggestions. It does not tell him what to do. It only drives him in a certain direction. But from what the Samaritan actually does we discover one important quality about the core imperative: it is extravagant. The Samaritan dresses the man's wounds with oil and wine, puts him on his beast, brings him to an inn, pays for his care, and tells the innkeeper he will pick up any further expenses on his way back. We are no longer on a head trip.

The lawyer answers Jesus' concluding question about who proved neighbor with the resigned remark "The one who showed mercy." The final, capstone comment is to go and do likewise.

But what is the lawyer to "do"? He is to live out of the religious experience of God's mercy which will make compassion not the logical motivation for his action but the very reality that carries him into action. In caring for the man in the ditch, he will be responding not only to the man but also to the grace of God as it flows through him. He will not be saving himself but responding to the free gift of divine love  by extending love to others.

Faith in God and charity toward others is the single dynamic of Jesus' experience of God. Christian action in concrete situations results from the triggering of the core imperative at the heart of the religious experience. The harsh truth of Jesus' religious vision is that only compassion knows how to act.

Our boy-turned-man has had the core imperative of his religious experience triggered in a number of situations. But, by his own admission, it has usually been activated because he has violated its intention. It seems his actual response to situations has difficulty in moving from belief to behavior. He usually forgets his belief in the fullness of the person and acts expediently.

But sometimes when he has tried to reduce people to their functions and manipulate them for his gains, the imperative has "come back" to remind him of their fullness. At these times, he has managed to reverse his action and find a new way to deal. He is surprised by the continual reemergence of the core imperative. From a developed theological perspective, the most appropriate comment might be that "grace does not give up easily."

But the more noticeable fact is that he has not integrated the imperative into his permanent style of relating. It is only a "sometime" thing, and his awareness of it usually arrives as guilt because he is actively working against it. Consequently, he has not developed the art of treating people in their fullness. The core imperative is not consistently overflowing into the specific situations of his life.

But there is some indication that when he does manage to act in accord with the imperative, he experiences a fullness of life that he cherishes. He touches once again the reality that touched him long ago. In the rarefied world of spiritual development, he is at a crucial juncture. He needs to grow more fully and appropriate more thoroughly the experience named Spirit that has been given him. If he does not, he risks losing it.

**Conclusion**

In the third century of the Christian era, the religious leader Mani predicted that his message would outlast the message of Jesus. The reason for this optimism had little to do with the quality of what he had to say. The reason was in the way he said it. Mani wrote books. His word would be preserved for all time. As Maurice Blondel has noted, Jesus wrote only once and then it was in the sand. The suggestion of that observation is that the depth of Jesus was not a message that could be captured in ink. Jesus was the bringer of a living relationship with God. It is this relationship which is his legacy. Blondel spells this out further: "It is in the hearts of men that Christ inscribes his living doctrine by the inner Word."[16]

But the disciples of Jesus wrote, and in the twenty centuries of Christian history, the People of Spirit and Memory have accumulated endless creations. These creations are the result of a ceaseless, dynamic process of relating both to God and the world, and they constitute the Christian heritage. An often-asked question about this inheritance is "What is essential and what is accidental? What can change and what must remain the same?"

We have scrupulously avoided this question, but have implicitly suggested a criterion. All the creations of the People of Spirit and Memory flow from the living relationship to God which is consciously appropriated in the experience named Spirit. Whatever is kept, is kept because it is perceived as essential to this relationship. Whatever is changed, is changed because it is perceived as hindering this relationship. This criterion may be hopelessly vague, but it understands the malaise that besets most established religions.

Religious traditions die because they lose touch with their God. M. Goguel states it this way.

> Religions usually degenerate in the end into a rationalistic theology, a formal morality, and a ritualistic cult. When in this way rites and practices are detached from religious experience, they can only survive as a form of restraint which the religious society exercises on its members . . . Sometimes a religion which is nothing more has ceased to live. To take religion in this state of existence and define it as religion is almost the same as taking a decomposing corpse and defining it as life and a living being.[17]

When people talk about the decline of faith in contemporary society, they are one step removed from the real problem. Faith is built on religious experience. If people are experiencing life religiously, they will be formulating faith responses. If a religious tradition facilitates religious experiencing, it is a vibrant reality. But if all its creations have become functionally autonomous, claiming importance independent of their service in bringing to mind and heart the living relationship to God, the religious tradition is in trouble.

The experience named Spirit is the founding religious experience of Christianity. It is not relegated to the past but is a present possibility. All the creations of the tradition are reflections of this experience. They flow from it and, when they are functioning properly, return to it. The most immediate expression of this experience is narrative, and that is what our next chapter explores. On the one hand, when we experience our relationship with God, we relate that experience in story form. On the other hand, the Gospels are the narrative renditions of the experience of God which Jesus made possible. Our concern is to map the interaction between our personal stories and the story of Jesus as they combine to facilitate and interpret the experience named Spirit.

## CHAPTER THREE

# STORIES OF THE SPIRIT

*All is imagery. Or, rather, all is experience which only
images can adequately convey.*[1]

*John V. Taylor*

*There can, of course, be no a priori proof of the critical
and liberating effect of such stories, which have to be
encountered, listened to and told again. But surely there
are, in our post-narrative age, story-tellers who can
demonstrate what stories might be today—not artificial,
private constructions, but narratives with a stimulating
effect and aiming at social criticism, dangerous stories in
other words. Can we perhaps retell the Jesus stories
nowadays in this way?*[2]

*Johann Baptist Metz*

*A* hundred years ago in the summer of 1961
when I was twenty, I was going to be rich. The source of my
wealth was going to be a construction job which paid the
smacking sum of $3.25 an hour. With this accumulated sum-
mer wealth, I was going to roll fat and sassy through the
upcoming school year.

The job fell through, and I was forced to do what I had done
for five previous summers: be a camp counselor. Of all the
undoubted joys of camp counseling, money is not one of them.

It was late in the season and I applied, with the help of the
seminary, to be head counselor at a camp connected with a
Catholic boarding school. This school took only those kids
who had attended the summer camp. The reason for this was

not disguised. The summer camp was staffed by eight nuns and four counselors. Part of their task was to observe the kids and sort out the saints from the sinners. The theory was that the best way to spot sociopaths is to watch them play baseball.

When I talked to the Head Sister, she was delighted. Not only did I have five summers of counseling experience, but in the fall I would start studying theology. She said it was the happiest day of her life. Before the summer was over, she was to regret that remark.

No camp season really starts until there has been a disaster. The campers arrived on Sunday night. On Monday morning someone was missing his hunting knife. By afternoon a baseball glove was nowhere to be found. By canteen time at nine, one of the campers reported losing $5. And you did not have to have "light years" of experience to know we had a thief.

It is difficult to know what makes kids eleven and twelve years old steal, especially if they do not really need what they are stealing. But one thing is for sure: they are really bad at it. So, by Tuesday afternoon, we had the culprit. Since I was the head counselor, I sat down with him.

"Why did you do it?" I asked.

"I didn't do it."

"We found the knife and glove in your locker. Why did you do it?"

"I didn't do it."

"Look it," I said, "this is only the second day of camp. We are going to forget this ever happened. No one knows you took the stuff. I am going to return the knife and glove—we are going to forget about the $5—and start over. We are going to wipe the slate clean and begin again."

"I didn't do it."

This kid was not afraid of me in the least. And all the time I talked to him there was absolutely no expression on his face. There was no light in this kid's eyes at all.

On Wednesday afternoon in a rowboat he stuck a fish hook in another kid's leg. And there we were again—me and the kid with no light in his eyes.

"Why did you do it?"

"I didn't do it."

"Stay here," I said. And I went to see the Head Sister, the one who was so happy to have me.

"Sister," I broke out, "we have a real problem on our hands."

"Before you tell me about it, Mr. Shea" (she was very formal), "I have a few problems I would like to discuss with you. About the record?"

"O yes, the record," I smiled. For you see I had been at many camps but this was the most Catholic camp of them all. Lights went out every night at ten o'clock, and to waft the little darlings into dreamland, they played Shubert's "Ave Maria" over the loudspeaker. I thought this was a bit much. So on the second night of camp I substituted a popular camp parody of the time by Alan Sherman: "Hello Mother! Hello Father! Here I am at Camp Granada."

The Head Sister wanted to know if perhaps I had acted rashly and introduced radical innovations into the life of the camp before I had sufficiently understood its spirit. I said that this was a possibility and that from now on I would consult with her. This was good training for dealing with bishops.

"But," I forged on, "we have a real problem. This kid is a flaming sociopath." I had not studied Mark Hart's *Five Words A Day To A Better Vocabulary* for nothing.

"Also about the keys." The Head Sister was still in control.

"O yes, the keys," I smiled. For you see the Head Sister

kept the keys to the truck and the car on her person at all times. And if you wanted to go anywhere you had to find her and beg for the keys. And she would say, "I hope this isn't for beer, Mr. Shea." And then I would have to lie. Well on the second day of camp I wanted the keys. The sisters lived in a semi-cloistered area above the refectory which had an old rickety staircase leading up to it. I stood at the bottom of the stairs and yelled up, "Sister, I need the keys."

"I'll be right down, Mr. Shea."

"That's okay, Sister. I'll come up and get them."

"Don't come up here, Mr. Shea."

"I'm coming, Sister."

And then I stood at the bottom of the stairs and pounded my feet, producing the effect of climbing the stairs.

"Mr. Shea, don't you dare come up here."

And then she arrived at the top of the stairs, habit somewhat askew and car keys in her hand. She saw that I had not moved from the bottom step and she glowered.

"You're a very cruel young man, Mr. Shea, a very cruel young man."

I apologized for baiting her with the keys.

"But, Sister," I finally got in, "we have a kid who steals stuff and hurts kids. We have to get rid of him. If the other kids don't kill him, I'm going to."

She said that it was impossible to send him home. His parents had dropped him off and then taken off for vacation. They were going to return in two weeks to pick him up. She had the telephone number of an aunt in case of emergency, but she would not feel right in sending the kid home to the aunt.

"So," she concluded, "we'll give him to Sister Ruth Ann."

"Sister Fix-it?" I asked. For this is what the kids called Sister Ruth Ann. She was a retired nun whose only concession to old age and arthritis was a pair of red gym shoes which peeked out from under her habit as she shuffled along. Her father had been a janitor, the rumor mill had it, and she could repair anything, and that was what she did. She went around the camp, painting, planting, and plumbing.

I did not think it was a good idea to give the kid with no light in his eyes to the old nun, but I had just lost twice, so I said okay.

The next morning at seven, Sister Fix-it shook me awake. "Which one?"

"Top of the last bunk."

She walked down to the end of the cabin. I could hear her say, "Wake up. Come. I need you."

Then it started. We would be playing baseball, and you would look up, and out past centerfield would be the old nun and the kid planting something in the earth. We would be swimming, and you would look over and see the old nun and the kid painting the side of the chapel. We would be in eating, and you would look out on the pier and there would be the old nun and the kid having lunch—two baloney sandwiches and two Orange Crush. Wherever you saw the old nun, you saw the kid, and wherever you saw the kid, you saw the old nun.

The two weeks passed and the parents returned. They parked their car at the back and were walking up to the refectory where the Head Sister saw everybody. The Head Sister suddenly appeared on the porch of the refectory and saw me sitting on the hill watching the parents.

"Mr. Shea, come down here."

"Yes, Sister."

All four of us—two parents, one Head Sister, and one counselor—sat down together. The parents asked what parents have asked since the dawn of time.

"How is our son doing?"

The Head Sister launched in.

"You lied to us. You told us this boy was doing all right. He is not doing all right. He has stolen other boys' property and viciously hurt one boy. Your son is very troubled."

The mother began to cry, and the father began to plead. "We know. He has been arrested for stealing, and he has been put back a grade in school. But we thought if we could get him into the academy, he might straighten out."

"Well," said the Head Sister, "it is Sister Ruth Ann's opinion that we should keep the boy another two weeks." She looked over at me and smiled, and in one "fell swoop" got me back for both the record and the keys. "But," she went on, "he will not be playing with the other campers. He will be working around the camp with Sister. Nevertheless, you will pay as if he was one of the campers."

"Anything," the father sighed.

Now this was a "clean cup" camp. Two weeks of campers were dumped, and another whole new batch brought in. The new ones didn't know the history of the kid with no light in his eyes. They asked me, "Who is the kid who hangs around with the old nun with the gym shoes? Think he wants to play baseball?"

"Ask him."

They asked him. He looked at the old nun. She said, "You go play at baseball, and when you are done, you come back here and we will hoe in the garden."

We would be going out to go horseback riding. The old nun and the kid would be "reconstructing the ark" which was at the entrance of the camp. The kids would yell from the back of the truck, "Wanna go horseback riding?" He would look at the nun. She would say, "You go play at horseback riding, and when you are done, you come back. here and we will paint the bench down by the lake."

# An Experience Named Spirit

We would be having swimming races, and he would be standing there watching with those lightless eyes. "Wanna swim?" He'd look at the old nun. "You go now and play at swimming, and when you are done, you come back here. We have much to do."

And so it went for the second two weeks. She let him out, and she reeled him in; she let him out, and she reeled him in. And at the end of the two weeks, the kid was integrated into the life of the camp.

His parents came for the second time, and they parked in the back and made their way toward the refectory. From the hill I watched them. The Head Sister didn't call me in. So I don't know what happened. After about a half-hour, the parents came out and went back and waited by the side of their car.

I think I saw them at the same time the parents did. The old nun with gym shoes and the kid with no light in his eyes were coming up the path that led down to the lake. Even at twelve, he was taller than she was. She had her arm around his waist and a glow on her face like a woman who had found a coin she had long looked for, and with each step, she pulled him against her. She was hip-hugging him as they walked toward his waiting parents. And he let her do it.

In Chapter One, we characterized the Church as a People of Spirit and Memory. At the center of these people was an ongoing experience that sustained and transformed their identity. This was the experience of God that Jesus of Nazareth made possible and which continued among his followers even after he was gone.

A shorthand name for the diversity and complexity of this experience is the word many were compelled to say when they interacted with Jesus—Spirit. Chapter Two suggested that the creations of the Christian tradition are parented by this foundational experience and, when they are functioning properly, lead people back to it.

We tried to explore this dynamic dependency in the development of myth and ritual, belief and theology, imperative and behavior. In this chapter we want to further explore an observation hinted at earlier.[3] The silent strivings of the Spirit find a Voice in the Memory of Jesus, and when the Memory of Jesus is heard, the Spirit stirs.

Men and women of today undergo events which, with the eyes of faith, are authored by the Spirit. But the religious significance of these events often goes unheralded. The Spirit is the permeating energy of the experience, but it is not recognized. The experience is appropriated in purely secular terms and its God-power does not break into consciousness. We find ourselves in the position of Eliot's impoverished people: "We had the experience but missed the meaning."

In this situation, the Memory of Jesus is brought forward to uncover the deepest meaning of the experience. Since the story of Jesus is associated with the Sacred, to use it to interpret experience is to disclose the Sacred dimension of that experience. The Spirit is notoriously silent; the Memory of Jesus becomes its voice. The first half of this chapter deals with contemporary experience told in story form and proceeds to the Jesus story. Although storytelling and story listening can never be separated, the concentration will be on personal storytelling.

In the second half of the chapter we will focus on what happens when we hear the Jesus story. The oldest Christian appreciation of the origin of faith is "fides ex auditu," faith comes from hearing. In hearing the story of the life, death, and resurrection of Jesus of Nazareth something happens. The hearers are shocked, stunned, turned around. Their lives are seen in a new light, and they must choose for or against the

God that is breaking into their awareness as they hear the good news.

What is happening is that the Memory of Jesus is triggering a new experience of the Spirit. The story of the Spirit-Giver stirs up the dormant Spirit in the lives of the listeners. The Christian code for this experience is "In remembering Jesus Christ, he becomes present." This procedure begins with the story of Jesus and moves to contemporary experience. In this section the concentration will be on story listening.

**Religiously Significant Experiences**

Our religious assumption has been that at birth people are initiated into a living relationship with God. The more immediate relationships of human living—self, family, friends, society, universe—mediate a deeper relationship to the ultimate Mystery of life itself. This relationship to God is alive and functioning even though we are not aware of it. We may be able to blot out other relationships by banishing them from our minds, but this is an ontological constant.

Two of the metaphors of divine presence from the Hebrew Scriptures are breath and blood. Divine influence is as subtle and as influential as the inhalation and exhalation of air and the rush of blood. The words on the wall at Delphi are eternally true: "Invoked or not, God is present. "

Religiously significant experiences are those times when we become aware of this omnipresent relationship and sense that some of the effects within us and within our situation have been stimulated by this relationship. Although we may not agree with Hobbes, who characterized life as "nasty, brutish, and short," much of our time is spent "getting through to Friday."

The practical demands of staying alive are the usual contents of consciousness. But there are moments which, although they occur within the everyday confines of human living, take on larger meaning. They have a lasting impact; they cut through to something deeper; they demand a hearing. It may be the death of a parent, the touch of a friend, falling in love, a betrayal, the recognition of what has really been happening over the last two years, the unexpected arrival of blessing, the sudden advent of curse. But whatever it is, we sense we have undergone something that has touched upon the normally dormant but always present relationship to God.

We have stressed Church and Tradition as the social context of people's experiences. In Chapter Two, we traced the ambiguity of a teenager's religiously significant experience as he encountered the creations of his community. But the arena of religiously significant experiences is much wider than interaction with the products of past Christian living. In fact, any interaction in life has the potential of becoming religiously significant.

Contemporary theology insists that grace is coextensive with creation. Grace is available to us in and through the events of ordinary life. Given this conviction, we sift our personal histories—events that occur in interaction with the products of Church and Tradition and events that occur independent of Church and Tradition—for the touch of God. Paul Pruyser focuses on this widened scope of religious inquiry: "The old question was: Which are the significant data of religious experience? The new question is: Which data of experience are of religious significance?"[4]

Another way to view this is in terms of what triggers religiously significant experiences. Church and Tradition have an enshrined set of triggers. Through hearing the story of Jesus, participating in the sacraments, attending Mass, meditating, engaging in certain prayer practices, people enter explicitly into their relationship to God.

But a second and more extensive set of triggers are the multiple life situations in which people find themselves. In situations of sickness and vitality, of questing for truth and struggling for justice, of loving and reconciling, of pondering the vastness of space and of traveling the inner, endless journey of the psyche. people come upon the reality of God. In fact, this seems to be the more traveled path to religious awareness today.[5]

The trigger power of the creations of the Christian tradition is seriously questioned. The presence that people used to find in the dark back of Gothic churches they now claim they find in the bright light of the secular world. Our interests are in bringing these two sets of triggers together.

But it should be noted that religiously significant experiences of everyday life are not completely tradition-free. There is a dual influence. First, the people we are concerned with were socialized into the Christian religious tradition. This socialization may have been more or less successful, but at a minimum, it opened their minds and hearts to the larger realities and questions of life. It initiated a sensitivity which is now operative as they sense the presence of God in their everyday living.

Second, the tradition is often called in to interpret the fullest meaning of the experience. The creations of the tradition do not trigger the experience, but as the experience is gradually interpreted over time, traditional forms are consulted to disclose the depth rhythms of what happened. The inherited faith acts as a interpretive tool. Memory becomes the voice for the silent strivings of the Spirit.

It is extremely difficult to categorize the different types of religiously significant experiences. The qualities of one type always seem to overflow into the qualities of another type. Any differentiation among them is never a complete disjunction. For our purposes, three interlocking categories are (1) mystery experiences which stress expanded consciousness, (2) conversion experiences which stress change of mind, heart, and behavior, and (3) revelatory experiences which stress the communication of a message. A brief rundown on these types of religiously significant experiences will lead us to our major concern: how people relate these experiences in story form.

Mystery experiences are times when we become aware of the larger Mystery within which we live. Usually our consciousness is narrowed to the immediate issue at hand, whether that is catching the train or getting the sink fixed. Times of mystery move our mind and heart to consider the wider, more encompassing reality of human living.

There are degrees of awareness in mystery experiences. Rodney Stark has delineated four possibilities.[6] Experiences are confirming when we simply sense the presence of God. In these moments our inherited belief has been empirically confirmed. Experiences are mutual when we not only notice God but God notices us. The relational flow goes both ways.

Experiences become ecstatic when the two-way relational flow is perceived as loving. That which I notice and notices me, loves me. Experiences become revelatory when God lets me in on the divine plan and solicits my participation. That which loves me has something for me to do. When most people think of religiously significant experiences, they think of some form of mystical awareness.

There may be expanded awareness in conversion experiences, but the major emphasis is on the process of change. The catalytic event of a conversion experience is seldom solicited. Something happens, and the person suddenly perceives her or his life as participating in what Tillich would call the structures of destruction. Something happens which throws new light on the person, and what the light shows is not flattering. The person then is free to change or remain in the destructive patterns that have been revealed.

If the person chooses to change, the conversion process is successfully completed. If the person hardens and refuses to change, the conversion process is aborted. The pattern of the experience could be laid out as destructiveness, catalytic occurrence, human freedom, movement toward new life. If this type of experience is to be religiously significant, God must be perceived as the energy of the entire process.

There may be expanded awareness and change in revelatory experiences, but what they stress is communication. Revelatory experiences are times when a truth about the ultimate Mystery of life has been received. In these experiences, the person responds, "This is what it is all about." Life may be about many other things, but it is at least about this. Although the experience took place at a certain time and in a certain place, what was revealed is applicable to all times and all places. The truth that was given in the experience is universal.

The truths that are experienced in revelatory experiences are not solutions to puzzles. They are rather felt insights into what it means to be alive. The camp story that opened this chapter would fit most comfortably into the category of revelatory experience. If this type of experience is to be religiously significant, the truth that is received must be perceived as given by God.[7]

These three types of experience become religiously significant for two reasons. First, either immediately within the experience or upon later reflection, a sacred power is discerned to be present and active. These are not just peak times or special moments. They can be investigated from a psychological point of view, and the mental and affective processes can be precisely detailed. They can also be pursued from the sociological perspective, and the cultural influences and social determinations can be persuasively laid out.

But for the person undergoing the experience what happened cannot be reduced to these two approaches. Psychology and sociology can illuminate what happened, but in the last analysis, they cannot determine what happened. The experience becomes explicitly religious when it is judged to be a time of contact with a transcendent otherness. Divine reality has made itself felt religious identity.

Second, these types of experiences are formative of our religious identity. Every person has multiple identities. We understand ourselves one way in the context of family, another way in the context of work, another way in the context of society, and still another way in the context of Church. One person is a father and husband, a plumber, a taxpayer, and a layman. Another person is a daughter, a counselor at a Family Life Center, a native of Kentucky.

Religious identity includes yet goes beyond these immediate forms of self-understanding. It concerns the ultimate self. As ultimate, this identity permeates all our other self-understandings. It colors or, in another metaphor, flavors our familial, work, societal, and ecclesiastical identities. Religious identity focuses on "who we are" in the final analysis and so influences, to some extent, who we will be in all the proximate situations of life. These three types of experience initiate, fund, nuance, or disorientate this ultimate identity. They are the real resourcing and conscious input into the living relationship with God.

## Telling Religiously Significant Experiences

We will use the story of camp which opened this chapter to explore the way religiously significant experiences are told and retold in story form. Although I have opted to use a personal life experience, I hope it does not restrict our reflections to my ego. Each person has religiously significant experiences that are idiosyncratic. They belong to him or her as him or her, and they find very little resonance in other people.

But other experiences are symptomatic of the human condition. They belong to the person, but not to the dimension of the person which is unique but to the dimension of the person which is shared with other people—the affirmations and conflicts of our common humanity. This story is offered with that hope, and like all true stories, in the hope that it will have a "Canterbury effect" and trigger the personal stories of the reader.

In general, three components of this storytelling process can be filtered out. In a certain sense, we touched upon these components in Chapter Two, but now we will consider them more personally and developmentally. First, people tell and retell experiences. Any religiously significant event needs more than one telling. Second, through the retelling of the experience, people form pervasive attitudes and outlooks about the mystery of life. Third, these enduring convictions and attitudes engender a certain sensitivity and precipitate certain moral struggles.

First, we tell and retell our significant experiences in story form. There is more in our experience than we are initially able to appreciate. So we tell it again and again until we are satisfied that all that was in the original experience is captured in our retelling of it. The experience has a density to it which will not be illuminated in our first halting and incomplete rendition. The surface of events may be easily remembered and narrated. But if an experience has religious significance, it is because of its inner impact.

# JOHN SHEA

It is the inner impact of an event which is gradually sorted out and claimed in the retelling process. We tell and retell it "'til we get it right." This makes it very hard on our friends. They sit there and listen, and in their honest moments say, "I've heard it." But the truth is that we have not heard it, or at least not all of it. So we must tell it one more time, hoping to bring to conscious awareness all that happened.

In "the time of its happening," a given experience may have religious potential. But this potential will only be actualized over time through a retelling process. It is important that the telling of the experience be in story form. If we give only the pattern of the experience ("I once found out that people only change because other people pay an ingenuous and creative price."), we cut short the process of personal appropriation of the experience through storytelling.

To tell the experience in a concrete narrative ("A hundred years ago in the summer of 1961 . . . ") is to reenter into the time of its happening. We reexperience in diminished form the feelings and insights of the event. In the reexperiencing we see it differently and "unpack" its meaning further. Storytelling has a power of involvement and appreciation that the mere noting of patterns or talking about experiences analytically does not have.

Another facet of relating religiously significant experiences in story form is that time is existential rather than chronological. This means that the person creates time units in terms of their personal impact with only a nod to the hours, days, weeks, months, and years way of counting. An experience may take place in five minutes or over five years. But however short or long, the time is unified in terms of its significance for the person.

The experience I told took place over four weeks. But I talked about it as a single experience. Many other things happened during those weeks which, if I was interested in pin-point accuracy, I would have to relate. But they had very little to do with the sequence of events that were intriguing me. Chronological time is a mere backdrop for the human process of demarcating periods in terms of their existential power.

During the last four years, I have told that story a number of times, in private conversation and in front of large audiences. Before that I seldom focused on those years of my life and only barely remembered that set of events. Why I should remember it, ponder it, and retell it suggests an interesting dynamic of personal religious storytelling: we remember past significant experiences when something in our current living resonates with them.

From a heavy providential perspective, it might be stated that we remember what we need. Anyone in midlife, as the teller of that story is, is dealing with the question of what is important and what is not, of where the remaining energies will be spent. This story focuses the question of time and energy for its teller. We tell the stories of the past to ground us in the present.

I have changed the story considerably in telling it. If we had a videotape of those four weeks, the recording would not sound and look exactly as I have told it. The main characters would all be walking around, and the essential flow of events would be happening, but the very words and exchanges that I have related might not appear.

If the story was told for historical purposes, this would be misrepresentation. But religious storytelling follows a different set of instincts. What counts is the revelation that goes on inside the person. The storyteller changes the surface of events in order to express and communicate this revelation. We are dealing with existential truth and not mere factual accuracy. The truth is built upon the facts and does not play "fast and loose" with them, but it has interpreted them in light of the inner revelation. This penchant of religious storytelling is extremely important for understanding both personal storytelling and the formation of the gospel narratives.

The stories of religiously significant experiences are as diverse as the experiences themselves. Yet despite the diversity, a pattern of reporting can be discerned. The report is usually an autobiographical or biographical narrative which carries, usually in a covert way, the fullness of what was communicated in the experience. But often an image emerges within the narrative which "kernelizes" the experience. This image does not replace the narrative, but it captures its core. As such, it functions as a code for the experience, anchors it in memory, and is the main linguistic medium through which it is shared with others.

In the story we are exploring, the image is "the old nun in gym shoes and the kid with no light in his eyes." These personal images, garnered from experience, become the secret name for God which each person consults. They are not naming an outside reality, but are construing the relational flow between God and the person.

To live within a religious tradition is to share the images of that tradition. The Christian tradition urges every generation to experience its living relationship to God through the images of Father, Mother, King, Creator, Crucified One, and many more. But as long as the relationship is living, new images will continually emerge. These images seldom function socially. They usually remain the private preserve of the individual. But they are necessary if the continuing personal and individual experiences of God are to be articulated.

A second moment of personal storytelling focuses on the pervasive attitudes and outlooks that emerge from the process of retelling. People are natural narrative beings. They love to tell the stones of the experiences that were important to them. But they also love to share the message they found in the experience.

Few people have the discipline to stay at the "basement level" of interpretation that the story, as story, provides. We move immediately to the first floor and with very little encouragement are on our way to the penthouse. "This is what I got out of it" flows naturally from "Wait til I tell you what happened." We supply a cognitive interpretation along with the narrative line.

At this stage, the attitudes and outlooks that have been formed in the retelling process are explicitly articulated. Since all religiously significant experiences either explicitly or implicitly concern the presence of a sacred power, the attitudes and outlooks that emerge from the telling often focus on God.

> After the experience of the sense of presence I knew, as Walt Whitman expressed it, that there was more to me than was found between my hat and shoes. It was up to me to find out more about that MORE; and so, as I see it, my minuscule will was linked up with the will that our forefathers called God. I don't know what that power is, nor do I call it God. But by it I live and in my slow, often frustrated effort to learn means of communication with it I grow, inch by inch, into a person more nearly resembling a human being than was ever imagined by me to be possible. This power beyond my own ego is not altogether beyond it or separate from it. It is as personal and "of me" as the color of my eyes, is friendly and reliable, resourceful and companionable. But on the far side of "me" it is a

mystery with respect to which I put my hand on my mouth.[8]

There is an aftermath to religiously significant experiences, a permanent residue in the subject. In this account, the person is formally stating the sensitivity that emerged from her experience. We do not have the actual narrative of the experience. We have the attitudes and outlooks that developed as a result of narrating the experience.

The attitudes and outlooks that are garnered from mystery experiences usually concern God. The attitudes and outlooks that flow from conversion and revelatory experience usually concern insights about people and life which God's presence illumines. The life truth that I have taken from the camp story is that people change, but only at great cost, and the cost is usually paid by someone else.

I am sure the old nun had shepherded many troubled kids before the one with the unlit eyes arrived. And I am sure it would have been fine with her if he had never arrived. But arrive he did, and so she took him on. I wanted to exercise that most venerable of Catholic options and excommunicate him. She exercised an even older option and was faithful to him in his sin.

I believe in change. I believe the destructive patterns that we, individually and collectively, get ourselves into can be reversed. But I also know that the reversal will cost. My own life, with its damnable balance of creativity and destruction, is where it is because of the price people have paid for me. The response to this costly redemption is reflected on by Hammarskjold: "The price you must pay for your own liberation through another's sacrifice is that you in turn must be willing to liberate in the same way, irrespective of the consequences to yourself."[9] In light of the camp story, this is really the kid's obligation more than it is mine. But even though I was more a watcher than an actor in the story, I feel compelled, as the Matthean Jesus puts it, to give as I have received.

The third component of the storytelling process is just the natural unraveling of the first two. The experience told in story form which creates pervasive outlooks and attitudes engenders a particular sensitivity and precipitates certain moral conflicts. Moral struggle begins with the move from numbness to sensitivity. It is only when we "sense"" situations in a certain way that we construe what must be battled and what must be promoted.

This sensitive response to present situations is at least partially determined by the past situations we have undergone. Who we are is prior to any situation we find ourselves in, and our past history functions as a stethoscope to hear the heart of the present.

Ethical sensitivity has many sources, but when it springs from personal experience, it exhibits a perseverance and power that is unmatched. Walter Gulick, in commenting on archetypal experiences, makes this connection:

> A person's archetypal experiences provide ideals and standards with power to motivate action. A person who has experienced the succor of redemptive love with archetypal intensity has an internalized sense of value which is quite different from the individual who has merely been taught that it is good to forgive and love others. The latter person knows that one ought to forgive and love others, but such a sense of obligation will be quite impotent when opposed by other stronger interests (especially if the other interests have an archetypal ground).[10]

Religiously significant experiences often begin in a receptive mode. The person undergoes a series of events. But these
experiences eventually influence behavior. People seek to live
out the meaning which the experiences revealed.

No one is long in the ministerial game before they know
that a big piece of it is fidelity to people in the grip of destructive forces. The old nun knew this, never sermonized about it,
and never knew she taught it to the counselor who watched
on the hill. The teenager dropping out of school has to be pursued; the grieving widow has to be "sat with"; the divorced
have to be patiently helped back to trust; the sick have to be
visited. What is important is the actual other.

The vast abstractions I so easily fall into are falsification of
the real. There are no poor students; there is only Mary who
needs some help. There is no problem of divorce; there is only
John who is hurting and needs to be put in touch with other
people. There is no drug problem; there is only Joan who by
noon doesn't see all that well.

For the storyteller, the ethical imperative which flows from
the experience is "pay attention to what actually is." All that is
important is concrete and actual. The abstractions are meant
to serve that. When the ethical imperative has been adopted,
the area where there will be need of repentance has also been
staked out.

As we mentioned, throughout this storytelling process
the tradition has been active. When a tradition is living, it
becomes the eyes and ears of people.

> Tradition is living because it is carried by living
> minds—minds living in time. These minds meet
> with problems or acquire resources, in time, which
> lead them to endow Tradition, or the truth it
> contains, with the reactions and characteristics of

a living thing: adaptation, reaction, growth, and fruitfulness. Tradition is living because it resides in minds that live by it, in a history which comprises activity, problems, doubts, opposition, new contributions, and questions that need answering.[11]

The tradition was obviously at work as I interpreted the events of that long-ago camp season. I suspect that only someone socialized into an understanding of love and sacrifice would read the events in the way I did. There is no escaping the "attention-directing" function of tradition.[12]

But the tradition also works in a more explicit way. It provides a language to interpret the depth of what is occurring. Language is a social phenomenon before it is a personal tool. People who want to express and communicate a religious experience inevitably reach for the language that is available within the culture. This language has a particular history, and any use of it plays upon that history.

Within a Christian culture, to "bring forward" the gospel language is to signal the sacrality of the tale. The story may be about toads, rattlesnakes, and rabbits, but if suddenly the phrase "brood of vipers" appears, a connection is triggered in the mind and heart of the hearer. It may be that a phrase is introduced for the fun of it or for purposes witty and urbane, or it may be that the teller is shifting the story to a new level, the level of sin and salvation. The introduction of the larger Christian story immediately contextualizes the individual story as a story of salvation.

The Christian experience as witnessed to in the gospel narratives can best be characterized as mythic history. The events recorded took place at a certain time and in a certain place. They are about Jesus of Nazareth and the personal, religious and political conflicts of the first half of the first century in Palestine. In that sense they are irrepeatable. They belong to the past; they have happened and are over. This is their historical particularity. But they are also revelatory events; they disclose what God is doing in relation to creation. This divine activity is not restricted to any one time or place. It is an activity that is eternally going on. What God made happen in Jesus of Nazareth, God is making happen today. This is the mythic dimension.

When phrases, images, and stories from the life of Jesus are interwoven with contemporary narratives the presence of God is being pointed to. When in Hemingway's *The Old Man and the Sea* the old man cries out and the author tells us that "there is no translation for this word and perhaps it is just a noise such as man might make, involuntarily, feeling the nail go through his hands and into the wood,"[13] we are being invited into a deeper level of participation.

For the simple and unartistic story of camp, the deepest interpretation is provided by the gospel story of the woman who lit a lamp and swept her house until she found the coin she had lost (Lk. 15:8–10). That is how the old nun holds the boy, the way a woman holds a coin she has found.

Telling religiously significant personal experiences moves beyond the idiosyncratic when they connect with the commonly shared sacred story. At this moment, the personal has "leapt out" of its individuality and is talking about everyone in relationship to God and one another. In terms of the images, God is the old nun and we are the kid with no light in our eyes.

Putting together our story with the story of Jesus is the way we discover the movement of the divine in our lives.[14] To return to a theme of Chapter One, the proximate players of human life are what are most obvious. Our stories always include the ingenuity and obtuseness of ourselves and others. When we discern an ultimate author at work beneath the fury of our intentions and actions, we talk about its presence by using the language of the event where this ultimate author was fully revealed.

But in order to be able to do this, there first has to be contact with the sacred stories. And more than just contact. We will be able and willing to use the inherited stories to talk about present experiences of God only if in hearing those stories the divine has been revealed. Only if we have found God in the Jesus story will we use that story to talk about the God of our own story. In the language of Johann Baptist Metz which opened this chapter, the Jesus story must become dangerous. It must be told so that life is imperiled and renewed.

## Ways of Contacting The Jesus Story

Most people initially encounter the Jesus story in a listening experience. Somewhere along the line someone tells us a piece of the Jesus story. Perhaps it is a mother who reads us a section of the Bible as we sit on her lap. Perhaps it is a catechist who first unravels the tale for us.

Subsequent encounters with the Jesus story also often occur in the listening mode: The deacon reads the stories to us Sunday after Sunday. The preacher tells them and comments on them while we sit and try to absorb. A friend has been born again, and we are on the receiving side of her rendition of the living Christ. Or we may have the good fortune to hear a professional storyteller fill our ears with the comedy and tragedy of the gospel story. Although we are in the age of the printed word (and many claim that even that is passé), significant contact with the Jesus story still takes place in oral-aural situations.

A second form of encounter is the reading experience. We may pick up the Gospels themselves and come in direct contact with the canonical version of the life, death, and resurrection of Jesus of Nazareth. This gospel rendition may be supplemented by a commentary to help us through writings that initially belong to another time and place. Or we may pick up a life of Christ by Endo, Goodier, Sheen, Prat, Guardini, Mauriac, Bishop, or others and, through their insights, find the story making inroads into our consciousness. If we are of an intellectual bent, we might encounter the basic story line in more speculative christological studies. But in all these cases, the dynamics of a reading experience, an individual in interaction with printed words, are operative.

A third form of encounter is the dramatic and cinematic experience. This is an extremely popular form of contact today. If people are asked for images of Jesus, they often respond by citing scenes from Pasolini's *The Gospel According to St. Matthew* or Zeffirelli's *Jesus of Nazareth* or the rock opera *Jesus Christ Superstar* or the musical *Godspell.* Many mainline church people feel this popularity is a misplaced emphasis. But the fact seems to be that these renditions are more fascinating and impacting than the staid socialization efforts of the churches. Also stage and film have peculiar powers of involvement and release which make them apt mediums for the rhythms of the Jesus story.

These are not the only ways of contact with the Jesus story, but they are the major modes. A common element among them which is worth noting reflects a theme we considered in Chapter One. It is people, always people, who are handing on the memory of Jesus. We have access to the Jesus story through a chain of mediation, a long line of personal appropriations and retellings.

It is through a parent's instructive voice or the evangelist's artful writing or Zeffirelli's camera that the story is made available. This does not deny the normative nature of the gospel rendition or the need for a teaching authority to correctly interpret it. It merely underlines the personal nature of community and tradition. The tradition thrives because people reexpress its core stories out of their own flawed experiences and in their own halting voices.

At a time when tradition is caricatured as an abstract burden and community slandered as oppressive conformity, the personal qualities of both need to be stressed. A story, courtesy of Reuven Gold and Hassidic tradition and drastically reworked by the current teller, is rich in suggestions:

> Once upon a time there was a very pious Jewish couple. They had married with great love and the love never died. Their greatest hope was to have a child so their love could walk the earth with joy.
>
> Yet there were difficulties. And since they were very pious, they prayed and prayed and prayed. With that, along with considerable other efforts, lo and behold the wife conceived. When she conceived, she laughed louder than Sarah laughed when she conceived Isaac. And the child leapt in her womb more joyously than John leapt in the womb of Elizabeth when Mary visited her. And nine months later there came rumbling into the world a delightful little boy.
>
> They named him Mordecai, and the sun and moon were his toys. He was rambunctious, zestful, gulping down the days and dreaming through the nights. He grew in age and wisdom and grace until it was time to go to the synagogue and learn the Word of God.
>
> The night before his studies were to begin his parents sat Mordecai down and told him how

important the Word of God was. They stressed that without the Word of God Mordecai would be an autumn leaf in the winter's wind. He listened wide-eyed.

Yet the next day he never arrived at the synagogue. Instead he found himself in the woods, swimming in the lake and climbing the trees.

When he came home at night, the news had spread throughout the small village. Everyone knew of his shame. His parents were beside themselves. They did not know what to do.

So they called in the behavior modificationists who modified Mordecai's behavior, so there was no behavior of Mordecai that was not modified. Nevertheless, the next day he found himself in the woods, swimming in the lake and climbing the trees.

So they called in the psychoanalysts, who unblocked Mordecai's blockages, so there were no more blocks for Mordecai to be blocked by. Nevertheless, the next day he found himself in the woods, swimming in the lake and climbing the trees. His parents grieved for their beloved son. There seemed to be no hope.

It was at this time that the great Rabbi visited the village. And the parents said, "Ah! Perhaps the Rabbi." So they took Mordecai to the Rabbi and told him their tale of woe. The Rabbi bellowed, "Leave the boy with me and I will have a talking to him."

Mordecai's parents were terrified. So he would not go to the synagogue but to leave their beloved son with this lion of a man . . . But they had come this far and so they left him.

Now Mordecai stood in the hallway and the great Rabbi stood in his parlor. He beckoned, "Boy, come here." Trembling, Mordecai came forward.

And then the great Rabbi picked him up and held him silently against his heart.

His parents came to get him and they took Mordecai home. The next day he went to the synagogue to learn the Word of God. And when he was done, he went to the woods. And the Word of God became one with the word of the woods which became one with the word of Mordecai. And he swam in the lake. And the Word of God became one with the word of the lake which became one with the word of Mordecai. And he climbed the trees. And the Word of God became one with the word of the trees which became one with the word of Mordecai.

And Mordecai himself grew up to become a great man. People came to him who were seized with inner panic and with him they found peace. People came to him who were without anybody and with him they found communion. People came to him with no exits and with him they found a way out.

And he often said, "I first learned the Word of God when the great Rabbi held me silently against his heart."

Contact with the Jesus story, no matter what form it may take—listening, reading, dramatic, cinematic—is a result of personal mediation. Effective communication within any tradition is always a matter of one generation holding the next to its heart.

## When a Story Works

To tell a story, especially one with religious ambitions, is risky business. Sometimes stories fall on deaf ears, as the storyteller at the foundation of Christian faith knew only too well. People hear and see and walk away. No impact is discernible. At other times, the story penetrates to the center of the receiver and "holds the soul in balance." People hear and see and stay to talk. Something has been touched.

But there are no guarantees. It is difficult to predict what stories will function religiously and what stories will not. As Ian Ramsey puts it:

The characteristic situation (in which God is known) may be evoked for some by telling casual stories, for others by telling wisdom stories, for others by telling creation stories, for others by telling purpose stories. In fact there is no word which, in principle, cannot lead to a story which might evoke the characteristic situation in which God is known.[15]

Storytellers work in the dark. Their hearers bring their beauty and blemish, their resistance and readiness to each tale. Who knows what will happen? Storytelling is always a wager.

Within the Christian tradition, the wager is that the stories Jesus told and the stories about Jesus will have religious impact. Two reasons we considered in Chapter Two make this a good bet. First, the stories of the Gospels are the chiseled result of religious experiences. The gospel narratives are the careful working out of the salvific impact Jesus had on people. As such, the hope is that the retelling of the stories will be re-creative of the experiences of which they are expressions.

What happened once will happen again. The dynamic sequence is original experience, creative expression, retelling, re-experience.[16]

Second, the stories are told within the larger tradition which provides the necessary atmosphere for receiving the stories creatively. Life within the tradition readies the hearer for a meeting with the Holy Spirit when the Memory of the Giver of the Spirit is remembered. The wager is reasonable.

Here is an account of a wager that paid off. The story of the death and resurrection of Jesus is told to a young boy.

> When I was a small child, perhaps five or six, my mother told me the story of the passion and death of Jesus. I had heard the story before and I knew Jesus would rise. But for some reason this time the story reduced me to tears. No, elevated me to tears. For the overall effect was that I was elevated. Soaring and crying at the same time. I don't remember how my mother told the story but the phrase that sticks in my memory is "out of love." Out of love the Son of God died for me. I also remember that at the time it was like a diamond was forming inside me. There was some sparkling, brilliant part of me that Jesus died for. I have never lost that diamond. My ultimate self-worth is something I never question. No, more than that. I call the "diamond" to mind whenever I am distressed. It reassures me.[17]

Here is an account of a wager whose payoffs are a little more ambiguous. The story of the death and resurrection of Jesus is told to a young girl.

# JOHN SHEA

My first religious experience, or rather the beginning of my religious experience (because I feel it is a religious experience to be alive, so I cannot say "this is a religious experience, that is just an ordinary one") was a very tragic one. I must have been 4 years old; I was sitting on a little footstool next to my mother, who read to me from a children's Bible about Jesus. I had no contact with my mother, but I loved Jesus, and the more she told me about him, for his kindness, wisdom and patience, for his being a perfect man, grew every Sunday. I was unaware, as his disciples had been, of the signs of coming disaster. I was totally unprepared when suddenly my mother told me about the crucifixion and what led up to it. I fell into an abyss of sheer black desperation. My misery was such as I have never since encountered in my life—which by the way has had its fair share of happiness and despair. If I had at that age known that there existed the possibility of ending one's life, I would have committed suicide. Some days later my mother must have told me about the resurrection, but the blow had been too heavy for me to recover in so short a time. What some people think of as necessary for us to reach an understanding of another life going on around and above and within our everyday life, this was the severest misery to me. I started to distrust the Bible, and what I heard in church. And at a very early age I discovered a difference between the Old Testament Jahweh and the loving father that Jesus taught us of. I remember that, although I was very sensitive to my surroundings, I discovered that real happiness exists independently of life's

situations, because there is in man an unchange-
able, inextinguishable source of happiness, a link
with the Universal Life. Although of course my
emotions, my knowledge and my capacity for
understanding have matured, I have the feeling
that my religion of today, my feeling of Unity with
all living beings, and above all the certainty of the
all-pervading Life and Love from which no-one and
nothing is excluded, is the logical outcome of a natural growth which began with this first desperate
moment of truth when I was 4 years old.[18]

These two different responses to the story of the death
and resurrection of Jesus highlight an essential factor of story
listening. The teller should check out with the listener what he
or she heard. The question that follows the story is "What are
you thinking? What are you feeling?"

Theories of narrative distinguish the implied reader and
hearer from the actual reader and hearer. The implied reader
and hearer should receive a meaning that the text embodies
and the tradition supports. The actual reader and listener may
receive multiple meanings, some in continuity with the meaning of the text and the larger convictions of the Christian tradition and some meanings that might be alien to the text and
the tradition.[19]

In story listening that is formative of faith, an extensive
and exploratory conversation must follow the story. A first
sign that the Jesus story is functioning religiously is that it
moves the mind and heart of the listener into the religious
zone, into the relationship to ultimate Mystery. In order to do
this, the story must cut deep, stop the hearers in their tracks,
grab the soul.

There are often physical signals that this is occurring.
Tears well up; attention is total; the eyes close to absorb the

impact; the hands hold the head which is suddenly heavy with thought. In the above examples, the story of the passion and death of the Son of God carried both the boy and the girl into a dimension of reality that suffuses yet transcends the everyday world. Both have been brought to a consideration of the ultimate Mystery of human life.

But more is required. The story must fill the "God space" it has opened up with feelings and insights that are sensed as salvific. The story not only has the process impact of placing the person in relation to the ultimate Mystery, but it also has the content impact of allowing the person to experience the qualities of that relationship.

The man who remembers his boyhood encounter with the story of Jesus talks of a "diamond." The metaphor seems to mean that he is valuable. The Son of God died out of love for him and that makes him a person of inestimable worth.

The woman who remembers her first encounter with the story also has a deep sense of an all-pervasive Love. But there is a quality to it that causes some hesitation. She might be finding this Love independent of life situations. The impact of the death of Jesus may have pushed her away from the conflicts of life into an "escape" love. It is difficult to tell from her account of what happened if this is the case. Further conversation is necessary.

The category of "over time" which figured prominently in our discussion of the retelling of religiously significant experiences is also helpful in understanding the impact of the retelling of sacred stories. There is "story-time" and "chewing-time." Story-time comprises the event of hearing or reading the story. Chewing-time is the subsequent reflection on what was experienced during story time.

Any ministerial effort which attempts to use storytelling must have structures for these companion activities. A religiously powerful story naturally unravels into insights and strategies. And many cherished insights and prized strategies can be traced to the impact of a religiously functioning story. Hearing, reflecting, and acting constitute the fullness of religious response.

Besides the awareness of Mystery and the qualities that "flow from it and into us," a religiously functioning story communicates an imperative. The natural imperative that flows from telling religiously significant experiences is also a component of hearing a story which has religious impact. The religious story has a "must" at its heart. We feel commanded to enact what we have experienced.

If we fail to respond to what we have found in interaction with the story, we do so at our peril. Religiously functioning stories communicate a sense of danger. We have been touched at our depths and we must respond from the depths. The man and the woman in our example stories do not tell of the imperative that flowed from the experience. But if they did, we would know more clearly the impact of the story on them.

We need a more action-oriented encounter with the Jesus story to underline the imperative dimension. This story was related at a conference on spirituality and the parables of Jesus: A couple, getting up in years, decided they needed some steady income-producing property to bolster their retirement years. They bought some land that had three houses on it. All were rented, and all the renters had a standard lease. One of the clauses in the lease was that if the renter improved the property, he or she could deduct that amount from the monthly rent. This, of course, was to be worked out with the owner.

One of the renters painted the house and began to deduct the expenses from his monthly payment. But he had not consulted with the owners before doing this. The first decreased check came as a surprise to the retired couple. On their way to church on a Saturday afternoon, they stopped by their property to talk to the renter and get things straightened out. They rang the bell. Inside a baby cried and dogs barked. The door opened. They went inside. Five minutes later they were in their car, fuming. There had been a brouhaha. They decided that as soon as this guy's lease was up they would oust him.

At church they head this parable:

> A man had a fig tree growing in his vineyard, and he came out looking for fruit on it but did not find any. He said to the vinedresser, "Look here! For three years now I have come in search of fruit on this fig tree and found none. Cut it down. Why should it clutter up the ground?" In answer, the man said, "Sir, leave it another year, while I hoe around it and manure it; then perhaps it will bear fruit. If not, it shall be cut down."
>
> Luke 13:6–9

Back in the car they decided that they would write the renter a letter explaining to him their difficulties. Then after a while, when he did not respond (and they were sure this hothead would not respond), they would refuse to renew the lease.

But he wrote a return letter.

And they wrote a second letter.

Then they got together on *their* property in *his* house. They said, "You shouldn't have done it without consulting with us." He said, "Just because you own this land, that does not mean you can come here unannounced and humiliate me before my wife and children." It always looks different from the other side. They said they did not mean to do that. He said perhaps he should have talked to them first. And the conversation went on.

When the couple told me this story, they ended it with: "Last week we baby-sat for the kids."

The story of Jesus is told. But who knows what response will be given? There is a need to determine if the response, both cognitive and behavioral, is appropriate to the story and the Christian way of life. In order to do this there must be a general understanding of the experience named Spirit. It is this experience that the stories are meant to evoke.

But this experience takes many shapes, depending on the concrete situation in which it is heard. What is needed is a normative understanding of the experience. This understanding will not solve the problems of what is a fitting or alien response in any minute detail. But it will set some broad parameters to know when a response has developed in a completely wrong direction. But before we investigate the actual contents of the experience named Spirit, we should look at two ways in which the story of Jesus is retold.

## Two Ways of Retelling The Jesus Story

We have been considering ourselves as hearers and readers of the Jesus story. But we are also tellers and writers of that story. What we have received, we pass on. We not only inherit a tradition, we contribute to it. What we have learned from the story we put into the story as we retell it. W. Benjamin says that the storyteller's tales are "based on experience, either his own or other people's, which he transforms into the experience of those who listen to his stories."[19] The life of each person enters into the retelling of the story. We become the living bridge between the past and the future. We become the tellers of the tales we have been told, and in telling them we tell ourselves.

The first and indispensable step to retelling a Jesus story is to ask "What redeeming power have I found in the story?"

There is no escaping this personal foundation for the retelling. Without it, all telling lacks persuasion and passion.

As we emphasized above, the story arrived in our lives through a chain of personal mediation which, when we retell the story, we join. Of course, we hope that the redeeming power that we found in interaction with the story is not so idiosyncratic that it has no resonance in the lives of others. We retell the story not only to express what we have found but to communicate and enrich the lives of others. But in order to do this, we must join the chain of flawed and halting storytellers.

Two ways of retelling the Jesus story are prominent. The first is to retell the story in companion language. The story is spoken or written in its more or less scriptural form and the salvific meaning is spliced into the narrative. This way of retelling seems to be available to all people. No special skills are needed. We simply speak back the religious meaning which we have found through the medium of the story in which we found it. This is a typical example:

> Jesus visited the house of Martha and Mary. It was a special occasion, as it always was when Jesus visited. Martha was busy about many things, not paying much attention to Jesus but scurrying about doing this and that. She looked into the living room and saw Mary and Jesus in deep conversation. She was envious and said to Jesus, really only to get his attention, "Tell Mary to come and help me." Jesus saw through it. "Martha, you are busy about many things, but Mary and I are sharing our souls." Whenever I tell this story, I always get pushed back into my priorities. The accidentals of my life are always getting out of hand. My "busyness" is always preventing my attending to the people I

love, and whenever I become aware of it, instead of changing I get jealous of those who take time for personal sharing and try to convince them they should be like me. It is a strange, perverted reaction, and the story always makes me aware of it and calls me to straighten things out. Life is more than scurrying about.

Interaction with the story pushed its teller into the question of life priorities. She came to some wisdom about life and expresses that wisdom by retelling the story which mediated it to her. She necessarily changes the exact scriptural form of the story to communicate her finding. The scriptural form, of course, remains authoritative. Hers is a spin-off. But it is a spin-off that is rich in insights and evocative for other people. She is the latest link in the chain of mediation.

A second way of retelling a Jesus story is to imaginatively recast it.[20] This requires the skills of a storyteller, either written, oral, dramatic, or cinematic. This way does not merely state the salvific impact intertwined with the enshrined narrative. It significantly rewrites or retells the story so that the redeeming power which was discovered shines through.

This is the more powerful way of retelling for it hopes not only to communicate what was found but to involve the listeners or readers to such an extent that they experience the power themselves. It is time to wager a retelling of two of Jesus' stories.

## All I Want is What is Mine

I never saw him. I never heard him. I never touched him. But there were those who did. And they told others, who told others, who told others still, who eventually told me. And now, in my turn, I tell you so that you, too, can tell others. And so, you see, there will never be an end to it.

Eventually they all came to Jesus. Even at night they sought him out. Perhaps better said, especially at night they sought him out.

He would be seated on the ground before a fire, teaching and telling tales. His disciples would be close around him, a bit officious, warding off the very people Jesus wanted near. They were always saying, "The Master thinks that . . . ," only to find out that the Master did not think that. Usually, in fact, he thought the opposite. But they never seemed to learn. That is why down to this day we call them disciples .

The influential would often drop by. They would stand, their robes unsoiled, at the outer rim of the fire's light. Their arms would be folded across their chest in grim listening. None could mistake that they were men of seriousness. When they spoke, their right arm would shoot out like a dagger thrust, then return to the sheath of their side. Jesus always said, "Come closer, we can barely see you." They never did.

The adulators would also crowd around the fire. "Hello, Jesus, remember me?" They would sit cross-legged, head in hands, their mouths open, their ears eager for every syllable. They would listen for hours on end, not understanding a word.

Of course, the ill were there. The sick flocking to the physician, as he would say. A man with an arm as gnarled as a washed-up branch on a beach. A blind woman feeling for the warmth of a fire she could not see. Sorrowing parents with a crazed son, tied round with ropes, his lips white with froth. The obligatory pallet bearers with paralyzed friend. It was quite a scene. It would be hard to say who, at one time or another, didn't make it.

And, of course, troubles. Always troubles. It was like each person was a secret tale of tears, and with him they had a chance to cry. A son who would not obey; a daughter who ran away. A husband who would not come to bed; a wife who would not talk at meals. A tax-collector without a heart; a priest without a soul. A land which would not yield wheat; a tree which would not bring forth figs. A lake without fish; a home without heat. Too little bread; too much wine. Troubles—and him there in the middle, the fire leaping, casting a circle of light in the dead darkness of the Galilean night.

Once, while Jesus was speaking, a young man pushed through the outer edge of the crowd and moved toward him. Although there was an urgency to his stride, there was no loss of poise or presence. He was robed in linen and purple. As he passed the fire, the signet ring on his right hand gleamed. He was obviously heir to more than the wind. All eyes followed him, including those of Jesus who had fallen silent the moment the man appeared.

He found a place to the right of Jesus and sat down. Then they found each other's eyes. "Yes?" said Jesus.

"Rabbi," the young man's voice was as imposing as his walk, "make my brother divide the inheritance with me. I want my share of the money."

"You are lucky enough to have an inheritance?" said Jesus. "I myself have nowhere to lay my head." He was playing with him.

The young man did not want to play. "I'm not an heir yet. My brother refuses to comply. All the rabbis since Moses have insisted that if one of the sons wants it, the inheritance must be divided. All I want is what is rightfully mine; what is rightfully mine is all I want. Tell him to give it to me."

Now Jesus did not want to play. "Friend, who made me a divider between you and your brother?" Then he looked beyond the young man at the gathering of people. "Am I now divider among you all?"

"Rabbi," explained the young man, "the more which I want is coming to me." His voice was as logical as a ledger. "I do not ask for what is not mine. Neither do I ask you to be a divider between me and my brother. I will be the divider. All I ask of you is to command the division."

All who heard him were impressed with the legitimacy of his claim and the clarity of purpose that informed his speech. All except one.

Jesus turned away from this petition and stared into the fire. He did not speak.

Now we Christians mourn because so many of the words of Jesus were lost. The words of the Word of God were carried away with the wind. But, Christians, trade them all, trade them all for the thunder of one of his silences.

When he finally turned back to the young man, the story was already on its way. "Once there was a rich farmer," said Jesus.

"He was well into his middle years. Not like you," Jesus gestured to the almost-heir, "still in the vigor of youth. He was rounded from the good life, as fat as a banquet calf. Not like you, lean and muscular."

One evening, while he was at table with his family and friends, the foreman of his farm suddenly stood at his door. Fearing something was wrong, he went outside to see him. "The wheat has sprouted in a strange way, tripling what we had expected," said the foreman.

"I must see this," said the farmer. He had a servant bring him a torch, and leaving his family and guests without a word, he and the foreman went out into the fields. The blaze of the torch pushed back the darkness enough for the farmer to see the superabundance. Somehow the seed had multiplied. Surplus was everywhere.

"The earth is generous, my Lord," said the foreman. "You are the heir of a miracle."

But the farmer did not hear him. Thinking to himself, having only himself to think to, he thought, "I need bigger barns to hold my more wheat."

"Tear down the barns and build bigger barns," commanded the farmer.

"Master," said the foreman timidly, "if we do that, the wheat already stored will be lost."

"Of course," muttered the farmer. "How foolish of me! All this wheat muddled my thinking. For a moment I lost my perspective. Keep the barns we have. What I need is more. Build more barns to house the more which is rightfully mine."

When the farmer returned to his house, his guests and friends were gone. His family had retired without kissing him.

The months that followed found the farmer anxious. Thinking to himself, having only himself to think to, he thought, "How will I keep all this more that is mine from the others who are not me?"

So he hired carpenters to build special locks for the barns. When they came to his land and saw the incredible abundance of wheat almost white for harvest, they told the farmer, "You are blessed."

"Will the locks be strong enough?" the farmer asked.

There was no celebration on the final day of harvest. As soon as the workers had finished, the farmer dismissed them. He wanted to secure the locks himself. When the last wooden bar slid into place, the farmer, thinking to himself, having only himself to think to, thought, "Now I will never be hungry again."

Now Jesus stared directly at the young man who was nothing like the farmer. "He never was hungry again. That night he died. Now tell me what will happen to all the more that was rightfully his? Whose inheritance will it be now?"

For the length of time it takes to rub mud on the eyes of the blind; for the length of time it takes to push spittle into the ears of the deaf; for the length of time it takes to breathe life into the mouth of the dead, there was silence.

"Then you won't tell my brother," the young man finally blurted out.

"No!" said Jesus. It was the only way he could say, "Yes!"

The young man stood and began to break through the circle of people, shoving them aside as he went. Jesus' eyes never left his back as he moved farther and farther away from him. Finally, he pushed past the outer edge. He was gone as abruptly as he came. The night swallowed him.

We might want to know more but more is not ours to know. The record is silent. Except that sometimes when Jesus was restless, he would tell his disciples, "Stay here by the shore of the sea. I will go to the mountains." Or he would say, "Stay here in this village. I will walk the desert." When he would return to tell them what the mountains whispered or what secrets the desert could not keep, he would often ask them:

"While I was gone," and his voice would trail off.

"If when I was away was there perhaps any word?" and his eyes would search the sky.

"Did you hear anything?" and he would fumble with words like a man afraid to ask but hoping too much not to ask.

"Is there any news about the young man who, more than anything else only wanted what was rightfully his?"

Peter hated to see Jesus like this—so tentative and beaten, not cutting his losses like a sensible man and moving on but worrying about what was over. So, as he tried so often to do, Peter consoled Jesus.

"Why bother?" Peter said. "He is gone. You have us."

The disciples were already seated around Jesus. They joined with Peter in telling him to forget the young man. The rich are like that, they assured him. The young man may walk away, but they would always be there. There was no need for him to brood. It was natural that some would not understand and reject his offer. He should not expect everyone to be receptive. Did he himself not say that some seed falls by the side of the road and is lost?

Jesus waited till they were finished. Then the Son of the Father spoke.

Once there was a certain man who had two sons. The younger son was a bird. He rode every wind, and played his life out against the sky where all could see him climb and fall. The older son was a rock, centuries could tear at him and he would withstand. He was as secret as soil. He made few mistakes, and those he made, he did not advertise. In his heart the father delighted in them both.

He would often watch them in the field. The younger son, stripped to the waist, would recklessly gather what he could. The row of wheat he harvested looked like the wind had reaped it. A village could eat for a week on what the ground still held. When he reached the end of a row, he would turn and yell, "I'm finished." Then he would run back to where his father was and say, "Look at all this wheat."

"Yes " the father said.

The older son, properly covered, moved over the field meticulously, like a man sensing a treasure was about to be unearthed. He missed nothing; lost nothing. When he finished, he walked silently back to where his father watched. "We still have the crops on the west to bring in," he said.

"Yes," the father said.

The day the father knew would come came. The younger son approached him. "Father, give me my share of the inheritance. All I want is what is rightfully mine." So the father called both his sons together, sat them down at table, and divided his money between them. When he was finished, he asked, "Is this fair?"

They both nodded.

"I have no more," the father said. "All I have is yours."

Within a few days, the younger son gathered together his belongings and inheritance and set out for a far country. At his departure the father threw his arms around him and wept. "O Father," the younger son said. He was embarrassed by this display of affection; his arms never left his sides. The older brother, who was watching this farewell, thought to himself. "If I was going, there would not be these tears."

Jesus stood now and walked around the circle of his disciples, touching each of them.

In the far country, Jesus continued, this younger brother was no Joseph. He was without his cloak in many a house, but it was not to walk naked and noble away from the lust of some Potiphar's wife. This younger brother was no Jacob who could mastermind two sheep into a herd. Under the guidance of this heir, the inheritance dwindled and disappeared. And when a famine covered the land, the king did not make him the overseer of the granaries, but a small farmer made him keeper of the pigs. And his fall was so great that he would have eaten the slop they fed the swine, but the farmer would not let him.

In this condition the son who once cried "See how much wheat we have!" cries "Who will feed me?" He knows. In his Father's house there is food, but he will have to beg for it. In his mind he writes the word of his disgrace. "Father, I have sinned against heaven and thee. Do not take me back as a son but only as a hired hand. " With only these words in his mouth, he moves toward home.

Jesus finished the round of his disciples. He had touched them all. He had missed none of them. He sat down again and waited a long time before he continued.

# AN EXPERIENCE NAMED SPIRIT

On the hill beside his home, the father waits. He has been there before. He sees his son coming from a distance, and lifting his robes above his knees, he runs to greet him. The servants who are out in the field watch the old man running past them, his breath short, his eyes never wavering. By the time the younger son sees him, the father is on top of him. He embraces his son and weeps down his neck.

"Oh Father," said the son, his arms never leaving his side.

"Bring the robe," said the father. The servants had gathered around.

"I have sinned."

"Bring the ring."

"Against heaven."

"Bring the sandals."

"And against thee."

"Kill the fatted calf."

"Do not take me back."

"Call in the musicians."

"As a son."

"My SON," and these words the father whispered into his ear, "was dead and has come back to life."

"But as a hired hand."

"My SON was lost and is now found."

The party had no choice but to begin.

The older brother was out in the fields. He had worked late as usual. The sweat of the endless day dripped down his face. When he drew near the house, he stopped at the top of the hill. He heard the sounds of rejoicing and dancing. He grabbed one of the servant boys and asked him what was happening. The boy said, "Your younger brother has returned, and his father has killed the fatted calf and is rejoicing."

"Go," said the older brother, "and tell my father I will not party with him."

The servant boy entered the house and within moments the father came out of his home. He pulled his robe above his knees and, out of breath but with his eyes unwavering, climbed up the hill to where his older son was standing.

"O my beloved son!" the father said, and embracing him, he wept upon his neck.

"All these years," said the older brother, his arms at his sides, "I have slaved for you."

"O my beloved son!" said the father. And with the sleeve of his robe, he wiped the sweat of the slave from his son's forehead.

"And you have never given me a calf so that I might party with my friends. But this son of yours comes groveling home having squandered your inheritance with whores, and for him, for him, you kill the fatted calf."

"O my beloved son!" said the father a third time. "You have been with me always, and all I have is yours. But if any son of mine was lost, surely this feast will find him. If any brother you know is dead, surely this party will bring him to life." Then the father kissed both of the earth-hardened hands of his oldest son.

Suddenly the father was old. He was a tired man. He turned and moved back down the hill. When he reached the bottom, he noticed his younger son had come out of the house. The robe he had put on him had slid off one shoulder. The ring he had given him had been too large for his starved finger and barely clung to the knuckle. The leather of the new sandals had already cut a ridge on his ankles. The father looked back up at his oldest son. He seemed to be frowning. The sweat of the slave was still on him. Between them both stood the father.

The music from the party that at the moment none of them were at drifted from the house and hung in the air between the three of them. Suddenly the father was no longer tired. He lifted his robes, and there between the son on the hill and the son outside the house, the joy of his heart overflowed into his feet. In broken rhythm he began to dance, hoping the music he could not resist would find the hearts of the two brothers and bring his sons, his true inheritance, back to him.

Jesus now looked at Peter and said, "Why bother?"

The man who once saw in the flesh of his friend the radiance of God saw it again. "Because a man always has two sons," Peter said.

Jesus lept up. A great cry of joy rang out from him. And from where Peter sat it seemed his hands touched the sky and his outstretched arms were wide enough to welcome everyone.

These are two of the stories which I must tell you because they have been told to me. And now that you have heard, you must tell others. But if all the forests that ever were were cut down and all the wood from those forests turned to paper and all the quills that ever were were dipped into all the ink that ever was and those quills put into the hands of all the scribes that ever wrote, even then not all that Jesus Christ did and said while he lived among us in the flesh could be recorded. But I tell you these things so that we may have life

## Love and Power

"What are you thinking? What are you feeling?" Two stories of Jesus have been retold. What they will evoke is determined by how they intersect the life of the hearer. And since hearers are always unique people, what happens in the wake of the story is very individualized. Someone fourteen will hear them differently from someone sixty-five. The rich will reflect and act in one way; the poor in another. Diversity of response is the name of the game.

But the story of Jesus in the Gospels is a witness to the experience named Spirit he made possible. When it is retold, it is supposed to evoke experiences that are in continuity with that original experience. The story of Jesus is not totally open-ended; it is not an ink-blot. It has some abiding concerns which should be present in every response to it.

The abiding concerns of the experience named Spirit are love and power. John Taylor's suggestion in the quotation that opened this chapter is that imagery carries the fullness of experience. Jesus' imagery for his experience of God was Abba and King. *Abba* is the familiar and intimate form of father. Although it plays upon the Hebrew tradition of father imagery for God, it seems to be unique to Jesus.

> The Abba experience would appear to be the source of the peculiar nature of Jesus' message and conduct, which without this religious experience, or apart from it, lose the distinctive meaning and content actually conferred on them by Jesus.[21]

*Abba* stresses the aspects of trust and intimacy. Most importantly, it is a word spoken in love.

*Kingdom of God* does not evoke tender feelings. Norman Perrin says that it was a symbol that evoked a myth, and the myth was that God was acting as king on behalf of his people.[22] King conjures up power. James Dunn sums up Jesus' use of language with the remark:

> With Jesus, in short, we see the freshness of an original mind, a new spirit, taking up old categories and concepts, remoulding them, creating them afresh, using them in a wholly new way in the light of his basic experience of God caring and commanding

him and of being bound to God by the closest ties
of obedience and love.[23]

The genius of Jesus was to hold together two images
which tend to go off on their own: God is a father who would
be king and a king who would be father. The abiding concerns
of the experience named Spirit are power and love.

A few remarks about how images function in relationship
to religious experience will help us explore this Abba-King
experience. First, the images are not the reality. The images
illumine the experience, but they do not exhaust it. It is an
experience of divine reality which the images seek to serve
and so there is always a transcendent dimension which
remains unexplored.

In other words, the images always break under the
weight of what is encountered in the experience. When this is
forgotten, the images no longer function as a pathway into
the mystery of God and people. Instead they take up residence
in the mind and link up with other ideas to form a worldview.
Although this in itself is not necessarily a bad move, it is
not a substitute for the image as a communicator of a
lived relationship.

Second, the images are drawn from certain areas of the
human condition in order to illumine the experience, but
also the experience is allowed to "talk back to" those areas.
Abba and King are drawn from the metaphoric fields of family life and government. To call God Abba is to try to experience and understand God from an analogy with the world of
parenting. To use this image is to bestow an honor on family living. It is so important a part of the human scene that it
can be used to understand the source of human life itself. To
call God King is to try to experience and understand divine

reality from an analogy with the world of governing. This is also a compliment. It points to the crucial importance of politics for human life.

But what begins as a compliment often ends as a critique. For to use the images of Abba and King means to draw the human world of parenting and politics into the experience of God. In this atmosphere, parenting and politics undergoes both affirmation and critique. What is happening in the human world that is congruent with the religious experience is supported. What is happening in the human world that is out of sync with the religious experience is critiqued with the divine command to change.

The flow between the world of the image and the world of the experience is two-way.[24] This is the key to understanding why Jesus took images from the patriarchal family and the ruling class. In that way he brought them under the experience of God and urged upon them the necessity to change.

Third, these images are open-ended and, therefore, are in need of further speech to express and convey the true meaning of the experience. In other words, what is the point of the comparison? Is to call God a potter to suggest that we are inert matter to be molded as a greater power wills? Is to call God a shepherd to designate ourselves as passive sheep? To miss the point of a comparison is to end up in either humorous or disastrous understandings.

> When the psalmist tells us that a united family is like oil dripping down Aaron's beard onto the skirts of his robe, he is not trying to persuade us that the family unity is messy, greasy, or volatile; he is thinking of the all-pervasive fragrance which has so deeply impressed itself on his memory at the anointing of the high priest (Ps. 133:2).[25]

In order to accurately express and convey the religious experience the image must be further specified by story; and the story must be held in constant tension with the felt perception of the experience.

The image of Jesus for his experience of divine reality is not just Abba, but the Abba unfolded in many mini-stories and one major parable. It is not just "any old father" but the father who appears again and again in the conversation of Jesus and to whom his prayer and the prayer of his followers is addressed.

The image of King is not just any King, but the King who banquets with the uninvited, gives money to servants, and freely forgives debts. Although Father and King are images rooted in human experiences that are relatively common, they cannot be interpreted in so general a fashion. It is the activities of the King and Father who are portrayed in the Gospels that give the correct content to the image. The words that this Father and King are made to speak, the attitudes he is said to have, and the actions that we are told he delights in are the clues to what the experience is like. We must allow the abiding concerns of love and power that the images evoke to be specified by the stories.

In the contemporary climate, the need to relate precisely the images of Abba and King to the religious experience which grounds them is particularly acute. For in these images many people see the distortion of the true nature of Christian faith and the source of endless oppression.

The main charge, among many, is that they have been used as the ideological bolstering of sexist and classist privilege. The Father and King God is the energizing source and validation for the second-class status of women and the maintenance of oppressive political structures. It provides a rationalization in the very nature of reality itself for some of the worst human instincts. To uncover the true religious dynamics of love and power present in these images does not answer the pastoral question of their use. It will only once again establish the insidious tendency of human nature to use what was meant to bind us together—an interlocking of love and power—to tear us apart.

In the next two chapters we will try to trace the dynamics of the experience named Spirit as it is expressed in the gospel witness. Abba and King have provided the framework for our exploration. The experience may concern many different feelings and insights, but its pervasive atmosphere will be the issues of love and power. Our ambition is a greater appreciation of how divine and human love and power interact. To gain this appreciation we will inhabit the story of Jesus to see what it discloses to us about God, ourselves, and our neighbor. What is this experience named Spirit that the last three chapters have flirted with?

## CHAPTER FOUR

# AN EXPERIENCE NAMED SPIRIT: DIVINE LOVE

*In religion there lurks the fear that we invented the story of God's love.*[1]

*Sebastian Moore*

*In vain, my Christ, in vain, two thousand years have gone by and men crucify You still. When will You be born, my Christ, and not be crucified any more, but live among us for eternity.*[2]

*Nikos Kazantzukis*

*T*he silent sky suddenly spoke love to Jesus in the waters of sin. This seems to be the symbolic essential of the baptism accounts in Matthew, Mark, and Luke. The sky is the primordial symbol of transcendence. In times when faith is strong, it is the home of God who watches and cares for all creatures. In times when faith is weak, it is a wasteland, alternately blue and stormy, which silently oversees the struggles of earth. The religious imagination paints pictures on the sky to communicate its overriding vision of the meaning and truth of human life.

In the baptism of Jesus, the last black hole at the end of our telescopic eyes has a larynx. The sky speaks. The divine initiates the communication. In matters religious, people are receivers before they are actors. In a primary biblical metaphor, before they can be sent, they must first be contacted. The

Word of the Lord has to arrive before the prophet can sally forth.

The sudden voice from the sky reverses a cherished pose of modernity—the human voice shouting at a silent sky and often accompanied by an angry fist. We fancy ourselves as constant communicators and God, at best, as a good listener. But the story implies a different flow to the divine-human relationship. The transcendent reality begins the conversation, not with pleasantries about the weather, but with direct address.

"You are my beloved Son. On you my favor rests" (Lk. 3:22). The word from the sky is *Son.* Although in this narrative we do not have Jesus' response, we have it elsewhere. As we saw at the end of Chapter Three, Jesus speaks back "Abba." This becomes one of his privileged images of God.

But it must be remembered that Jesus had the audacity to call God Abba because God first had the graciousness to call Jesus Son. Lest this image of Son go astray, the specifying adjective "beloved" accompanies it. The word from the sky is generative love.

The boldness of this communication often escapes us. Not only has the notoriously silent sky become loquacious, but it is saying what we deeply hope for but which we have great difficulty believing: we are loved by the transcendent reality within which we live. The evidence that this basic affirmation is true is exceedingly ambiguous. A good deal of our reflection in this chapter will be to explore this foundational conviction of Christian faith. But in this narrative, God is unburdening his heart, blurting out his love.

Jesus receives divine love in the waters of sin. The baptism of Jesus by John in the Jordan has high historical probability. Scholars think that the early Church would not have constructed a baptism story for theological purposes. In fact, the baptism of Jesus was something of a theological embarrassment. In the first place, if John baptizes Jesus, is not John greater than Jesus? Matthew is aware of this problem and in his version has John defer to Jesus: "I should be baptized by you, yet you come to me!" (Mt. 3:14).

But the deeper embarrassment comes with the development of the christological confession of Jesus' sinlessness. Why is the sinless Son of God receiving a baptism which signifies the forgiveness of sins? Under the influence of this high Christology, the Gospel of John omits the actual baptism. John the Baptist is the forerunner of Christ and witnesses to him when he arrives, but he does not encounter him in the waters of sin.

However these theological difficulties are resolved, the historical fact seems to be that Jesus was baptized in the Jordan. But this event was remembered not merely because it happened. Much that happened has been forgotten. James D. G. Dunn suggests that it was retained in the Good News because it was a major experience for Jesus.

Jesus' baptism by John was probably the occasion for an experience of God which had epochal significance for Jesus, even though that significance may only have been fully grasped after some reflection by Jesus.[3]

But the synoptic accounts of the baptism have all the earmarks of mythic history. They are at one and the same time a rendering of the religious experience of Jesus and a revelation of how God works everywhere. The story of Jesus' baptism reflects the stories of all people. In a more precise phrasing, the experience of Jesus, mythically expressed in the baptism narratives, is made available through Jesus to all people.

The interactive center of the baptism story is divine love encountering human sinfulness. That is the symbolic reason why Jesus is in the waters of sin. In order to take away the sins of the world, he first had to take them on. He enters the Jordan not to be cleansed, but to be stained. Unless the Son of God in Paul's language becomes sin, he will not meet us where we are.

The sober truth seems to be that the arrival of divine love always finds us, to some degree, loveless. The lovelessness of the life God encounters is not simply a brute fact. We may not have started the destructiveness that characterizes human existence. But at a minimum, we have "gone along," and at a maximum, we have actively promoted it. We have participated and extended the power of sin. That is why divine love is characterized as forgiveness, and the experience Jesus triggered in people takes the form of repentance and conversion. James Mackey spells out this dynamic:

> When first there is invoked in us the experience of being valued and cherished as a gift is valued, we are already in complicity with the destruction and decay which form the ambivalence of existence. We have already grasped at possessions or power for our security, thrown up the barriers, and sown the seeds of hatred, if we have not actually deprived others of the means of subsistence, or maimed or killed. We are already guilty, and to the guilty the sense of being valued and cherished and accepted comes across necessarily as a sense of being forgiven.[4]

Two sets of tears accompany divine love—tears of remorse for our sin and tears of joy for our acceptance.

But the voice is not the only visitor from the sky. The Spirit descends. As we saw in Chapter One, Spirit is the image for the sustaining and transforming power of God. The Spirit and the Voice together reveal the nature of the divine presence which Jesus will mediate. It will be powerful love. The love the Voice proclaims is not effete or sentimental, but the ultimate force of the world.

When this powerful love is at work overcoming sin, another image comes into play: we say the Kingdom of God is present. Kingdom happens when people respond to the power of divine love.

So far as Jesus was concerned, the exercise of this power was evidence that the longed-for kingdom of God had already come upon his hearers . . . The eschatological kingdom was present for Jesus only because the eschatological Spirit was present in and through him.[5]

Put simply, love is power. But what is this powerful love or loving power doing?

The Spirit descends as a dove. The dove image resonates with the narratives of creation and flood from the Hebrew Scriptures. The Spirit, imaged as a bird with outstretched wings, hovers over the water at the dawn of the world, and the dove returns with the olive branch of peace to Noah's ark. These function as clues to the Spirit's work. Through Jesus, God will be recreating and reconciling people to their divine source and to each other. The dove of Jesus may contrast with the fire of John. God's advent for John is judgment and separation; for Jesus it is healing and renewal. When divine love meets human sinfulness, the person is reconciled and recreated. Whenever this happens, the ultimate author of the event is the Spirit.

This poetic exploration of the baptism of Jesus has disclosed that divine loving power interacts with human sinfulness in the hope of a recreated person and reconciliation between people. These are the structural dynamics of the experience named Spirit. In Chapter One, we focused on the Christian origins of this experience in the life of Jesus and its continuance in the life of Church, the People of Spirit and Memory.

In Chapter Two, we construed the creations of the People of Spirit and Memory as flowing from this experience and ultimately trying to lead people back to it. In Chapter Three, we explored the story of Jesus as both the interpreter and catalyst of this experience. In this chapter and the next, we hope to trace the dynamics of the experience itself. This chapter will investigate the initiating divine love and the following chapter the responding human love. If the experience named Spirit could be compressed into a single word, it would be *love.*

In unpacking the experience named Spirit, what is claimed or, better, what is disclaimed should be made clear. It is not claimed that what will follow was the experience of Jesus, although something like it may have happened to him. The pitfalls of trying to uncover Jesus' self-understanding are well-known, and the impossibility of retrieving his actual consciousness is even better known.[6] Nor is it claimed that this was the experience of the disciples and the early Church, although something similar to this may have happened to them.

Our interpretation of the experience named Spirit is not an attempt at historical reconstruction. All that is offered is what the writer has found growing up and living within the Catholic, Christian tradition and interacting in a steady but not preoccupied way with the New Testament witness. It is a rendering of the living relationship to God which is indebted to the People of Spirit and Memory and which, hopefully, they will recognize as their own. Or if they do not see themselves with any clarity in these words, it is hoped that at least the instincts, impulses, and passions will not be totally alien.

### The Heart

Divine love encounters human sinfulness in the heart of the person. Anatomically, the heart is hidden in the cage of the ribs which is further covered by muscle and skin. It cannot be seen, but it pumps blood and is the source of life. When the heart is damaged in any way, the entire person is affected.

It is these physical facts that make the heart an apt metaphor for the relationship to God. The relationship to God is the invisible center of the person. When this relationship is properly ordered, the result is spiritual life. When it is disordered, the result is spiritual death. *The New International Dictionary of New Testament Theology* puts it this way: "The heart is that in man which is addressed by God. It is the seat of doubt and hardness as well as of faith and obedience. . . . it is the person, the thinking, feeling, willing ego of man, with particular regard for responsibility to God."[7] In language used earlier, the heart points to the ultimate relationship with God which is the permeating context of all other relationships.

The heart is God's special concern and the arena of battle. God knows the hidden heart (1 Cor. 4:5), examines hearts (Rm. 8:27), and tests hearts (1 Thes. 2:4). God wants more than lip service with hearts far from him (Mk. 7:6). God does not trust appearances, but looks at the inner reality of the heart (2 Cor. 5:12). The circumcision of the flesh is nothing if the heart remains uncircumcised (Rm. 2:2 9; Acts 7:51).

It is also the heart which Satan seeks to possess. He enters into the heart of Judas (Jn. 13:17) and fills up the heart of Ananias (Acts 5:3). In one interpretation of the temptation narratives, it is the heart of Jesus that Satan seeks.[8] The heart, then, is the locale where the divine and the demonic solicit human freedom. In refusing the divine, the heart becomes "hardened" and "stony"; in opening to the divine, the heart becomes "fleshy" and "repentant."

God wants the heart because it is the source of action. On the one hand, "a good man produces goodness from the good in his heart (Lk. 6:45). On the other hand, "wicked designs

149

come from the deep recesses of the heart; acts of fornication, theft, murder, adulterous conduct, greed, maliciousness, deceit, sensuality, envy, blasphemy, arrogance, an obtuse spirit—all these evils come from within" Mark 7:21–22.

The radical ethical demands of the Matthean Jesus stress interior renewal. "You have heard the commandment, 'You shall not commit murder.' What I say to you is: everyone who grows angry . . . You have heard the commandment, 'You shall not commit adultery.' What I say to you is: anyone who looks lustfully at a woman. . ." Matthew 5:21–22; 5:27–28.

In a similar manner, Jesus is concerned about the filth on the inside of the cup which shines on the outside (Mt. 23:24) and the dead men's bones on the inside of tomb that is whitewashed on the outside (Mt. 23:27). Evil and good are not just in behavior but in the interior heart which promotes good and evil behavior.

This emphasis on the unity of the person, interior and exterior, heart and action, is necessary to counteract two serious distortions of the divine-human relationship. The first stresses that the real concern of salvation is the inner healing of the isolated individual's relationship to God. In the past, this impression has led to a privatist form of Christian faith and the anomaly that people proclaim an interior salvation in relationship to God while their external relationships to other people remain destructive.

This is not a matter of our inability to adequately embody the love of God which has saved us into the love of neighbor. If that were the case, we would live the Christian life of repentance and struggle, never forgetting the salvation we have received and never ceasing to concretely extend it to others. Rather, what occurs is a disjunction, a separation of inner purity and outer action. The intimate bonding of God and neighbor is broken, and it is thought that these two relationships can be pursued independently of one another. Salvation becomes interior and unearthly and is able to be claimed even though the world of flesh and blood is alienated and broken.

A second distortion that often creeps in when the heart is construed as the target of salvation concerns the distinction between analysis and strategy. What we are engaged in is an analysis, an attempt to point to the core of the dilemma. Our suggestion is that by itself no behavioral modification or systemic revolution will bring salvation. Any behavioral change can be quickly undone once the controls are lessened, and any social reform is easily manipulated by those who know how into new and clever forms of injustice. The brutal fact is that no salvific change endures that does not change the heart.

But this analysis does not mean that the strategy is "First change of heart and then behavioral and systemic change; first interior conversion and then new action." Any in-depth appraisal of the human predicament should suggest multiple approaches. Perhaps the more effective strategy is social change which creates the possibility of a salvific, individual restructuring or behavioral change which gradually leads a person to a change of heart.

Although Jesus' ultimate target was the person's relationship to God, his proximate targets were self-serving behaviors and ingrained customs and laws that perpetuated oppression. To use a military metaphor in line with New Testament imagery, to name the battle is not to determine the mode of attack. We are engaged in a religious analysis which should be considered in the Christian struggle for personal and social salvation. We are not proposing step-by-step approaches to the total topic of change.

### The Panicked Heart

A Matthean passage about the heart has come under considerable fire:

Do not lay up for yourselves an earthly treasure.
Moths and rust corrode; thieves break in and steal.
Make it your practice instead to store up heavenly
treasure, which neither moths nor rust corrode nor
thieves break in and steal. Remember, where your
treasure is, there your heart is also.

Matthew 6:19–21

It has been pointed out that treasure is treasure.[9] The
same greedy spirit hoards heaven as hoards earth. What we
have in this piece of advice is only a change in the objects of
acquisitiveness. There has been no transformation of the
human spirit from "take and hold" to "give and receive." It is
now spiritual coins that are counted alone in the dead of night.

There is little doubt that this passage has inspired this type
of spiritual greed in many frightened Christians. But perhaps
this passage is not about investment counseling. Like other
imperatives of the Gospels, it is not a concrete demand to
act in this way. It is meant as an imaginative shock to reorient
the heart.[10]

We obviously lay up treasure on earth, not merely in unre-
alistic attempts to totally secure the future but in realistic
attempts to provide for the needs of tomorrow. The initial
statement, which suggests we cease this practical planning,
offends our common sense. The dangers of moths, rust, and
thieves are part of the risk of earth and not serious reasons to
quit the survival game. It is only with the final "Remember"
that the target of the saying comes into view. The saying concerns the heart and its penchant for false attachments which
make it vulnerable. If a house should not be built on sand, a
heart should not be left to rust.

The heart, in Augustine's famous phrase, is restless until it
rests in God. Its natural love is the divine, and when it seeks

love elsewhere, it is destined to suffer rust and plundering. A person may treasure many other people and possessions. But the person as person, the heart of the person, is ontologically oriented toward God.

This is the structure of created existence, and although the human person is an open-ended reality in many ways, this is the area that the Bible articulates with the words, "Hear and obey!" It concerns the necessary foundational orientation for creative living. When the heart of the person treasures God, all the other treasures are treasured correctly. The deep question of the heart can be phrased "either-or"—either heaven or earth. But the more inclusive understanding is "both-and"— both heaven and earth. The heart authentically set on God is appreciative of all creation.

Theories of revelation often begin by constructing the human condition so that it is open to God. In the metaphoric language we have been using, they examine the heart. This openness to God is characterized as the capacity to receive but not to grasp. It is an ascending movement which, by itself, can never attain that toward which it ascends.

But God, in an outpouring of love, descends to meet the ascending human spirit. This is the experience of revelation, a human reaching that cannot reach is met by free, divine descent. To keep divine initiative always in the forefront of revelation, it is often stated that the very reaching of the human person is inspired by the grace of creation. The grace of creation provides the possibility of the grace of revelation.

But what is often lacking in these theories, as in most metaphysical renderings of the God-humankind relationship, is the note of passion and panic. Waiting for God to descend is, for most people, not a time of quiet patience. It is a time of furious search, and the banner phrase "You would not be searching for me if I had not already found you" is not as consoling as it is meant to be.

The heart thrashes about, frantic that what it was made for either is not or does not want it. When Burt Lahr, who played Estragon in *Waiting for Godot,* was asked to sum up his part, he replied, "Hunger!" The heart is a hunger and a thirst, and it needs the food and drink of God. But if this food and drink is not forthcoming, it will find substitute nourishment. To uncover the heart is to uncover desire, and the desire does not merely burn, it rages.

A good guide to the heart as a structure of desire is Sebastian Moore.[11] He asks the question "Is there some state of being which everybody wants?"[12] He answers that we all desire to be desired by the one we desire. If we do not desire someone, we are not unduly disturbed if we are not desired by that person. But if we desire someone, we desperately want to be desired back. When we kiss, we want to be kissed back. Charlie Brown has put it both poignantly and flippantly: "Nothing spoils the taste of a peanut butter sandwich like unrequited love." No one escapes this structure of desire. It is universal to the human condition.

But is there also a common object of desiring? Moore suggests that there is. We all want to know we are significant for the unknown reality that is our origin and our destiny. "If our human self-absorption is at root our dialogue with our unknown origin, it is not the self-absorption of the lover awaiting the news that the other is interested."[13] This is the "pre-conscious" love affair with God. At first we may not be aware of this desire. What seems more immediate and real is our desire for human love. But upon reflection, we may perceive that "our questioning of the human beloved is perhaps powered by and modeled on that questioning of God which is the very heart of a person's life."[14]

But does the ultimate Mystery of life, out of which we came, in which we subsist, and back to which we will go, desire us? No one of us asked to enter this Mystery, and few of us will ask to leave it. But enter we did and exit we will. Now does this strange reality, this other-than-we-are which is intimately involved with us, cherish us in our coming and staying and going? For we surely cherish this Mystery.

The evidence is ambiguous. At one moment, time, which is at the core of the Mystery of life, seems to be a friend, holding out the possibilities of fulfillment. At another moment, time appears as an enemy, contributing only to our diminishment. Add to this the steady bounty of nature and its sudden fickleness, providential deliverance from danger, and freakish chance destruction, the history of human goodness, and the chronicle of moral evil—and the enigma deepens.

The reality that sums up this ambiguity is death. Our best smile at the graciousness of life is met by the smirk of death. We are inescapably bound to the processes of diminishment, but we are not reconciled to this destiny. Is our desire to be desired by the Mystery within which we live ultimately thwarted?

This ambiguity—that life is given but not guaranteed and therefore perhaps not returning our love—is the abiding sensitivity of religious awareness. In the midst of this ambiguity, what we often do is choose certain events as revelatory of an answer to the question of desire. If we choose gracious events, our sense is that we are desired, and we integrate all the horror of life into this fundamental sense of our desirability. We struggle with the problem of evil.

If we choose destructive events, our sense is that we are indifferently considered, if we are considered at all. In this posture, we reduce all the graciousness of life to momentary but not lasting reprieves from its true hostility toward us. We struggle with the problem of good. The options often become nihilism or faith.[15]

But our exploration will take us into different territory. We will not look immediately at the various events people choose as revelatory of an answer to the question of the heart's desire. We want to trace the strategies that the heart employs in the face of a nonanswer. The heart, with its desire skyward but the sky silent, is panicky, unsure, shaken. This panic may induce momentary paralysis. But soon, consciously or unconsciously, protective plans are devised.

**The Rejected Heart**

F. Scott Fitzgerald is cited as saying that "the three worst things in life are to lie in bed and not to sleep; to wait for one who does not come; to try and please and not be able." The atmosphere of the heart we are considering lies in bed, but it does not sleep. It is the heart that cannot find rest. But its sleeplessness is not inactivity. Rather. in its sleeplessness. it takes two different but complementary tacks: The first is to court the attitude of waiting for one who does not come and to live in rejection. The second is to try and please and not be able and to live in envy.

The heart that waits for one who does not come lives in the secret yearning for love to arrive. But it has waited for so long that it begins to revile itself for waiting. It seems to stand watch through a night that has no dawn. Like all realities that wait and watch, the heart talks to itself: "Fool, you are spurned! Settle for it."

But no matter how much common sense tells the heart to stop hoping, it will not stop. The very fact the yearning will not go away makes the heart feel a dupe of its own desires. It begins to rage and strike back at the Mystery it loves but which will not love it in return. It proclaims itself the Rejected One and plays out this rejection in all it does. But deep down, unquenchable, it cries out, "Come to me!"

The Gospel of John, remembering Isaiah, suggests that the heart and eyes are closely connected:

> Hc has blinded their eyes
> and numbed their hearts,
> lest they see
> or comprehend
> or have a change of heart
> and I should heal them.
>
> John 12:40

And Matthew has an instructive passage on the spiritual significance of eyes.

> The eye is the body's lamp. If your eyes are good, your body will be filled with light; if your eyes are bad, your body will be in darkness. And if your light is darkness, how deep will the darkness be!
>
> Matthew 6:22-23

The foundational orientation of our heart becomes the way we perceive the events of life. We do not see "neutrally." We select and choose on the basis of disposition and attitude. The old jingle "Two men looked out from prison bars/ One saw mud, the other stars" reflects this fact. The heart sees, and what it sees reveals both its pain and joy.

What does the rejected heart see? It sees everything in its devalued form; it reduces everything to the lowest common denominator. Nothing true, good, one, or beautiful flourishes in its sight. In sexual love, it perceives lust; in sacrifice and dedication, guilt; in charity, condescension; in political skills, manipulation; in the powers of the minds, rationalization; in peacefulness, ennui; in neighborliness, self-interest; in friendship, opportunism. The vitality of the old is pathetic; the exuberance of the young is immature; the steadiness of the middle-aged is boredom.

The rejected heart lives in resentment and demeans all it surveys. And when in the course of events, as often happens, sex falls to lust, sacrifice is grounded in guilt, charity reveals condescension, political skills manipulate, the mind vacillates, peace sleeps, and neighborliness and friendship turn ego-centered, the rejected heart gloats. It does not grieve that life has been devalued; it dances that it has been proven right. All of these realities are as empty as the heart itself.

As we see, so we act. The spurned heart strenuously acts out its rejection in destructive behavior. Since its self-worth is lacking, everything is permitted. It approaches the situations of life out of an inner hostility, and so creates hostility in every interaction. It is not coerced by the sanctions of society or moved by appeals to human dignity. Human dignity is a category for people whose eyes have not been opened to their fundamental rejection, and the right ordering of society is merely the protective covering the weak need for meaning. Any behavior is acceptable, and the most unacceptable behavior is the best. Each act that tears down and destroys symbolizes the unloved center which the rejected heart takes as its premier truth.

In the Gospels, the rejected heart energizes the behavior of Mary who is a whore, Zacchaeus who is a thief, Matthew who milks his people, the adulterous woman, and the whole class of people known as "tax collectors and sinners." But no matter how hardened this heart appears, there is still in it a hunger and thirst for one who does not come.

But there is also a more passive acting out of the rejected heart. This way does not strike back at the Mystery of life it desires. It accepts its rejection by being nobody. It seeks out situations where life is lacking, for it loves the lack of life.

This strategy of rejection attempts to crush all desire. The spurned heart compounds the ignominy of poverty by deigning it appropriate for one so unlovable. It willingly makes itself the footstool for the feet of those more worthy. It bows its head in obedience, not because it hears the Author of life, but because a nonassertive self is the natural meekness of a heart that is not cherished. It makes a home in the places where life is perishing. It embraces diminishment but does not understand the paradoxes of which Paul sings:

> We are called imposters, yet we are truthful; nobodies who in fact are well known; dead, yet we are alive; punished, but not put to death; sorrowful though we are always rejoicing; poor, yet we enrich many. We seem to have nothing, yet everything is ours!
>
> 2 Corinthians 6:8–10

The rejected heart that resigns itself to rejection lies down and dies long before breath is gone.

In the Gospels, the heart resigned to rejection is symbolized by the poor, the sick, the forgotten, the insignificant, the outcast—those who are sure they are not loved and lead lives of quiet lovelessness. But their surface resignation is not the whole story. The longing to be significant in the eyes of the beloved is never totally dead. This diminished acting out of rejection suffers the same inner agitation as the strenuous acting out of rejection. This heart may appear to have lost its appetite for life, but there is still in it, deep down, a desire for the one who does not come. The ear is cocked for his footstep; the eyes dart about for his face.

## The Envious Heart

There is a second complex response of the heart that cannot sleep. Unlike the heart who waits for one who does not come, this heart does not strike back at the rejection or resign itself to lovelessness. This heart begins a process of beautification. It says to itself, "Perhaps at the moment there may be some doubt about God's love for me. But I am going to make myself lovable. When I am done, I will be so desirable that God will not be able to resist loving  me." This heart launches a campaign to prove its desirability. The lack at the center of this heart is quickly filled with attention-attracting schemes. This is the heart that tries to please and is not able.

The means that this heart chooses to make itself desirable is, quite simply, whatever is available. It may be a radiant smile, an "A" on a report card, new clothes, a promotion. The classic "objects" we seek and then use to establish our self-worth are wealth, power, sex, and fame. All these things are good in themselves. It is the service they are put to that is questionable. The panicky heart uses them to entice love from a reluctant God. Their message is "How can you not love me when I am so personable, bright, well-dressed, rich, powerful, sexy, well-known?" This heart takes whatever it has and whatever it can get and parades it before the sky—which remains silent.

It is trying to please, but it is not able. Once our panicked hearts begin this process of preening and strutting, we are on our way to a life of anxious striving, self-deception, and oppression. If it is wealth that will make us lovable, we notice we never have enough. A Rolls-Royce tools by our Cadillac on the expressway, and suddenly we feel poor. That certain amount of wealth and possessions that we thought would satisfy us never does. We need more, but as we acquire it, even more looms before us. Our infinite appetite devours every finite appeasement. There is always somebody with more, and whenever we are with them or hear of them, we feel less desirable.

Feeling less desirable, we redouble our efforts at gaining the possessions that promise us "self-worth at the center." But when this new acquisition is proudly in our hands, it does not quiet the question in our heart. So we look around and begin again. We live a life of anxious and hopeless striving.

This dynamic of making ourselves desirable is closely associated with idolatry. Idolatry is often stated as making a finite reality the object of ultimate concern. The finite reality takes up residence in the "God-space" that is the heart of the human person. It promises what God promises but fails to make good on those promises.

In our analysis, God remains God and the "object" of the heart's ultimate concern. The question is how to attract divine attention and love. The display of talent and possessions is the strategy employed. But when we do this, we unconsciously equate our self-worth with that part of us we put on display. The totality of the person is tied to one segment of the person. The mystery of who we are in relation to all there is is restricted to the "stuff we strut." It is the classic situation of getting more and more of less and less. That is why when the heart is liberated from this confining process, it experiences life as enlarged, and the image most often used is "freedom from bondage."

The anxious striving is never over and life becomes narrowed to what we strive for. But that is only the beginning of the bondage of the heart that tries to please and is not able. The next stage is self-deception. Wealth is the perennial whipping boy of religion, but the Gospels are equally interested in the way we use "goodness." When being good makes us lovable and constitutes our self-worth, we dare not do wrong.

Wrong threatens the very essence of who we are. Yet, inevitably we do wrong. Sin runs deep in us and breaks out in ways we do not expect. The generous deed is done for self-serving motives. We are silent in the face of unjust systems we are benefiting from. There are no innocents east of Eden.

Yet the heart that has prided itself on purity cannot admit to any wrongdoing. It would threaten the very foundations of its loveability. So we protect ourselves by denying the wrong we do. We hide from the light and rationalize away the evil we are involved in. Since we have identified ourselves so thoroughly with our goodness, we cannot stand the void we would face if it were stripped away. Flannery O'Connor portrayed the terror that this unmasking brings:

> His heart constricted with a repulsion for himself so clear and intense that he gasped for breath. He had stuffed his own emptiness with good works like a glutton . . . His image of himself shrivelled until everything was black before him. He sat there paralyzed, aghast.[16]

Rather than the terrible truth, we settle for the comfortable lie.

Anxious striving and self-deception move outward in oppression. This heart knows who it is only when it knows who it is not. If it is our knowledge that makes us lovable, then we have a vested interest in other people's ignorance. If it is our wealth, we have a personal stake in other people's poverty. If it is our goodness, then other people must be designated sinners. If it is prestige, then other people must be downtrodden. We know ourselves as lovable only when other people do not have the possessions or qualities that makes us lovable.

Making ourselves lovable means making other people unlovable. All our efforts to build ourselves up mean that other people are automatically put down. At one level of our consciousness, this life of chronic comparison is too distasteful to admit. But at a deeper, and usually suppressed, level it flourishes. We are now at the insidious center of this heart, the energy source of its strivings, deceit, and oppression. We live in envy.

The heart that tries to please and is not able sees everyone else as more or less pleasing. The more pleasing are "beating out" this heart for the minimal amount of love that the Mystery of life is willing to give. And so it schemes to take their pleasing qualities or possessions away from them. We torch a reputation for goodness to secure our own self-righteousness. We climb the economic ladder delighting in the fact we leave people behind on lower rungs. Those perceived as more pleasing we struggle to surpass or demean; those perceived as less pleasing we keep in their place.

This heart is ingenious at actions that are continual reminders of its own superiority. We flaunt our higher position so other people do not forget their lower status. We preen our beauty to remind the ugly of their mirror. We parade our learning so the empty headed will not presume to question us.

Ego maintenance and defense is now our full time activity. And we stand before the silent sky and pray the only prayer we can:

> I give thanks, O God, that I am not like the rest of men—grasping, crooked, adulterous—or even like this tax collector.
>
> Luke 18:11

In the Gospels, the envious heart energizes the wealthy, the political authorities, and the religious elite. In particular, the Pharisee symbolizes the envious heart. The front the rejected heart puts up is "I don't care whether you come for me or not. In fact, I am not worthy of your love, am I? And to prove it I will kill or whore or rob. Or I will wallow in all the diminishments that surround and suffuse life; a lacking person loves life where it is lacking." But the deep center of the heart that waits for one who does not come hungers and thirsts and cries out "Come to me!"

The front the envious heart puts up is "There is none like me. I have done well where others have not. Other people look at me with envy. They acknowledge my accomplishments and know that I am someone to be reckoned with. This is not just anyone you are dealing with but a person of distinction."

But the deep center of the heart that tries to please and is not able cries out "None of these things is me. Find me and love me!" The energy of both the rejected and envious hearts is its raging desire to be desired by that which it desires. If this desire could be met, all the destruction that this unmet desire unleashes might be redirected. The question would no longer be "How does an empty heart deal with its emptiness?" The question would be "How does a full heart overflow?"

Jesus initiated the experience named Spirit by filling the heart, by revealing that the divine desire for the human not only matched but exceeded the human desire for the divine. He bared the human heart in its fear and panic and exposed the divine heart in its overwhelming love. We must explore how he did this.

## The Impact of Jesus
"He needed no one to give him testimony about human nature. He was well aware of what was in man's heart" (Jn. 2:25). Mainly, Jesus was aware of what was not in the human heart. Divine love was missing. If it arrived, a new way of see-

ing and behaving was possible. But God seldom makes independent interventions. The way divine love would embrace
these twin distorted hearts was through the human love of
Jesus. James Mackey spells out the logic of this divine-human
conspiracy.

> In the end the only way to give people the experi-
> ence of all life and existence as enabling and inspir-
> ing grace, the only way to give them the experience
> of being themselves grace and treasure, is to treat
> them as treasure and to be gracious to them.
> Human kind as a class, of all species of object on
> this earth, is very class conscious The sun may
> indeed rise on the evil and the good, and the same
> rain refresh the just and the unjust (Matthew 5:45),
> but the lesson will likely enough be lost on me
> unless the warmth of another human being envel-
> op me, unless some other human person refresh
> the weariness of my defeated days. I simply will not
> feel my own life, my own self, as grace or gift of
> God, unless someone values me. That is presum-
> ably why the gospels can make Jesus describe the
> whole experience of the reign of God, which it was
> his whole mission in life to give us, In terms of
> serving the needs of others. It may seem, at first
> blush, to stand the whole logic of the experience of
> the reign of God on its head, putting the effect
> before the cause. The logic should surely read: first
> feel all life and existence as gift or grace, then feel-
> ing the grace of God, be gracious to others. Not,
> first feel the grace of some human presence, feel
> forgiven, accepted, served, then begin to feel all life
> and existence a grace, and then feel inspired to be

gracious to others. But it is really a universal human idiosyncrasy that is operative here, not a matter of logic. It may well be that some rare individual, perhaps Jesus himself, followed the former logic, having a power of perception and evaluation and acceptance far beyond the ordinary. Indeed in the case of Jesus, it is very likely that his power to value went far beyond anyone's ability to value him. But for the rest of us, we can only sense ourselves and our world valued and cherished by God when we feel valued and cherished by others.[17]

Divine love is perceived through the struggles of human love. The arms of God embrace us through the human arms that hold us.

In those rare moments when we are in the grip of logic, it is undeniable that, as John says it, "God first loved us." But we come to this conviction by a circuitous route. It is in and through people's love for us that we sense a greater love. We intuit that their love is not merely of their own making but that they are symbols of "something greater."

Once we have this awareness, we can select out the "something greater" and claim that the unconditional care of this reality is the necessary grounding and motivation for our love for one another. But first we had to have had the appreciation of the divine, and this, for most of us, is the gift of loving, transparent persons.

Mackey intimates that Jesus might have been an exception to this process. Historically reliable material has always been lacking in this area, but Christian piety has been quick to fill in the gaps. Jesus found love from the woman who treasured him in her heart. He was the beloved son of Mary who experienced himself as the beloved Son of God.

It is also speculated that Joseph taught Jesus the path of love. If Jesus was to use the image of father for his relationship of love and election with God, his relationship with his earthly father must have been life-giving. John the Baptist also enters the picture. Although their messages are quite different, all the Gospels stress the connection between Jesus and John. When Jesus hears of John's death, he "withdrew by boat from there to a deserted place by himself" (Mt. 14:13). This may have been to size up the new political situation, but it also may have been to grieve for a friend. If Jesus was truly human, the social fabric of human mediation must have been an influence, but perhaps not the sole influence, in his awareness of divine love.

But if the Gospels are relatively silent about who mediated God's love to Jesus, they are eloquent about Jesus mediating God's love to other people. This mediation did not occur independent of or alongside of Jesus' human love. The divine worked in and through the human in Jesus. Jesus loved people with such intensity and perspicacity that he drove the ambiguity out of their heart. Their relationship with him became the event which they took as disclosive of ultimate truth and meaning. Under the impact of his love, people replied, "Yes! This is the reality I desire desiring me!"

Part of this response was generated by the fact that Jesus loved people in the very "place" they could not love themselves—their hearts. He did not do this by denying their sin, by accepting them in a gush of romantic blindness. He became the revelation of God by unflinchingly incorporating all the nonlove into the power of the ultimate Love he radiated. Any event which qualifies as a revelation of God does not pick and choose in order to appear inclusive. It gathers in everything and through this universal embrace transforms it. Such was the love of Jesus as it sought out the rejected and envious hearts.

This human mediation of divine love is the beginning of a response to what Sebastian Moore in the quote opening this chapter suggests is the lurking fear of all religion: we fabricated the story of God's love. Our need was so great and our pain so unbearable that we fantasized a divine lover to hold us. We are caught in wish fulfillment, daydreaming love without the backing of reality. We need the courage to face the indifference of the universe and, as Freud so provocatively put it, leave heaven to the sparrows.

A major way to put this fear to rest is to point to an event of human loving that broke the bounds of the humans involved, an event that was not individual heroism against the grain of a graceless Mystery, but a revelation of the true rhythms within which "we move, and live, and have our being" (Acts 17:28). Such was the event of love that Jesus made possible.

Human love that is revelatory of the divine is nothing if not concrete. It meets the need of the other person as an actual other, not as a projection of itself. It attends to the other person on the terms that will open that person to divine love. It discerns the escalating value of every encounter and promotes it.

The art of loving is adaptation to the redemptive power of God already at work in the other person. It necessarily employs diverse strategies. These are not coldly calculated plans or unfeeling ploys. They begin with passionate resonance to what is actually happening in the person and evolve into creative responses. Love in the concrete is an act of imagination which knows when to hold a sobbing body and when to let it sob.

Jesus loved concretely. He approached the rejected and envious hearts in different ways. To the rejected, he became an event of inclusion; to the envious, he became an event of unmasking. To the bereft, he became a banquet; to the self-

righteous, a mirror. His acceptance of sinners with their rejected hearts and his anger at the Pharisees with their envious
hearts were two stratagems of a single love. He did not love
one group and hate the other. He loved them both in ways he
hoped would open their hearts to the love of God.

It is easy to see love in the acceptance of the rejected heart
of the outcast, but it is difficult to see it in Jesus' rage at the
envious heart of the religiously righteous. But in Chapter 23 of
Matthew after Jesus' anger is spent and the litany of woes
over, the force behind his tirade is revealed:

> O Jerusalem, Jerusalem . . . how often have I
> yearned to gather your children, as a mother bird
> gathers her young under her wings, but you
> refused me.
>
> Matthew 23:37

The vulnerable love of the Son of God is showing.

The ultimate aim of the human love that mediates the
divine is to heal the heart in relationship to God and bring the
people together. The ambition of divine love is human peace.
Some contemporary scholars have surmised that the guiding
purpose of Jesus' ministry was the restoration of Israel.[18] He
wanted the divided house of Israel to be whole. This meant
reconciling the multiple warring factions. The broad categories of the Gospels divide them into the religiously outcast
and the religiously righteous.[19] They are actual historical people, but they also symbolize permanent temptations of the
human spirit. The religiously outcast embody the rejected
heart; the religiously righteous em-body the envious heart.
Although both suffer from the same malady, they are not
friends. The ways that they have responded to their inner
panic of unworthiness keep them apart. But their surface
antagonism for one another hides a deeper mutuality.

The social interaction of these two hearts provides subtle reinforcement for their peculiar distortions. They live with one another in a sick symbiosis. The envious heart delights that there are people who are less than it. Social outcasts and diminished people are sources of the continual reassurance it needs. It whispers this comfort to itself: "There but for the grace of God go I. I am not like them, therefore I am somebody. They are reprehensible, therefore I am approved."

This unveiled contempt is just what the rejected heart finds supportive. What it knows about itself—that it is not worthy of love—is confirmed by the envious heart's disdain. And the more the rejected heart acts out its foundational sense of unworthiness, the more the envious heart is justified in inflating its virtue. The sinner and the pharisee help one another maintain their separate distortions. This is what Jesus saw so clearly.

Jesus' twin strategies of love are aimed at the distinct distortions of each heart and are meant to bring them together in common recognition of their sinful grounding and common gratitude for God's healing. The story of the woman taken in adultery shows the "lightening fast" process at work. The sinful woman is brought to Jesus. "In the law, Moses ordered such women to be stoned. What do you have to say about the case?" Envious hearts have found a rejected heart to reassure their virtue.

Jesus holds up the mirror of love to the envious. "Let the man among you who has no sin be the first to cast a stone at her." As Jesus scribbled on the ground, they sulked away. When he looks up, his first words are "Woman, where did they all disappear to?" Then Jesus comments that since they have not condemned her, neither will he. To the rejected heart the strategy of love is acceptance. She is to go, but sin no more. In

Augustine's magnificent comment, "Only two are left: misery and mercy."

But the divine love that flows through the human love of Jesus wants everybody there. This is not a narrative about the victory of mercy, but a story of love reaching in two directions at once. Jesus' observation "Where did they all disappear to? Has no one condemned you?" can be read as a mere statement of fact. Or perhaps it is an ironic comment. Since Jesus knows they are sinners, he knows they will depart, and he is feigning surprise. And then in mock reversal, he suggests that he will follow their compassionate example and not condemn the woman either.

But perhaps he expected a different response from them. Perhaps when he exposed their own sinfulness, he expected them to stay and embrace the adulterous woman with the words "My sister!" And perhaps, if we could peer into the heart of Jesus (which we cannot), he dreamed that she would embrace them back: "My brothers!" And he would take them all to his table of bread and wine and teach them to say "Our Father!"

Perhaps the greatest story of the twin strategies for the twin hearts and the hope of reconciliation is "the man with two sons" (Lk. 15:11–32). The wayward son has created the classic script of the rejected heart. It knows it is worthless and it minces no words. "I have sinned against heaven and against you; I no longer deserve to be called your son. Treat me like one of your hired hands." The father's art of love is pure extravagance:

> While he was still a long way off, his father caught
> sight of him and was deeply moved. He ran out to
> meet him, threw his arms around his neck, and
> kissed him . . . "Quick! bring out the finest robe

and put it on him; put a ring on his finger and shoes on his feet. Take the fatted calf and kill it. Let us eat and celebrate because this son of mine was dead and has come back to life! He was lost and is found!"

The rejected heart that has cultivated its rejection comes to cherish itself as spurned. The only chance love has to penetrate this listless pity is abundant and overwhelming welcome.

The stay-at-home son speaks the classic script of the envious heart. "All these years I have slaved for you. I never disobeyed one of your orders, yet you never gave me so much as a kid goat to celebrate with my friends."

The older brother knows who he is only when he knows who his younger brother is not. The life of envy needs the rejection of others to flourish. The father holds up a mirror to his resentment. "My son, you are with me always, and everything I have is yours."

The older brother has lost nothing but the necessary foil for his self-righteousness. The final lines of the father are a second mirror to this anxious and oppressive heart. "But we had to celebrate and rejoice! This brother of yours was dead, and has come back to life. He was lost, and is found."

This is reminiscent of the unmasking question which closes the parable of the workers in the vineyard:

I am free to do as I please with my money, am I not?
Or are you envious because I am generous?
Matthew 20:15

I recently had the pleasure of telling this story of "a man had two sons" to a young woman who had never heard it before. She was a natural story listener and followed closely every nuance of the tale. When I finished, her first question was "Did the older son go in?" I told her the story ends without telling us. Then I asked her, "Would you go in?"

She did not speak for quite some time and then said, "I don't know. Would you?" I was about to flippantly reply "Sure, I like parties" when the question of the heart and not social expectations hit me. Would I rejoice and party from my heart, forgive my brother from the heart? (Mt. 18:35). I thought for quite some time and said, "I don't know. Would you?"

Our hesitancy is not without precedent. The Gospels seem to indicate that Jesus' wholehearted welcome of the outcast produced wholehearted disgust on the part of the in-group. Jesus as banquet was received; Jesus as mirror was rejected. The total art of Jesus' love was to make the first last and the last first, so that all would be middle. It was to make the in out and out in, so that all would be together. It was to tell the ones who knew they were sinners that they were loved and to tell the ones who were loving themselves destructively that they were in sin.

In this way, both hearts could come together in their common need of repentance and their common openness to the free offer of divine love which Jesus was making available. This art of loving did not work. And it was not only that the envious heart decided not to join the feast; it decided to break the mirror. But before we look at the shattering of the mirror, we must explore further Jesus' total but differentiated offer of divine love.

### A Story of the Rejected Heart Accepted

The electricity of Jesus' presence was that the love that flowed from him was free. It was given before the person was known and without soliciting promises of change. The source of the love was God, and although God wanted response and grieved when response was lacking, the lack of response did not stop the flow of love.

This is a reversal of how things are usually done. The standard path of acceptance is change your ways and we will accept you. This, in fact, was the structure of conversion in the Judaism of Jesus' day. The procedure was that the sinner was converted first and then became part of the community. Conversion first; communion second. "The novum in the act of Jesus was to reverse this structure: communion first, conversion second."[20] This freely available love, more than anything else, is the folly of God made manifest in Jesus.

The divine love of Jesus accepts us just because we are creatures, in spite of our failures that prove we are not worthy (the rejected heart) and in spite of our efforts to prove we are worthy (the envious heart). As James Mackey puts it,

> [this type of forgiving love] had nothing to do with previous acts of contrition or promises of penance, much less with penance actually performed or sacrifices already made. It was the sense of our acceptance by God, not despite what we were, or because of what we were, but as we were.[21]

This love tells the uninvited and unworthy "Come eat with me!" And with that offer communicates the depth of love. This love tells the worthy "You don't need all that to be loved!" And with that suggestion communicates the depth of love.

We are not accustomed to this. Up-front and unconditional love is not "the way the world works." We are trained in cautious and limited acceptance of ourselves and others. We know there are "things that make us good" and "things that make us bad." If we parade the good before others and bury the bad, we have a good chance of finding acceptance.

On the other hand, if we are known by all to be bad and the very structure of society ratifies this judgment, then we can be assured the rejection we feel is "coming to us." What we do not expect is a love that cuts through these rather clear and commonsense regulations to embrace us at a level deeper than human thought and action. When this happens, the prized assumptions of our heart about what makes us worthy and unworthy are called into question.

Jesus fell upon the obviously unworthy, not with pity for their bereft lives or cunning allegiance with their sins, but with a call to act out the greatness of who they were. To stand before all that diminishes human life and bless those that are suffering it is an act of mind-boggling boldness. "Blessed are you poor . . . you who mourn . . . you who suffer . . . "

Even if the blessedness is in light of a future vindication, it is a present proclamation based on a perception of their inestimable value. To stand before those who have pretended to lose the desire for life and hype desire—"Seek! Ask! Knock!"— is to love them in a way they cannot love themselves. But by far the best way to communicate this love is to gather them together in table fellowship. Their hearts are hungry, so feed them with so much bread and fish that there will be baskets left over. Their hearts are thirsty, so make more than enough wine to slake it.

The abundance of the meals which Jesus hosted communicated God's overwhelming love to starved hearts. And when the banquet-giver had to leave, the way he wanted to be remembered was as bread that was more than itself and wine that was more than itself.

This message of divine acceptance communicated to the rejected heart certainly appears to be "good news." And the Gospels indicate that many welcomed it and, in the light of it, changed their lives. But there are also indications that there was resistance to this liberation from hidden self-hatred that Jesus brought.

The simplest statement of the depth of sin is that we avoid with a passion the things that will save us. But this resistance to divine love is met by Jesus' persistence. Jesus is haunted by the agony of loss. The widow will hunt until she finds the lost coin; the shepherd will leave the many and search until he finds the strayed sheep; the father will run down one hill to meet the runaway and climb another hill to meet the one with no party in his heart. In order to catch the flavor and the cost of communicating divine love to the rejected heart, we must tell a story.

Those who have ears to hear, hear this story. Those who have eyes to see, see this scene. *Anything can happen at a well.*

The man who was sitting on the small stone ledge that circled the well slid off, turned to the woman who had just arrived, smiled and said, "I'm thirsty."

She had seen him at a distance. She had stopped to readjust the yoke which straddled her shoulders. A bucket hung from both ends of the yoke and when her steps were not perfect, and they seldom were, the wood cut into the flesh along the nape of her neck. She took the pain for granted, but from time to time she stopped to shift the weight to more callused skin. From bruise to bruise, she thought. It was as she straightened from her bent posture, to gauge the last ground left before the well, that she saw him. He appeared to be waiting for her.

Her mind raced. She thought of turning around and making for the village. But if he wanted to, he could easily overtake her and take what he wanted. Then, she cursed. Why did she not come earlier in the day with the other women? She knew why. But right now that humiliation looked better than this danger.

Then a plan formed out of her panic. She could see by his dress that he was a Jew and he would probably walk away.

Most likely after some quick insult and with a great show of disdain. If not, she could make him go. She would steel herself, hide her mind, harden her heart. She knew how. She had been there before. It was not the first time.

."I'm thirsty," the man said again.

It was so blatant it took her back. At a distance she could manage him in her mind. Up close his presence was almost too much. But she recovered quickly. "Who isn't? This sun would fry a lizard's tongue."

"Give me a drink!"

"You—a Jew and a man—ask me—a Samaritan and a woman—for a drink?" I have a simpleton on my hands she thought.

"Thirst makes friends of us all," the simpleton said. "I will help."

Before she could protest, he moved the lid off the top of the well and stood waiting for her to give him the bucket.

"I'll do it," she said.

She let the bucket fall down the well. The splash rang up from below. She swung the rope sideways till the bucket at the bottom tipped and filled. Then with quick, successive jerks she pulled it to the top.

The man waited at her side. He said nothing.

If he thinks he is going to be first, she thought, he thinks wrongly. This is our well and it is my bucket. He will learn who he is here.

She rested the bucket on the ledge, hunched over it and splashed water toward her mouth. She drank like an animal that had been worked too long in the sun. All the time her eyes darted from the water to the silent man at her side. He was smiling. The simpleton has missed the meaning, she thought.

When she was done, she stepped back. The man did not move. She waited, then, finally, jerked her arm toward the bucket. Slowly he cupped his hands, dipped them deep into the bucket, and brought the water to his mouth. As he drank, his face was turned up into the sun and the water ran and glistened in his beard. He drank like a bridegroom, loving the first cup of wedding wine.

With his lips still wet from the water the man turned to her. "If you would ask me, I would give you living water."

"The well is deep." Her tone was instructional. She felt as if she was giving a child a lesson in logic. "You do not have a bucket. Therefore, how do you propose to fetch this water?"

"Yokes and buckets are always the problem, aren't they?" said the man. His arms flew up in the air in exasperation.

A smile popped open her eyes, but her lips stayed tight and disapproving. Not a simpleton, she thought, a child. Just a child.

The child had a question. "Do you have a husband?"

The question slapped across her face. Not a child, she thought. A man, just another man. "I have no husband."

"True enough," said the man. "For you have had, ah, five husbands and the husband you have now is not your husband."

"Do you have a wife?" she spat back.

"I have no wife," said the man

"True enough," the woman said. "And the woman you had last night was not her either."

The man laughed, like someone had taken him and turned him upside down. He is enjoying this, she thought, but not for long.

"Besides, prophet, the number is not five but twelve."

"I was never good at numbers."

"One for each tribe of Israel," she said and thought that that would do it.

"Very pious of you," said the man. "Very pious."

AN EXPERIENCE NAMED SPIRIT

This time she could not catch the laugh in her teeth and swallow it back. It escaped and howled out loud like a prisoner finally free in the sun.

"You are very hard to get rid of," she said, but now she wasn't sure whether she wanted him to go.

"Everyone says that," said the man.

One more try, she thought, and this Jew, like every other man, will surely leave me. "Tell me, O prophet who is not very good at numbers, where should we worship the living God? On the mountain or in the Temple?"

The man grew silent and closed his eyes. He seemed to be traveling deep within himself to some sanctuary where she could not follow. So this is it, thought the woman. It will be in the name of the living God that he will spurn me.

When the man opened his eyes, he caught hold of the woman's hand. "God is not on the mountain, but in your thirst. God is not in the Temple, but in the scream of your spirit, and it cries to me. Ask me, ask me for a drink."

Not just another man, she thought. Not just another man.

She pulled her hand back. "I don't ask." She said it as if her whole life was in every word.

"Even without a bucket—if you ask me, I will give you living water."

So they sat on the ledge of the well under the sun which shines on good and bad alike. They spoke no words. Finally, he reached out for her hand. She let him take it.

"Give me a drink," she whispered.

"What," said the man, "you—a woman and a Samaritan—ask me—a Jew and a man—for a drink?"

"Thirst makes friends of us all," she said and smiled.

The man took her hands in his and formed them into a cup. Together their hands dipped deep into the bucket and brought a cradle of water to her lips. She drank it slowly, with her head back, her face open to the sky. She drank like a deer with the thirst of summer, like a field parched by drought, like a desert wanderer finally at home.

With her lips still wet she said to the man, "Sometimes the yoke and buckets cut into my flesh so bad I want to yell with pain, but I never do."

"I know."

Then she told him all about the husbands who were not husbands. She told him everything she ever did. Everything she ever did she told him. All the time she spoke, she cried.

When she was finished, he said, "I know." Then he told back to her everything she ever did. Everything she ever did he told back to her. All the time he spoke, he rubbed the nape of her neck where the marks of the yoke were the most punishing.

It was just as he had finished his revelation of her to herself that she saw the other men. His friends were coming towards them. "They will be scandalized to see me here with you." By now he held her in his arms.

"Probably," the man said.

"I must go." She eased out of his embrace and moved gracefully away from him. As she walked away, she turned often to look at him. Whenever she did, she always found him looking at her. Even when his companions gathered around him, he stood on the ledge of the well and watched her go. Finally, she was so far away she could not watch him watching her.

Then she could not get to the village quickly enough. Once there, she went from house to house and told people about a man who was not just another man who taught her how to drink. It was only after she had stirred up the entire village that she realized she had left her yoke and buckets at the well and for the first time in memory she was not thirsty.

The curious villagers formed a circle around her. She stood in the middle and proclaimed: "I met a man who told me everything I ever did—except how many times." And she laughed high and long. Some of the villagers said it sounded like she had a fountain of living water springing up inside her.

Let those who have ears to hear, hear this story. Let those who have eyes to see, see this scene. Anything can happen at a well.

## A Story of the Envious Heart Unmasked

The envious heart prefers a love surrogate to the real affirmation that comes with the acceptance of divine love. The importance of this love surrogate has to be maintained, for if the surrogate itself is devalued in any way, it cannot confer self-worth. Therefore, a great deal of psychic energy goes into defending the glory and prestige of the surrogate. Also, a great deal of anger is unleashed when the surrogate is relativized in importance.

But unless the "choke hold" on the love surrogate is loosened, the heart will never open onto a new grounding. The envious heart thinks that it possesses the love surrogate—wealth, righteousness, fame, and so on. But the truth is that the surrogate possesses the heart. First, the heart must be freed from its addiction before it can move toward its creator.

The love that manifests itself in Jesus shows the heart in its actual situation. There can be no love without truth. Love always discloses the reality of the human condition. The love of Jesus that came as unexpected acceptance revealed the facade of the sinner. The loveless behavior was really a cry for love; the resignation to diminishment was really a hope for abundance.

The love of Jesus which moves toward the envious heart will be no less revealing. This heart must see itself as it is before it can become anything else. The art of love that Jesus employed to open the eyes of the envious heart was both direct and indirect. The indirect strategy was to tell stories that overturned assumptions and offered an alternative way of being-in-the-world. The direct strategy was to shout out loud its distortion in the hope that those with ears would hear and those with eyes would see.

Paul Ricoeur suggests that the existential impact of the parables of Jesus can be appreciated in terms of orientation, disorientation, reorientation.[22] People construe the world and their role in it in a certain way. They then sort out their experiences in terms of this worldview. Along comes a story that this personally constructed world cannot make sense of. This disorients the hearers, forces them to look at the basic foundations of their life.

But this does not lead to automatic reorientation. It leads to existential choice. The story does not so much shatter the world of the hearer as profoundly question it. If the question is accepted and pursued, new possibilities of living are disclosed. If the question is resisted, the construed world tightens and vigorously defends itself. The heart can see the Kingdom yet fear the cost of entering it. "The light came into the world but men love the darkness rather than the light" (Jn. 3:19).

If it is the accident of birth that bestows worth on us and bestows disgrace on others, then listen to the story of the Good Samaritan (the disgraced other) and wonder. If wealth makes us somebody and poverty makes others nobody, listen to the story of Dives and Lazarus and wonder. If we pat ourselves on the back for fidelity and wag our finger at others for fickleness, listen to the story of the Man with Two Sons and wonder.

If it is hard work that has got us where we are and laziness that keeps others in their place, listen to the story of the Workers in the Vineyard and wonder. If it is our spotless purity that gives us a hearing before God and other people's sin that closes God's ears, then listen to the story of the Tax-Collector and the Pharisee in the Temple and wonder.

If it is our social position that makes us wanted and other people's lack of prestige that makes them abject, then listen to the story of the Invited Becoming Uninvited and Uninvited Feasting at the Banquet and wonder. The stories that Jesus told targeted the love substitutes and unmasked them as the anxious strivings and oppressive holdings of an envious heart.

Stories do not attack directly; they insinuate. They leave the hearers free to discover the criticism which is being directed at them. They are not a club over the head, but a mirror to the heart. They allow the hearers to look at their falseness and destruction in a gentle and relatively nonthreatening way. In this sense, they are a wager on the wind. They are spoken and are over. Their full impact is never known. If they are effective, it is always with the participation of the hearers.

Story telling and story hearing are a cooperative venture. It is difficult to tell if a story hits home, if it is doing its religious work of uncovering the heart. Two reactions that are, in general, signals of effectiveness are exterior anger and interior musing. Both these responses usually mean that the point, or at least *a* point, has been made. But stories often leave hearers befuddled. The story has had no impact, and the nonplused hearers demand: "Speak plainly!" (Jn. 16:29).

If there was ever anyone who could speak plainly, it was Jesus:

> What will you use today to bolster yourself at the expense of your brother and sister? Will it be lineage, glorying in the fact that you are a son of Abraham? God could raise up sons of Abraham out of these stones.
>
> Luke 3:8

What will you use today to bolster yourself at the
expense of your brother and sister? Will it be family? Unless you love me and the love I bring more
than mother and father and brother and sister, you
will not enter the Kingdom of Heaven,

Mark 10:7

What will you use today to bolster yourself at the
expense of your brother and sister? Will it be your
piety? Will you say long prayers in public places so
that others will see you and whisper of your sanctity? Then go to the closet and pray there. And my
Father who sees in secret will hear you.

Matthew 6:4

What will you use today to bolster yourself at the
expense of your brother and sister? Will it be your
wealth and inheritance? Then leave it all and follow me, for a camel has a better chance of passing
through the eye of a needle then you do of entering
the Kingdom of God.

Mark 10:25

What will you use today to bolster yourself at the
expense of your sister and brother? Will it be your
almsgiving? Will you pass your pennies to the blast
of trumpets so all will know that you are a generous person? Then do not let your right hand know
what your left hand is doing.

Matthew 6:3

What will you use today to bolster yourself at the
expense of your brother and sister? Will it be your
knowledge? Then become a child.

Mark 10:15

What will you use today to bolster yourself at the expense of your sister and brother? Will it be your power and authority? Then take this towel and wash the feet of the road-weary.

John 13:1–11

What will you use today to bolster yourself at the expense of your brother and sister? Will it be the dismal look on your face while you make known to all that you fast for the sins of others? Then comb your hair and smile, but inside starve.

Matthew 6:16

What will you use today to bolster yourself at the expense of your brother and sister? Will it be the honor you are held in? Then move from that first seat to the last.

Luke 14:7

You use everything you are and everything you have to strengthen yourself and weaken others. Give it up and the Kingdom will be yours!

Indirect storytelling and direct confrontation was the art of how Jesus loved the envious heart. Both of these activities were mirror operations. But the deeper unmasking reality was the person of Jesus himself. He came at life out of an inner fullness which exposed their inner emptiness. He would not grasp at the things they thought conferred significance, and he would not grovel in the lack of life or spread destruction like the rejected. He was the free spirit whom those in chains either admire and follow or loathe and kill. In the last analysis, it was the freedom of Jesus that made him intolerable.

We told a story of how God's love in Jesus pursued a rejected heart. We need a story of how God's love in Jesus pursues an envious heart. It is told in the first person by *a man who once met Jesus.*

My mind wanders off more now. It is like a child who has strayed from the safety of his father's hand and is running through a meadow of flowers intent on something in the distance. Every so often the child looks back at me to see if he should go on. And I am torn between issuing a stern parental order to return or following him to some wondrous discovery. I cannot do either and I begin to wonder what is wrong with me. It is then that the child fades, and I see Jesus again, turning, forever turning, never turning away and never turning back.

That is why I have come to this deserted olive grove and sit with my back against the bark of this ancient tree. Its leaves shield me from the heat, and the sky filtered through the branches is strangely calming. I need time alone to sort things out. Even my friends agree.

Just yesterday at a meal which I hosted, with Levi and Benjamin bantering in argument the way I love it, my mind suddenly unmoored from the debate and drifted back to Jericho. I was inside myself again, going over what happened, piecing it together like a potter trying to mend a pot. Then the background buzz of the conversation died down, and I came back to the faces around the table. They were staring at me.

"Bored, Nathaniel?" Benjamin said.

"Sorry. "

"The man of 1,000 opinions has nothing to say? What has happened to that famous razor mind of yours? Gone dull?"

"Cutting elsewhere," I mumbled. Cutting myself, I thought.

"Like last week in court," Benjamin snapped.

"Benjamin! Let's not go over it again." It was Levi's usual suggestion. Avoidance.

"No. He needs to hear it."

So he told me. I did not need to hear it. I already knew.

In court I was unfolding what I thought to be the core of the case, what more and more I see as the core of everything—how God, the law, and human frailty are locked in an eternal embrace. We love the law for it is the only hope of a weak people. But the holy law we love only whispers to us that we are unholy. And God remains God. Unapproachable. The judge interrupted me.

"The application, please."

"What?"

"The application. We all know everything in Israel is based on God's law." He was telling me I was tedious. "And we thank you for reminding us." Not only tedious but arrogant. "But the question is the connection? Where are you going with all this?"

So I followed my mind—run, child, run—discovering connections as I went, growing excited at what I was finding. Then I became afraid like a deer who leaves the hills for water and suddenly finds lions by the pool. I wound down, hoping the connection was somewhere in all the words I had spoken. I looked around for the nodding heads and appreciative faces. Heads were bowed; faces studied the floor.

"Undoubtedly," replied the judge who was now visibly annoyed. "But the case before us has to do with the division of an inheritance." His voice was insistent; his finger was jabbing a message at me. "We will take it up again tomorrow when we are all better prepared."

"Unprepared!" Benjamin's voice broke into my own remembering. "Well, it's not all that bad. More embarrassing than anything else, I suppose." That was Benjamin's way, make it harsh then take it back, hit then console. "But it doesn't do your reputation any good. Some are saying this sudden—what is it Nathaniel, looseness? drifting?—in you is because of that debate with the Galilean teacher."

187

"It wasn't a debate."

"Take my, no, take all of our advice. Forget him." Levi said nothing. He agreed.

"How? "

"You are a lawyer. Think it through. Make it work for you. Turn it around."

Benjamin was right. That is the only way. And that is why with this tree at my back to steady me, I am going over it again. I know how it will end. With Jesus turning, forever turning, never turning away and never turning back. But maybe by the time I get to him turning I will find something new and know what to do.

It started when Caiaphas sent for me. Many knew about it. I made sure of that. I just told Simeon that I would be late for our appointment because the high priest wanted to see me. Simeon was owed the courtesy of an explanation, and he could be counted on to tell others.

When I entered his chambers, Caiaphas was alone. That was unusual. I took it as an honor to me and that our meeting was important. He began by saying that he had heard of me, and even though I was a young man I had "already distinguished myself" as a lawyer. He was obviously referring to the case of the priest Jude.

Jude had a reputation for being pious. At dawn and dusk he could be seen praying in the Temple. The pilgrims always quieted down and pointed at him as they passed by. But according to the accusation, between these times of pious prayer, he had been reselling the animals which the pilgrims had brought to the Temple for sacrifice. He would accept the offerings but would never offer them. Instead he would sell them to other pilgrims who were looking for atonement sacrifices. The specific charge was that he sold the same goat five times. There were many witnesses to this double-dealing and they came forward, outraged and scandalized, and pointed their righteous arms at him all the time they spoke.

First, I gathered testimony from his fellow priests as to Jude's sanctity. One was more eloquent than the next. When they were done, Jude was the holiest Jew next to Moses. Then I cited the famous saying of the Honored Rabbi Hananiah: "No man denies the derivatives unless he had previously denied the Root." If one breaks the commandments, it is because one has broken with God himself. The argument flowed: If Rabbi Hananiah is correct, the reverse is also true. No man in touch with the Root, can deny the derivatives. If the sanctity of Jude has been attested to, can his moral righteousness be doubted? Can a man in contact with God break God's law? The iron logic bound the judge. Jude was acquitted. My name became known.

I had "already distinguished myself" by saving a priest, and the high priest had taken note. "I have a mission for you, Nathaniel. You have heard of the Teacher from Galilee, Jesus. We need more information about him. He is now beyond the Jordon in Bethany with friends of his. He is preaching there. Go, observe what he has to say, and report back." I had heard that was the way it was with Caiaphas, direct with always hints of more.

That night I told my wife that Caiaphas had said that even though I was a young man I had "already distinguished myself" as a lawyer. The next day she told the other wives. That night they told their husbands. And the next day I could sense a new respect in the street for me. The greetings seemed a little more respectful; the other lawyers seemed a little more eager for me to notice them. It worked.

It was not hard to find Jesus in Bethany. Everyone on the road seemed to be moving toward the house of Lazarus. When I got there, he was teaching. I thought it best not to hide myself but to become part of the crowd and sit like the others. One more Jew come to learn. Of course my clothes obviously spoke of position and importance. But I would let the people whisper their own conclusions later. Never show too much.

His message seemed mainline enough. It was about retribution, about the way sin subtly entraps the sinner. He knew the teachings of the rabbis and he had a way with words. For his finale, he twisted the great Elazar. "For by the measure with which you measure, it will be measured back to you." The customary silence was on us all, allowing the teaching to sink in. Finally, a choked voice, old and oozing urgency, spoke up.

"But, Teacher, what is the measure?"

Jesus lit up. His arms began to tear at the air like he was pulling treasure from it. "The Kingdom of God is like a poor woman in the marketplace. She carries her few coins in a purse which hangs from a string around her neck. If anyone wants the coins, he will have to take her head as well." We all laughed. We knew her well.

"She has her basket with her; sackcloth is tied all around the inside. She will lose none of the wheat she has come to buy. She is determined to get her full measure. No merchant will cheat her. As the seller fills her basket, she shakes the wheat together to make sure it settles tightly. But she does not stop at that. She then presses it down with her hands and forearms so more can fit. She will get all that is coming to her." They all nodded. They had been there.

"When suddenly under the pressure of her pressing, the wheat reverses. What was pushed down, pushes up. The basket becomes a fountain of wheat, running over into her lap. It shows no signs of stopping and the last we see of her, she is up to her waist in wheat. Both her purse and bushel basket are lost. That is the measure."

I remember the looks on the faces of the people. Some sat in stunned silence; some were laughing; some were laughing and crying the way people sometimes do when the long-hoped-for happens before their eyes; some walked away to be by themselves. They all seemed to be moved by the story, to understand it instantly.

But I was confused. Wheat can't bubble like water. A child's fantasy. It made no sense. So I did what I was sent to do. I observed.

When I reported to Caiaphas, I made the mistake of keeping the story for last, adding it as an afterthought with the comment that it seemed a simple diversion. For a long time he weighed me on the scales of his eyes. Then he turned and with his back to me he spoke: "He is insinuating that there is no measure and the careful, studied way of life of which we are the guardians must give way to this enthusiasm. The target of this diversion in case you missed it, my distinguished lawyer, is us." I remember the rush of shame. It was like I was a little boy who had to be told the importance of things.

"But you are right about one thing," Caiaphas turned back toward me. "Stories are of little help to us. We need a clear confrontation, a stubborn statement of his mind. He needs to be tested."

"I can do it." I never thought about the words. They were just there. I needed to prove myself in Caiaphas' eyes, to find my true weight on those scales.

"Good. I will send for you." And he left the room.

I thought it would be soon, but it wasn't. Still, no day passed that I did not hope that he would ask for me. I wanted to redeem myself.

Finally, the word came. When I arrived to see him, he was with Annas and two other priests. They never left the room as we talked.

"Jesus is in Jericho, ' Caiaphas began without introducing me. "From our reports," he widened his arms to include his fellow priests, "it seems he has come out in the open. Less stories, more direct speech. He needs to be skillfully pushed, and he will say the intemperate words we know are in his heart. Push him for us, Nathaniel."

"Yes." Exactly what I had hoped for.

From Jerusalem to Jericho is always a dangerous trip. Thieves love its twists and turns. But on the way down my head was too busy with strategies to worry. I imagined every possible scenario and walked through each one a victor. I tested him, showed him up for what he was, and justified myself and, with me, all who stood for the law. On the way down I did not give danger a thought for all my thoughts were on the contest to come.

On the way back the worst had already happened.

I found him in the small valley outside the city. There were about a hundred people around him. I remembered that I wished there were more. The moment he stopped his preaching I stepped forward. There would be no being one of the crowd this time.

"Teacher," I began. Always honey before vinegar, the kiss before the slap. "What must l do to gain eternal life?" Sincere questions are the best test. I remembered the poignancy of "Master, what is the measure?"

He was in no hurry to respond. He looked at me for a long time. I forced myself to return his stare. I never looked down.

"What does the law say?"

Clever, I thought, the tester tested. He knows the game. I will show him.

In the purest tones I recited:

Love the Lord, your God,
With your whole mind,
With your whole heart,
With your whole soul.
And your neighbor
As yourself.

Approval rippled across the crowd. It pleased me.

He spread his arms out, signaling to me to receive the recognition of the people, nodding to himself all the time. "You have answered well. Do this and live."

Then there was silence again between us. I had been tested and had justified myself. But there had to be more. No one had won.

"Who is my neighbor?" It was a question worth a week of arguments, but it showed too much. The people stirred. The sincere seeker was now unmasked as the heresy hunter. A slight smile danced around Jesus' mouth.

He came across to where I stood. He grabbed both my shoulders, steadying me on my feet, squaring me off like he was readying me for a blow. He locked my eyes into his.

"A certain man went down from Jerusalem to Jericho," he began. He did not go on until he saw in my eyes that I knew I was that man. Then he moved away from me to tell everyone what happened to me on that journey.

The first blow was the easiest to take. Being left for dead is not dead. Skin heals. I would mend. I still had clothes and money and prestige in Jerusalem. All I needed was to get back there.

A priest on a donkey came by. I could barely make him out. The blood was crusting over my eyes. But even naked, he recognized me. "Nathaniel, is that you?" I had no strength to speak. I could not even move my hands to signal him.

"O my God!" The priest held his head. "You, of all people, will understand. I have just finished service in the Temple. If I touch you and you are already dead or if you die in my arms, I will be ritually impure." He paced back and forth on the road above me, hunched in thought and panic.

"They will force me to stand in shame at the Eastern Gate, and go through the long process of purification. It would be a scandal to myself, my household, and the priesthood. " He rose to his full height and did not look at me. "In this case, as you well know, the law entitles me to  pass by." I watched him go. He took with him more than the thieves had taken.

A Levite came next. As soon as he saw me, he jumped off the road down into the ditch. "Thieves," the hoarse sound came from deep within his chest. He looked quickly around but not at me. In my heart I yelled, "Help!" He  never heard it. He stayed low in the ditch, and when he was sure the thieves were no longer lurking about, he returned, running, to the road.

I now had nothing, so nothing came to me. Even through the blood I could see he was a Samaritan. But in his eyes were my tears.

The damnable thing about it was that it took so long. If only he would have cursed, thrown me on his animal, dropped me in a heap at an inn and gone his way with a slur "More than you would have done for me." But he cleaned me like a mother bathes a child, rubbed oil in my wounds, tore his own robe for bandages. He put me on his donkey and walked beside it, steadying me. At the inn he laid me on a cot and placed his blankets over me. I could hear him paying the innkeeper and saying he would be back to take care of me if it was needed. All that time, that endless time, he never spoke to me. Except for the tears.

The next thing I knew Jesus had me by the shoulders again. He, too, had my tears in his eyes. "Who proved neighbor to the one in need?" It was the only question I have ever heard that was not a test.

And for once I just spoke, not worrying right from wrong, not breathless for approval. I uttered sounds that were not recitation. My sounds, halting, like a child speaking for the first time. "The one who showed mercy."

"You . . . " and the place inside me that just spoke heard the word.

"Go . . . " and it was like an invitation to a feast.

"And do the same." And I found tears in my eyes, but I did not know for whom I cried.

Then he began to turn, and that is how I always see him. Turning, forever turning, never turning away and never turning back.

The next day I returned to Jerusalem. I went immediately to see Caiaphas. His chamberlain came out to meet me in the antechamber. "The high priest has asked me to tell you that he has already been told about what happened."

At my house Benjamin was waiting. "I heard it was quite a battle but ended in a stand-off."

"It was not a battle."

"I heard he cleverly changed your question and you cleverly slipped out of having to say the Samaritan was neighborly."

"At the time there were no Samaritans. Or Jews. Or Gentiles. Or Priests. Or Lawyers. Only those who cry and those who pass by." That was the beginning of my thinking about it, of trying to understand what happened.

I'm still at it. In this deserted olive grove, with my back against this tree, under this luminous sky, it all comes back to me. I know now it is not over. My wounds have not healed. Perhaps they are not supposed to. The cost of my healing is still going on. So I know he will come back for me. He said he would.

## The Crucifixion of Love

The lawyer of the story is struggling. He has opened himself to the experience named Spirit and is gradually being transformed by it. But Jesus was not so successful with others. The truth he held up for the envious heart to see did not make it repentant but turned it to stone. Divine love in Jesus moved toward both hearts at once, but the historical record seems to say that this love was received by the lowly and the sinners and rejected by the powerful and the self-righteous.

But this fact should not lead us to facile judgments about the openness of the rejected heart. It would be too one-sided to characterize the envious heart as entrenched and the rejected heart as receptive. Self-hatred and self-importance are equally resistant to the new grounding which divine love offers.

But the Gospels do stress the endless machinations of the envious heart. The moment the rejected reached toward the love of God in Jesus, the envious turned their back. The welcome extended to sinners was an immediate insult extended to them. They perceived themselves as pure and would not join the table fellowship with those they perceived as impure.

To share bread was to share peace, trust, and life, and to share bread with everyone was to blur the boundaries between right and wrong, good and bad. More to the point, it was to break down the cherished structure of righteous division and to suggest a common creaturehood, equally sinful and equally capable of redemption. There was a more appropriate response to Jesus than to eat with him and his friends:

> When the Pharisees went outside, they immediately began to plot with the Herodians how they might destroy him.
>
> Mark 3:6

The exact path of this plotting and who was involved is difficult to trace. The Romans most probably cooperated with the execution of Jesus because they thought he claimed a political messiahship. "King of the Jews" is a seditious title, and that is the charge tacked to the cross.

From the religious side the death of Jesus is pursued because he is perceived as violating God's law. He is a blasphemer (Mk. 2:7), in league with Beelzebub (Mk. 3:22), a violator of the Sabbath (Lk. 13:10–17), and a false prophet (Mk. 14:65). His cleansing of the Temple (Mk. 11:15–19) shows his disrespect for the spiritual and moral center of Judaism and his association with sinners shows his disregard for the law. But however the death of Jesus is construed, one factor should not be forgotten: in the last analysis, the death of Jesus is a theological murder.

From a highly developed Christian theological viewpoint, it is the sin of the world which kills Jesus. But from the point of view of the religious authorities of Jesus' day, God's law orders Jesus' death. A divine command is behind the whole thing. The validation of the plot to do away with Jesus is a certain understanding of God and how God deals with creatures. His death is pursued in the name of one God, and he goes to his death in the name of another God. The utterly transcendent God whose law is absolute and unyielding condemns him; Abba who whispers in his ear affirms him. It is the depth of sin that murdered the love of God in Jesus. But the depth of sin is a lie about the nature of God.

In Genesis 3, the serpent lies about the divine intention. God is not the endless lover of created life but only the subtlest of self-seekers. God has forbidden the eating of the fruit to protect divine power. The snake says:

> No, you certainly will not die! God knows well that
> the moment you eat of it you will be like gods who
> know what is good and what is bad.
>
> Genesis 3:4–5

This God that is sef-defensive and oppressive of others is the projection of sinful human instincts. God is like us, only stronger. This God ratifies human alienation and justifies divisive behavior. It is this God, enthroned in the rejected and envious hearts, who wants the blood of Jesus. The other name for this God is the one who first told the earth couple of this God's existence—Satan. The lie about God in the human heart seeks to kill the truth about God in Jesus.

This perspective is important to maintain. When the story of Jesus reaches its final stages in the arrest, trial, and crucifixion, the focus often shifts from Jesus and other people to Jesus and his relationship to God. Will Jesus abandon his faith and "curse God and die?" Will God intervene on Jesus' behalf and save him from the hands of his foes?

The drama is being played out on the level of transcendent relationships. This is a necessary plot development. The Christian sensitivity that produced the passion narratives was convinced that the cross was the supreme moment of revelation. The relationship between the father and the son and, by extension, between God and humankind was being disclosed.

But it must be remembered that the death of Jesus is the "hour of the power of darkness" (Lk. 22:53). To forget this is to become ethereal and remove the cross from the conflicts of history. Whatever is happening between Jesus and God is happening because the sin of the human heart is in the ascendancy. The cross of Jesus is first and always, but never exclusively, horror.

In the resurrection of Christ, the truth about God vanquished the lie about God. God raises Jesus from the dead and thereby validates his life and message. The ultimate trustworthy Abba who grounds all creation is indeed trustworthy. What appeared to be defeat has been turned into victory.

This simple contrast was probably the earliest interpretation of the resurrection.

> Then you must realize that it was done in the name of Jesus Christ the Nazarene whom you crucified and whom God raised from the dead . . . They killed him, finally, hanging him up on a tree, only to have God raise him up on the third day.
>
> Acts 4:10; 10:40

God vindicates Jesus and, in doing so, reveals the truth about God. The real God is not the plotting God behind the death of Jesus. The real God is the God ahead of Jesus, opening up to him a new and transformed existence.

But the simple proclamation of vindication is not adequate enough to interpret the complex experience of Jesus' death and resurrection. Too much is left unanswered. Is the cross, then, only something that happened on the road to glory? Granted that it is a sign of the depth of human sinfulness, is that all it is? Is there a neat division between the death and the resurrection—the death revealing sin and the resurrection revealing love?

In meditating on the death of Jesus in the light of the resurrection and with the aid of the Hebrew Scriptures, new understandings of the cross emerged. The death of Jesus was seen to fit into a divine plan. It was not merely the temporary frustration of divine purposes but it was necessary for the accomplishment of salvation. "Did not the Messiah have to undergo all this so as to enter into his glory?" (Lk. 24:26).

This is the infamous "divine must" of the crucifixion. Simple contrast between death and resurrection yields to a sense of continuity. The God who raised Jesus was also, mysteriously, involved in his death. This mysterious involvement of God in the death of Jesus is further explored in the light of Isaiah 53 and the myth that the death of a just man atones for sins:

> But he was pierced for our offenses, crushed for our sins; upon him was the chastisement that makes us whole, by his stripes we were healed.
>
> Isaiah 53:5

This passage connects the death of Jesus with sin in a new way. Sin remains the secret energy of the plot against Jesus and his ultimate executioner. But a reversal, so favored in the parables of Jesus, has been envisioned. In the very act of the sinful heart rejecting divine love, divine love has healed the sinful heart. This interpretation links the death of Jesus with his entire mission. His whole life was the mediation of divine love to human sinfulness.

Now the cross is seen to be the place where that mediation was most powerfully present. Not only is the cross the result of sin, it is the event that heals sin. The cross now cuts two ways: it reveals the human resistance to divine love and the divine persistence in soliciting human love.

The interpretation of the death of Jesus has come full circle. It began as a tragedy about the triumph of evil, and in the light of the resurrection, the experience of the Spirit, and meditation on the Hebrew Scriptures, it has become a comedy about the outpouring of divine love.

Each gospel reflects the conviction that the death of Jesus is a statement about God. In Matthew, the earth quakes, boulders split, and tombs open. These are signs of a theophany, an unveiling of God. In Mark, the Temple curtain which hides the divine presence is ripped in two and the centurion proclaims "Clearly this man was the Son of God." God is now out in the open for all to see.

In Luke, the crucified Jesus offers divine forgiveness to his executioners and hands his spirit over to his Father. His death is more a time of faith than of terror. In John, the last words of the dying Jesus are "Now it is finished." The cross ties up the work of the Word Made Flesh rather than fundamentally threatening it. The truth about God not only asserted itself in the rising of Christ, it was also manifest in the dying of Jesus.

The early followers of Jesus scratched crosses on walls and medallions, forged iron and tied sticks in cruciforms, and gathered around tables to break bread so they would not forget his broken body and drink wine so they would not forget his outpoured blood. The centuries of humdrum liturgies have dulled us to the radical nature of this activity. Time has tamed both its oddity and novelty. Why take the cross of Jesus as the sign of faith and eat a meal in the memory of his death?

The central proclamation was that love brings life out of death. The catalytic experience was the resurrection. Without that experience, as St. Paul says, faith would be in vain, and Jesus would have been forgotten, one more mutilated body in the history of "dumb suffering." The image of it all should surely be the glorified Christ. Ultimately there was victory. Why not take Jesus at the right hand of the Father as the "compressed picture" of faith? In the interest of theological accuracy it would seem a different image should have been chosen.

Practical reasons would reinforce this. The cross was a symbol of execution, a punishment reserved for enemies of the state. To follow the way of the cross would be to advertise yourself as a threat to established authorities. But more than that, the sight of a cross immediately produced repulsion. It carried the feel of death, not as a natural end to long life, but as the brutal and arbitrary intrusion of power. It was the most concrete reminder imaginable of the fragility of human life and the oppressive threat that each person is to every other. Would people be attracted to a symbol that was geared to evoke terror? If apologetics or proselytizing urged the early Christians to adopt the symbol of the cross, it was a poor strategy indeed.

The reason for the centrality of the cross is that somehow it said it all. It captured the experience named Spirit in all its uniqueness and power. The cross articulates the interactive flow that characterizes the God-person relationship. This is the ultimate Mystery of Christian faith and it is not reducible to a single insight. In Tillich's language, it is not an accidental mystery which can be solved, but it is an essential mystery which, the more it is known, the more mysterious it becomes.

Our hope is to explore it in the light of the rejected and envious heart and so connect it to Jesus' overall concern. In order to do this, we must pursue the ancient question that is the instant overflow of contact with Jesus: "What think ye of the Christ?" The experience of the risen Christ forced the question of Jesus' identity with new urgency. From the first moment of his ministry, "who Jesus was" was the question lurking behind the tumult of events.

But Jesus seemed reluctant to address his own identity except in relationship to the Kingdom of God. His interest was in what God was doing in human life and how he and other people should respond. As we discussed in Chapter One, "who he was" was the ultimate grounding for "what he was doing," but what "he was doing" was so fascinating that it was getting all the time and attention. With the resurrection, the emphasis shifts from Jesus' saving presence to his personal identity. In

Bultmann's famous phrase, "the proclaimer becomes the One Proclaimed." The era of Christology begins in earnest.

The articulation of Jesus' identity is an extremely complex development. In many ways it will be the abiding concern of the Church for the first five centuries. It will achieve, not closure, but stability at the Council of Chalcedon in 451. In this process, the image that will emerge as the most provocative revelation of his mystery will be "Son of God."

The resurrection experience brings Jesus' ultimate reality "into the clear," but it does not confer an identity on Jesus that he did not have prior to his rising from the dead. In the Spirit-guided reflection of the early Church there seems to be a steady retrogression. Jesus is the Son not only at the resurrection but on the cross; not only on the cross but at the baptism; not only at the baptism but from birth; not only at birth but from all eternity. The life, death, and resurrection of Jesus of Nazareth is the life, death, and resurrection of the Son of God. From this perspective, Jesus is not only the revelation of humanity in relationship to God but also the revelation of God in relationship to humanity.

With Jesus' identity established as Son of God, a high Christology is firmly in place. In mythological language, it is now the fullness of time when "Son of God will become man" and "the Word will become flesh." It is often pointed out that the problem of all high Christologies is that the humanity of Jesus suffers. In the downward movement of God to humanity, Son and Word never quite make it. The Son almost becomes man; the Word almost becomes flesh. This is certainly the major danger of articulating the event of Jesus Christ in the images of "Son" and "Word."

But there is also a major advantage to this approach. From the perspective of religious experience, salvation is always inaugurated by the divine. The human person is a receiver and a responder to the divine initiative. When the life, death, and resurrection of Jesus is appreciated as a "top down" movement, we keep this experiential dynamic in the forefront. In the next chapter, Jesus of Nazareth stretched on the cross will tell us something about the perils of human response, but in this chapter the Son of God stretched on the cross tells us something about the perils of divine love.

But it must be stated that the cross as a revelation of God does not replace the cross as a revelation of sin. In the gospel accounts, the two are held in tension. This juxtaposition focuses the twin elements of the experience named Spirit—divine love and human sinfulness. The literary device used to maintain this tension is irony. The passion and death in the Gospel of John is a masterpiece of irony, but all the Gospels deal ironically with Jesus' death.

In John, Caiaphas proposes the advantage of having one man die for the people. The hearers know that it is Caiaphas' envious heart that generates this proposal, but they also know this is true in a way Caiaphas does not surmise. In Luke, the soldiers mock Jesus by placing the inscription THIS IS THE KING OF THE JEWS over his head, but they do not know they are telling the truth. In Mark, the priest and scribes jeer:

> He saved others but he cannot save himself. Let the "Messiah," the "king of Israel," come down from the cross here and now so that we can see it and believe in him!
>
> Mark 15:32

But the hearers know that it is in Jesus' staying on the cross that salvation comes. Matthew adds to these insults the taunt "After all, he claimed, 'I am God's Son." But it is precisely as God's Son that he remains on the cross. What is this irony intended to convey?

In the crucifixion of Jesus, the Son of God, human sinfulness is at the height of its powers. It is raging out of control. Jesus' friends have deserted him; the mob has turned against him; the religious authorities have engineered his crucifixion and mock him; the soldiers torture him; and the state condemns him. The demonic has broken loose. Satan has entered not only the heart of Judas but also the heart of the world.

Yet this marshaled campaign of evil against divine love is subverting itself. It is attempting to kill the Son of God, and its very success will be its downfall. The wholehearted (rejected and envious) expulsion of divine love will establish it as the ultimate truth of human life. In imagistic language, the cross of agony becomes the throne of glory. Or in the developed reflection of the Johannine Christ, " . . . and I—once I am lifted up from the earth—will draw all men to myself" (Jn. 12:32). How is this possible?

It may be a wicked and adulterous generation that asks for a sign, that tests the love of God, but as so often in the past, God will provide a sign. But it will not be a sign that ratifies the rejected heart in its worthlessness or the envious heart in its righteousness. They will receive a sign, but not the sign their sinfulness craves.

The Gospel of Mark is carefully constructed so that the reader or hearer is led to the true sign which God offers. In Mark, there is the phenomenon of the messianic secret. The devils are orthodox; they know Jesus is the Son of God. But every time they shout out his identity, he silences them. When Jesus heals the deaf and the blind, he forbids the new ears and new eyes to reveal what has happened. Mark is afraid that these exorcisms and miracles will be taken as the "much-requested" sign.

Although the Son of God has the power to spectacularly overturn the work of Satan, he is not revealed in that power.

# JOHN SHEA

The Son of God is revealed in the power to die. An illuminating way to explore this faith conviction that the love of God is revealed in the willingness to die is to process it through the "testing" tradition. This tradition has a long and winding history, but for our purposes two perspectives are helpful.[23] First, the truth of relationships is known only through the trials that test them. If the relationship undergoes no difficulties, the fidelity of the partners is always in question. In the Hebrew Scriptures, Yahweh tests people to find out if they love him. He tests his covenant son, King Hezekiah, "to know all that was in his heart" (2 Chronicles 32:31). After the successful testing of Abraham, Yahweh concludes, "Now I know . . . " (Gn. 22:12).

This is an experiential truth of all relationships. Once they have survived difficult times, the bonding is more intimate and the people involved know each other more deeply and trust each other more thoroughly. The harsh truth seems to be that trials successfully undergone strengthen relationships because they expose the hearts of the people involved.

Second, sin is the source of the testing between God and people, and the successful completion of the test strips the tester of its power. The thoroughgoing monotheism of the Hebrew Scriptures cannot imagine anything outside of divine control. Therefore, the trials that tested the people's faith in the covenant were seen to be sent by God to find out "what was in the heart."

A later development of this theme saw Yahweh sending Satan to play the role of tester. The Book of Job is the classic example of this dynamic. By New Testament times, Satan appears to be working on his own. Satan can never be envisioned as completely outside God's power for that would come dangerously close to the heresy of dualism. Two co-equal principles, one good and the other evil, battling over the world. But neither is Satan God's obedient servant. In the Gospels, Satan does not seem to be on a divine leash. He appears to be, as Cyril of Jerusalem described him, a dragon who sits by the side of the road seeking whom he may devour.

This development is extremely important. When Yahweh was imaged as a tester, he was not far from a tyrant. On the one hand, he afflicts his most faithful of servants in order to satisfy his slightest doubt. He appears as an insecure lover, continually putting up obstacles to see if he is really loved.

On the other hand, Yahweh allows no testing of himself. Although the creature was always accountable, God was never to be questioned.

> The prohibition against putting God to the test reveals an important element in the Old Testament conception of Jaweh's covenant relationship with his people. The reciprocal promises and obligations do not have to be balanced out and accounted; indeed, the concept of God's covenant obligation is in the last resort an irrational one, losing itself eventually in the inscrutability of the all-holy, sovereign God.[24]

This way of dealing admirably maintains the transcendence of God, but over a long period of time, we question whether this covenant is a loving one. The thundering voice from the whirlwind may silence Job momentarily, but it does not shut him up forever.

It is theologically possible to see the relationship between God and God's people being tested by sin. Neither partner seeks a testing. Temptation is not to be played with; it is truly a threat to the relationship and could destroy it. But temptations and trials are inevitable. Sin is deeply embedded in the

human condition, and its principle work is to disturb the cre-
ator-creature relationship.

This double sentiment of not wanting the test but knowing it will arrive is succinctly expressed in the ending of
Matthew's version of the Our Father: "Subject us not to the
trial, but deliver us from the evil one" (Mt. 6:13). Also, in this
understanding, sin tests both partners in the relationships. It
tests the love of God for humanity, and it tests the love of people for God and for one another. Sin is the enemy of both God
and humanity. Against this background, the cross as the sign
of divine love is illuminated.

The death of the Son of God is the testing of divine love by
the sinful human heart. The sinful heart that Jesus encounters
does not believe the message of divine love. The rejected heart
has waited so long for the one who does not come that when
at last he comes, he is not accepted. It would rather live in
cynical rage at the fact it is spurned than to receive the burden
of significance. The envious heart has tried to please for so
long and has been unable to do so that it has come to love its
own standards of pleasing. It will not receive the other-centered love that will free it, for it has learned to love the
self-centered love that imprisons it.

The school of sin educates us in fear and teaches us to
maintain the lovelessness we have learned to love. The Son of
God has offered the love of the Father, but who can believe it?
It needs to be tested. And the arena of testing should be the
place where we are most sure we are not loved.

It is death which panics the heart and tells it it is worthless. From the shaken and unsure center of the person come
the strategies of rejection and envy. If divine love is to radically reconcile the person, it must encounter the terrorized heart.
The basis of these terrors may be rooted in our finitude, in the
natural death that flows from birth.

But human mortality is a "relatively neutral" foundation compared to the destruction people have erected on it. Death is most terrifying when it is inflicted on us by our fellow human beings. What we fear most is desertion by our friends and being handed over to our enemies. It is the fear of this abandonment and the loneliness and humiliation of this perishing that convicts us that we are nothing.

This type of death, then, becomes the test of the love of God mediated through his Son. Dialogues between God and the heart are a traditional form of religious expression. It seems a good way to explore this dynamic.

> *God:* I made you and I love you.
> *Heart:* You have a strange way of showing it. If you love me, make me Like you. Immortal. Above it all.
> *God:* I love you as mortal.
> *Heart:* But I do not love myself that way. I hide from it day and night.
> *God:* I will join you in the brightness of day and the darkness of night.
> *Heart:* In the brightness of day maybe.
> *God:* And in the darkness of night.
> *Heart:* As you?
> *God:* No. As you. I will send my Son.
> *Heart:* You will back off. You will not hand him over. You do not know the terror.
> *God:* But I know you and I love you. Where you are I want to be.
> *Heart:* But I don't want to be where I am.
> *God:* When I am there, we will go through it together; we will not lose love.

*Heart:* You will not go through it. You will play God
   and run. Take me with you.
*God:* I would rather be with you so that you can be
   with me.
*Heart:* When the time comes, you will climb down
   from that cross and leave me on it.
*God:* Is that what you want?
*Heart:* Part of me, yes.
*God:* And the other part?
*Heart:* God, I hate you.
*God:* Why are you crying?

To the question of the panicked heart—"Am I significant in your eyes?"— comes the answer it is not sure it wants, but the only answer divine love in Jesus offers: "Enough to die with?"

When the Son of God died on the cross, the test was successfully passed, and the power of the tester, the sinful heart, was broken. In its place, the liberated heart lives in the paradoxes of God. "What died upon the cross was death." "In his dying we are reborn." "Sin killed the Son of God and was, in turn, killed by the Son of God." "We soiled our hands with the blood of Christ, and it cleansed them." "We crucified Love, and Love raised us from the dead." The cross of the Son of God is the final, and most powerful, mediation of divine love to human sinfulness.

The life of the Son of God tried to embrace the panicked heart and was, on the whole, tentatively received. The death of the Son of God broke through this rejection and envy in a new and ingenious way. God died the death we fear and so freed us from the fear of death. Sin runs deep in us, and the only love we will believe is the love that lays down its life. It is the only love we can be sure we did not make up.

It goes on still. As long as we wait and do not know the one we wait for has come; as long as we strive, deceive, and oppress and do not know we do not have to, the Son of God stays on the cross. He stays there because to come down would be to ratify the inner energy of our sin and leave us unredeemed. He stays there so that the hardness of our hearts will encounter the outpouring of divine love. He stays there so we will not settle for the world as it is but continue to ask the question of redemption which his cross, forever concrete and unyielding, focuses: "In vain, my Christ, in vain, two thousand years have gone by and men crucify You still. When will You be born, my Christ, and not be crucified any more, but live among us for eternity?"

## CHAPTER FIVE

# AN EXPERIENCE NAMED SPIRIT: HUMAN RESPONSE

*He said that a man should be able to lie at the bottom of
a hill with his throat cut, slowly bleeding to death, and if
a pretty girl or an old woman should pass by with a
beautiful jug balanced perfectly on the top of her head,
he should be able to raise himself up on one arm and see
the jug safely over the top of the hill.*

*Zooey thought this over, then gave a mild snort, "I'd like
to see him do it, the bastard."[1]*

*J. D. Salinger*

*Some Israelites reviled Jesus one day as he was walking
through their part of town.*
*But he answered by repeating prayers in their name.*
*Someone said to him:*
*"You prayed for these men, did you not feel incensed
against them?"*
*He answered:*
*"I could spend only of what I had in my purse."[2]*

*Attar of Nishapur*

*I*t is known by everyone who cares to know
that the Lord Jesus and St. Peter used to repair to the local
tavern after a hard day of ministry to break bread and drink
wine together.

On a certain rainy night, St. Peter turned to the Lord Jesus
and grinned. "We're doing real good."

"We?" said the Lord Jesus.

Peter was silent. "All right, you're doing real good," he finally said.

"Me?" said the Lord Jesus.

Peter pondered a second time. "All right, God's doing real good," he finally admitted.

But the Lord Jesus saw how reluctant St. Peter was to admit the source of all goodness. He laughed and hit the table with glee.

It was the laugh that got to St. Peter. He pushed his face toward Jesus and blurted out, "Look it! I was somebody before you came along. You didn't make me. I know now everybody says, 'There goes the Lord Jesus and his side-kick St. Peter. Jesus cures them and Peter picks them up. But it wasn't always that way. People knew me in my own right. I was respected and looked up to. They would say, 'There goes Peter, the greatest fisherman in all of Galilee.'"

"I heard that you were a very good fisherman, Peter," said the Lord Jesus who was always ready to praise.

"You're damn right I was. And tomorrow I am going to prove it. We are going to go fishing, and you will see how the other fishermen respect me and look to my lead."

"I would love to go fishing, Peter. I have never been fishing," said the Lord Jesus who was always looking for new adventures. "But what will we do with all the fish we are going to catch?"

"Well," Peter smiled the smile of the fox. "We'll eat a few, store the rest, wait till there is a shortage, then put them on the market at top dollar and turn a big profit."

"Oh!" said the Lord Jesus, who had that puzzled and pained look in his face that Peter had often observed, as if something that had never crossed his mind just made a forced entry. Peter wondered how someone as obviously intelligent as Jesus could be so slow in some matters.

The next morning at dawn the Lord Jesus and St. Peter were down at the shore readying their boat. And it was just as St. Peter had said. When the other fishermen saw Peter, they sidled over. "Going out, Peter?" they asked.

"Yeah," answered Peter, not looking up from the nets.

"Mind if we come along?"

"Why not?" shrugged Peter, pretending to be bothered by them.

When they left, he glared over at the Lord Jesus and said, "See!"

St. Peter's boat led the way. The Lord Jesus was in the prow hanging on tightly for he was deeply afraid of the water. Now St. Peter was a scientist of a fisherman. He tasted the water, scanned the sky, peered down into the lake—and gave the word in a whisper: "Over there."

"Why isn't anyone talking?" asked the Lord Jesus.

"Shhhh!" Peter shook his head.

The boats formed a wide circle around the area that Peter had pointed to. "Let down the nets," Peter's voice crept over the surface over of the water.

"Why don't they just toss them in?" asked the Lord Jesus, who had hopes of learning about fishing.

A second shhhh! came from St. Peter.

The fishermen let down their nets and began to pull them in. But something was wrong. The muscles of their arms did not tighten under the weight of fish. The nets rose quickly; the arms of the men were slack. All they caught was water.

The fishermen rowed their boats over to St. Peter. They were a chorus of anger "The greatest fisherman in all of Galilee, my grandmother's bald head. You brought us all the way out here for nothing. We have wasted the best hours of the day and have not one fish to show for it. Stick to preaching,

Peter." And they rowed toward shore, shouting curses over their shoulder.

The Lord Jesus said nothing. St. Peter checked the nets. He put on a second parade, tasting the sea, scanning the sky, peering in to the depths. At long last he looked at the Lord Jesus and said, "Over there! "

No sooner had he said, "Over there!" than the Lord Jesus was at the oars, rowing mightily, the muscles of his back straining with each pull.

And all day long under the searing sun the Lord Jesus and St. Peter rowed from place to place on the sea of Galilee. And all day long under the searing sun the Lord Jesus and St. Peter let down their nets. And all day long under the searing sun the Lord Jesus and St. Peter hauled in their nets. And all day long under the searing sun the Lord Jesus and St. Peter caught nothing.

Evening fell and an exhausted St. Peter raised the sail to make for shore. The weary Lord Jesus held on tightly in the prow. It was then, as the boat glided toward shore, that it happened. All the fish in the sea of Galilee came to the surface. They leapt on one side of the boat and they leapt on the other side of the boat. They leapt behind the boat and they leapt in front of the boat. They formed a cordon around the boat, escorting it toward shore in full fanfare. Then in a mass suicide of fish, they began to leap into the boat. They landed in the lap of the laughing Lord Jesus. They smacked the astonished St. Peter in the face. When the boat arrived at shore, it was brimming, creaking, sinking under the weight of fish.

All the other fishermen were waiting. They gathered around Peter and slapped him on the back. "Peter, you scoundrel. You knew where the fish were all the time and never let on." They hit him on the shoulder. "Peter, you rogue.

You put us on. You surely are the greatest fisherman in all of Galilee."

But St. Peter was uncharacteristically silent. He only said, "Give the fish to everyone. Tonight, no home in this village will go without food." After that, he said nothing.

But later, at the tavern with bread and wine between them, Peter looked across the table at Jesus and said, "Go away from me. You go away from me. I wanted the fish to be over them not with them. I wanted the fish to rule them not feed them. You go away from me. I am a sinful man. "

But Jesus smiled, not the smile of the fox but the smile that swept over the waters at the dawn of time, the smile that moves the sun and the stars. And he had no intention of going away. There were other fish to catch.

*　　*　　*

The experience named Spirit has been our concern all along. We uncovered its interpersonal origins in Jesus of Nazareth and its interpersonal continuance among the People of Spirit and Memory. All the creations of this people emerge from this foundational experience. To inhabit these creations with an open spirit is to be led, slowly but truthfully, into the labyrinthine relationship of God and the human person.

We focused on a single creation—narrative—and explored the storytelling process. People tell their religiously significant experiences in story form and interpret them through the sacred story of Jesus, but they also hear the sacred story of Jesus and are urged to ponder and respond. In these two processes, the experience named Spirit gets under way. It is an experience that meets each person in their individuality, and so there are great surface differences. But if the story of Jesus is normative, there are some abiding concerns. The fullness of the experience named Spirit entails divine love, human sinfulness, the re-creation of the person and the reconciliation between people.

We have explored the encounter between divine love and human sinfulness. What must be looked at more extensively is the recreation of the person and the reconciliation between people. What will be the human response to the divine initiative? The story of Jesus and Peter "goin' fishin'" gives us a start.

The story begins with Peter in the classic posture of the envious heart and ends with him in the initial posture of the forgiven heart. His opening line is a statement of self-justification, "We're doing real good." Jesus' critical rejoinder "We?" makes Peter think that Jesus, like the secret desire of his own heart, wants to take all the credit. Peter gives him the glory.

But Jesus has no need to claim credit for the good that is happening. With the second response of "Me?" Peter realizes that Jesus is leading him into deeper waters of God. Peter reluctantly admits the source of all goodness, but Jesus catches the unconverted tone of this admission. With Jesus' laugh, Peter reverts to envy and asserts himself: "I am the greatest fisherman in all of Galilee" translates into "You, whoever you are, are not." Peter will now prove his importance at all costs.

The Lord Jesus is guileless. He is enthusiastic over the fishing expedition, tells Peter that he has heard of his fishing skills, and is an eager, if somewhat pesky, learner. He is also, like many Jews of his day, afraid of the water. Yet, vulnerable as he is, he is also the master and Peter will learn this day that God is a love that does not need his crowing and strutting.

The fish have proved elusive; they are not available to the skills of the greatest fisherman in all of Galilee. The other fishermen abandon Peter in his failure. Jesus does not. He is the first to the oars to continue the search. It is the moment when both are exhausted, when all their efforts have been expended and found wanting that the gift of fish arrives.

The miracle of the suicidal fish leaping into the boat is the work of an ironic God who abundantly gives us what we desperately want but not in the way we want it. Peter wants the fish as a conquering achievement, and they arrive as a comic gift. Through the mediation of Jesus, divine love is offering Peter a new possibility of being human.

Peter's initial responses to his personal event of grace show that he is tentatively moving toward accepting the gift. He does not bask in the emulation of the other fishermen. He knows that the old style is no longer appropriate. "Eat them. Store them. Make a killing" is replaced by "Give the fish to everyone. Tonight no home in this village will go without food."

Whatever has happened, it has released: other-centered energies in Peter. But at this moment. Peter's giving away of the gift of fish is impulsive. It is neither understood nor integrated. The more brooding response occurs at the tavern: "Go away from me. I am a sinful man."

**The Liberation of Love**

The first response to the inrush of divine love is the recognition of sinfulness. We have grounded ourselves wrongly, and that wrong grounding has brought pain into the world. There will be no possibility of a new grounding and a new life unless the past is confessed.

Christian conversion is not a movement from one stage of innocence to another. It is a movement from a struggle wrongly conceived to a struggle rightly conceived. We have become aware of our wrongly conceived struggle ("I am the greatest fisherman in all of Galilee") because the rightly conceived struggle initiated by divine love ("How will we feed one another?") has infiltrated our consciousness. God has not done this for the purposes of condemnation but for the purposes of transformation.

But, as we intimated in the last chapter, the sudden exposure that we are sinners is extremely painful. It is not easy to say, "I wanted the fish to be over them not with them." At this moment we need a Love that loves us more than we love ourselves. That is why Jesus does not go away but smiles the smile of creation for the new life of Peter is about to be born.

Personal re-creation entails surrender. William James has stated that "self-surrender has been and always must be regarded as the vital turning-point of the religious life."[3] E. D. Starbuck explores this moment insightfully:

> . . . he must relax, that is, he must fall back on the larger Power that makes for righteousness, which has been welling up in his own being, and let it finish in its own way the work it has begun . . . The act of yielding, in this point of view, is giving one's self over to the new life, making it the center of a new personality, and living, from within, the truth of it which had before been viewed objectively.[4]

The act of surrendering is really a process of recentering, a free acceptance of ourselves as constituted by a larger Power.

This recentering is a long and arduous process. The event of grace which reveals our sinfulness and offers the possibility of new life can usually be circumscribed quite neatly in time. "It happened when I was . . . " is a typical beginning when people relate conversion experiences.

But the response to these catalytic occurrences takes place over time. We only gradually see the implications of what has happened and, even more gradually, find the personal courage and community support we need to change. We engage in the process of recreation that we mapped out in Chapter Three. We tell and retell the experience; certain attitudes and outlooks become dominant; certain moral struggles begin to appear. Although the regrounding in God is a lifelong adventure, the general path of advance can be mapped. Surrender to divine love is the liberation of human love. The story of Jesus at the house of Simon on reveals this.

Jesus was on his feet; and he was angry. Turning to the woman, he said to Simon, "You see this woman" (Lk. 7:44).

But Simon sees no woman. Simon sees a sinner, a theological category created by his own self-righteousness and maintained for his own importance. Simon is a portrait of self-enclosure. He thinks to himself that Jesus is not a prophet. A prophet is supposed to know the hearts of people and "if this man were a prophet, he would know who and what sort of woman this is who touches him—that she is a sinner."

But Simon does not venture to speak this opinion. He keeps it to himself but that does not mean he keeps it away from Jesus. The man he does not think is a prophet knows his inner thoughts. "In response to his thoughts, Jesus said to him, 'Simon, I have something to propose to you.'"

The cautious response is, "Teacher, speak." The story of the two debtors—one forgiven fifty coins and one five hundred—ends with the simplest of questions: "Which of them was more grateful?" To the simplest of questions comes the most hesitant of responses, "He, I presume, to whom he remitted the larger sum." The "I presume" is the classic hedge of opportunism. Simon ventures nothing, neither his thoughts nor his values.

Jesus uncovers Simon's hidden heart by contrasting it with the heart of the woman. Simon has given Jesus no water for his feet; the woman has washed his feet with her tears and dried them with her hair. Simon has not given him a kiss of greeting; the woman has not ceased kissing his feet. Simon has not anointed his head with oil; the woman has anointed his feet with perfume.

The picture is complete: Simon is a miser. "He is like a person who holds on to the air inside his lungs, refusing to exhale it lest no more be available."[5] His whole life is one of "not giving." The woman, on the other hand, is total giving. She is pouring herself out on Christ. Her other-centered style is the polar opposite of the ego-centered style of Simon. Simon is a wary man in a wary world; she is a luxuriant woman in an extravagant world.

Jesus does not leave us in the dark about the source of these two different ways of being alive. The most acceptable understanding of what Jesus says is that she is capable of loving because she has been forgiven; little love flows from those who have been forgiven little.[6] When divine love meets sin and the person recognizes her sinfulness and surrenders to the love, the result is the release of human love. The one who has not found forgiving love, gives nothing. The empty heart of Simon only allows him to take; the full heart of the woman allows her to overflow. Simon stands back and judges; the woman embraces and cherishes.

A common characteristic of the envious and rejected is self-preoccupation. The rejected heart is obsessed with its insignificance; the envious heart is obsessed with its importance. But both are obsessed with themselves. Divine love is the release from this chronic egocentricity.

> Love is, therefore, on the one hand, the only salvation of the spiritual man and, on the other hand, unattainable by his own efforts. The spiritual man can only love when he is freed from the necessity of love, that is, when he knows himself already loved in his self-preoccupation. Only if man finds

that he is already accepted in his sin and sickness, can he accept his own self-preoccupation as it is; and only then can his psychic economy be opened toward others, to accept them as they are—not in order to save himself, but because he doesn't need to save himself. We love only because we are first loved. In this way, and only in this way, can the spiritual man genuinely and purely love.[7]

This dynamic underlies the woman's freedom. The experience of divine love becomes the possibility of human loving.

Divine love is not only the capacity for human love but its inner energy. The concrete situation receives the emerging love of the forgiven person, but it does not control it. This is the thrust behind the story of Attar of Nishapur which opened this chapter. The ones who revile Jesus, he prays for. Their hostility cannot control his response.

Jesus can give only what is in his purse. He is coming from the experience of divine love, and the resistances to embodying that love do not ultimately destroy it. The human love which divine love releases is free. This freedom is not indifference. Whenever love goes out, it is vulnerable. A person can be deeply hurt when his or her love is not received and returned. But when divine love is the force that suffuses human love, lack of response does not totally determine the flow of love. The sustained attitude of love is generated more by the experience of divine liberation than by the human reception.

The inner origins of Christian love are most clear in the command to love one's enemies. A situation of hostility would seem to dictate a hostile response. Yet the response suggested is the opposite of hatred—positive care. In the Gospel of Luke, enemy love is contrasted with situational love. "If you love those who love you, what credit is that?" (Lk. 6:32).

If a receptive atmosphere is not the stimulation to love, what is the incentive? It is said that the nature of the divine is to be diffusive of itself. "It cannot not pour out." Whether the earth receives the water or not, the fountain continues to spring. When human love is released by divine love, it takes on this characteristic. It continues to move from inner abundance. It is co-loving all things with the ever outward love of God. Chardin suggested that when this energy of love is released, the human race will have discovered fire for the second time.

**Toward God**

But what does the person who has accepted divine love *love?* What are the "objects" of love? The compressed answer of the Gospels is the double commandment of love:

> You shall love the Lord your God with all your heart, with all your soul, with all your strength, and with all your mind, and your neighbor as yourself.
>
> Luke 10:27

This double commandment suggests two directions—toward God and toward neighbor. From the sheer amount of words devoted to love of God, it would seem to have some priority. Yet the depth of Christian life is to envision these two directions as flowing from a single, responsive love. The continual task is to hold them together in a dynamic, mutual relationship, neither separating one from the other nor reducing one to the other. The reciprocity of love of God and love of neighbor is what we want to explore.

Responsive human love immediately moves toward the mediator of divine love. The outpouring of the forgiven heart is on the one who forgave it. The woman lavishes herself on Jesus, but not just on Jesus. She is loving Jesus as the bringer of forgiveness. Most commentaries on the story speculate that this is not her first encounter with Jesus. She has heard him preach, and the preaching reached her heart and stirred the Spirit of salvation. She has come in gratitude and praise to love the one who brought the Love. This is a natural movement of the redeemed heart. It loves the source of its redemption.

Although we have used a Scripture story to illustrate it, we do not have to resort to the Bible for examples of responsive gratitude. This is not an arcane truth; everyday life gives ample evidence of it. When someone brings us a love that liberates us, we respond with gratitude and commitment. We say, "I can't thank you enough."

We also feel a deep need to repay so unpayable a gift and we say, "If there is anything I can ever do for you . . . " Even time does not diminish our instinctive affective response to the love that loves us. Whenever we remember the people who have loved us and through their love redeemed us from destructiveness, our heart immediately goes out to them. From a religious perspective, we are first of all receivers of love, and the simple uncomplicated response is to love the love we have received.

We have stressed that divine and human love always come together, and although they can be distinguished, they can never be separated. But this ability to distinguish is important. In Jesus Christ we have a full and perfect mediation of divine love. The mediated and the mediator have fused together so completed that to love one is to love the other.

The Gospel of John emphasizes this identity of Jesus and God. There is no instance in the Gospel where we are commanded to love God. But there is often the command, either implicitly or explicitly, to love the Son.[8] Jesus the Son has brought the love of the Father. Therefore, to return love to the Son is to return love to the Father. All Christians are urged to love Christ because through Christ they have encountered the plenitude of God's salvific love.

But besides Jesus Christ, there are the "other Christs" of the Christian tradition. These are the concrete persons who constitute the People of Spirit and Memory and who, in their finest moments, have communicated divine love. They are usually parents, spouses, friends, and even, if the gospel stories are to be credited, those we perceive as enemies.

Our response is to love them. But in them the fusion of the divine and the human is not what it was in Jesus. It is here that our need to distinguish comes into play. We recognize that their loving was co-loving. They were loving us with the love of God.

This does not diminish them or make them mere vehicles of grace. They are not dispensable channels of divine love, but cherished communicators. The divine moves through their uniqueness, ingenuity, and creativity. They are the human face of God. But this does not mean that their own features are distorted. Their distinctiveness comes into its own beauty by being in union with divine beauty.

But human mediation, outside of Jesus, is flawed mediation. When we pretend this is not the case, we are ripe for disenchantment. We have turned the ones who have loved us into idols, and all idols have clay feet. The saints are the first to admit they are sinners. They know, as Francis of Assisi made explicit, they have become instruments of divine peace, but they also know at certain times and places, they are instruments of human war. The parent who loves us at one moment we see in a rage of spite and anger at another. The spouse who beheld our weakness and loved us anyway now berates us in front of others. The friends who were there when we needed them are now nowhere to be found. Human loving is fragmented and partial. Yet in its mediating impact it reveals unconditional love. It is this divine love that remains even if its human mediation fades.

Therefore, our responsive love encompasses the mediators but goes beyond them. When this recognition occurs we say "We love God." We perform a mental act of disengagement. We focus on the divine presence that comes through multiple created presences, but at this moment we are not consciously focusing on the created presences.

This is a natural procedure. A divine reality is perceived in the human reality. This divine love is truly other than the mediating human love. Therefore, a genuine option open to human perception is to focus on this divine love. Since it is this love that has cherished us, it is this love we wish to enter into a relationship with. Our response is to be attentive to it, engage it in dialogue, learn more about it. When liberated human love moves toward God, it begins to pray. "Thus praying is inseparable from love of God—it is the language of love which completes the relationship God initiates."[9]

The traditional analogy for prayer is a dialogue between two people who love one another, and this is a helpful way to explore the prayer life that arises from an encounter with divine love. In the first meeting, all the lovers know is the basic fact of their love. Their individual lives are "saved" when they are together and "lost" when they are apart.

With more encounters, there come greater intimacy and a deepened appreciation of what their mutual love is accomplishing in them. There also develops a sense of responsibility to their love. They become aware of the conditions under which it will grow and the conditions under which it will atrophy. Prayer is the cultivation of the relationship which was consciously established in the experience named Spirit. Its purpose is to deepen, appreciate, and become more responsible to the reality of divine love.

This procedure of "segmenting out" the divine and pursuing a relationship with it may be natural, but it is also extremely dangerous. The danger lies in forgetting the roots of the relationship. The relationship came to be in a free, divine act of love which was mediated by other people. Any further communication within the relationship must not lose these qualities of divine initiative and relatedness to other people.

Yet the history of many people's prayer life reads like a chronicle of the solitary self's strenuous striving to gain the attention of a reluctant God: Prayer is not response to the reality of God that has chosen to engage us, but unaided assertion toward the reality of God that is constantly avoiding us. Prayer does not lead us into the depth of our encounters with other people but provides an alternate reality for us to occupy ourselves with. In prayer we come to love a heavenly God while we are disdaining an earthly people. In order to understand the style of prayer that is appropriate to the experience named Spirit, we need to look at the prayer of the Giver of the Spirit.

### The Prayer of Jesus

Before Jesus was an advocate of prayer, he was its most thoroughgoing critic.[10] He mocked the prayer of the righteous with its pompous boasting before God: "Thank God I am not like the rest of men" (Lk. 18:11). He brutally uncovered the real reason behind the public display of prayer—self-advertisement (Mt. 6:5). He outrageously linked outward piety with acts of injustice: "Beware . . . men who swallow the property of widows, while making a show of lengthy prayers" (Mk. 12:40).

Jesus attacked the core assumption of all professional pray-ers that more is better: "In your prayers do not babble as the pagans do, for they think that by using many words they will make themselves heard" (Mt. 6:7–8). Finally, and most scathingly, he took up the ancient prophetic denunciation of substituting prayer for just action: "It is not those who say to me, 'Lord, Lord,' who will enter the Kingdom of Heaven, but the person who does the will of my Father in Heaven" (Mt. 7:21). In the light of this consistent critique it is not an idle question when one of his disciples asks, "Lord, teach us to pray" (Lk. 11:1).

The reason that Jesus so vigorously attacked the prayer practices of his day is that they contradicted the Abba-King experience of God. The prayer practices show frightened and panicky people before an all-powerful presence they cannot be sure of. These people alternately boast and babble, doing anything to get the attention of a God who is basically bored with them. Their prayer is just one more strategy in the over-all campaign of ego glorification. To pray in public for atten-tion and rip off widows in private for security is perfectly com-patible. Both flow from the shaken self, desperately grasping something to hold on to. In short, these prayers are not a response to the inrush of divine love but a sign of the stubborn resistance to accept our lives as given from beyond ourselves.

Prayer that is a loving response to divine love takes many different forms. But there is a definite "coloration" to the activ-ity. There is an atmosphere to the relationship, a feeling-tone that permeates all the interactions. Whatever the particular content of prayer might be, these qualities are present and influential. We will try to point out three characteristics of this type of prayer. Our guide will be Jesus' classic prayer: the Our Father.

> First, the divine and the human are held together, and the bonds between people strengthened. The first line of the Lord's prayer is "Our Father in heav-en." Although prayer may be said in solitude, it

always addresses the reality that binds people together. The opening word must be *our.* If it is not, we are in danger of creating a private God, one who looks after us but is neglectful of others. Prayer would then foster division because some would have the ear of God and some would not. But the God encountered in Christian prayer is the grounding of human solidarity. The divine love that is dialogued with talks to more than me, and so through it, I am related to all others. As the poetess Anne Sexton put it: "To pray, Jesus knew,/is to be a man carrying a man."

Although the Father is characterized as in heaven and so transcendent to the affairs of earth, the very fact that we can say "Father" indicates divine presence. The portrait is definitely different from the Oriental Potentate God who lives in the sky and can be contacted only through the bribes of slaughtered cattle and burnt wheat.

The God of Jesus' prayer has already made contact, and his contact has brought life. So he is called Father. The life that has been given comes from beyond ourselves, from an Otherness that is the source of all created reality. So we say "in heaven." But the perception is clear. The divine and the human are not alienated, but in intimate communion.

This interaction of the divine and the human is considerably deepened in the "forgiveness" section of the Lord's Prayer. This petition seems to say that the proper response to the experience of divine love is to transform it into human love toward one another. The energy and inspiration of this human love will be perceived as divine:

> Your light must shine in the sight of men, so that,
> seeing your good works, they may give the praise
> to your Father in heaven.
>
> Matthew 5:16

If we have been forgiven, we are to forgive in turn. When we do this, we do more than merely "give as we have received." In the fact of loving others, we enter more deeply into our own experience of divine love. As Norman Perrin puts it:

> In the context of God's forgiveness men learn to forgive, and in the exercise of forgiveness toward their fellow man they enter ever more deeply into an experience of the divine forgiveness.[11]

The atmosphere of the prayer "which passionately pursues the divine love that has passionately pursued the person" is the intimate bonding of God, self, and neighbor.

A second quality of the prayer that cultivates divine love is that it is other-centered and strategic. After the initial address in the Lord's Prayer, the priorities are set out: "Your name be held holy; your Kingdom come; your will be done, on earth as in heaven." The concerns are not those of the one praying, they are those of the one prayed to.

These petitions purify the desires of the person before God. The one praying has experienced love and expressed it as "Our Father." The response to this love is to espouse the concerns of the Lover. This is the true maturity of prayer. Prayer is not pleading with an unfeeling Higher Power to do our bidding. It is not a begging of God to do for us what we cannot do for ourselves. This procedure, all too common in prayer, subtly places us at the center of the universe and reverses the creature-creator relationship. Prayer is for the purpose of discerning the cause of God in human life and marshaling our energies to serve it.

In prayer, we lay ourselves open to the cause of God. Nikos Kazantzakis opens his autobiography, *Report to Greco,* with three prayers: "Three kinds of souls, three prayers: 1. I am a bow in your hands, Lord. Draw me, lest I rot. 2. Do not overdraw me, Lord. I shall break. 3. Overdraw me, Lord, and who cares if I break."[12] In prayer we become available for the divine mission. We must be careful of this. It easily turns to fanaticism. The only check is the reminder that the divine cause is love.

Prayer then is for plotting. In the overall story of Jesus, the rhythm of prayer and action is firmly established. Jesus prays at times of important decisions—when he chooses the twelve, when he sets his face toward Jerusalem, when the influential and powerful decide against him, when he faces the possibilities of suffering, when death finally comes. In the middle of a whirlwind ministry and in the face of growing opposition, Jesus retires to desert places to pray. The implication is that the path of love is not all that easily discerned.

And if prayer does not complement action, action will go its own way, breaking loose from divine love and inevitably betraying it. Nowhere is this more evident than in the Gethsemane prayer:

> Abba! Everything is possible for you. Take this cup away from me. But let it be as You, not I, would have it.
>
> Mark 14:36

In prayer we gauge our situation and project the path that will most serve God's cause.

This fact that prayer is other-centered and strategic means that it can never be divorced from experience and action. On the one hand, prayer flows out of the experience of divine love we have undergone. It is meditation on the implications of that experience and the cultivation of the relationship which was established at that time.

On the other hand, prayer looks to the further embodiment of that experience. It envisions actions that will be congruent with it. Any type of prayer that does not stem from experience or has no overflow into action is too isolated. Prayer may provide times of ecstasy, but as long as that ecstasy is experienced by people in the throes of sin and grace, it cannot be an end itself. The touch of God always means personal and social transformation.

The third constant quality of praying out of the experience of divine love has to do with the affective flow of the relationship. Divine love initiated the relationship, but mutual love sustains it. Prayer is a conversation between hearts. It includes the traditional praise and gratitude, an occasional scream for help, a fervent petition now and then, and some hard-nosed bargaining for a better deal.

But prayer does not stop there. It encompasses the confiding of secrets, the admission of fears, the free flow of tears, and ecstatic dance. When you start a conversation with "Abba," anything is liable to happen. Divine love is abundance, and in relationship to it, abundant feelings and insights emerge. And if you are steeped in the anthropomorphism of the Bible, God is an avid conversationalist.

Prayer that is more than duty includes religious affections. It is a nurturing activity which provides "bread for the day." The qualities of trust, intimacy, warmth, delight, and exuberance are often present. But this God is not a chum or a mere fellow traveler. The transcendence of God always remains.

This is the God whose ways are not our ways and whose uncovered face spells death. Yet the majesty of the divine does not mean coldness. Can there be such a thing as friendly transcendence and warm majesty? The poets think so.

> I'm mooring my rowboat
> at the dock of the island called God.
> This dock is made in the shape of a fish
> and there are many boats moored
> at many different docks.
> "It's okay," I say to myself,
> with blisters that broke and healed
> and broke and healed—
> saving themselves over and over.
> And salt sticking to my face and arms like
> a glue-skin pocked with grains of tapioca
> I empty myself from my wooden boat
> and onto the flesh of The Island.
> "On with it!" He says and thus
> we squat on the rocks by the sea
>  and play—can it be—
> a game of poker.
> He calls me.
> I win because I hold a royal straight flush.
> He wins because He holds five aces.
> A wild card had been announced
>  but I had not heard it
> being in such a state of awe
> when He took out the cards and dealt.
> As he plunks down His five aces
> and I sit grinning at my royal flush,
> He starts to laugh,
> the laughter rolling like a hoop out of His mouth

and into mine,
and such laughter that He doubles right over me
laughing a Rejoice Chorus at our two triumphs.
Then I laugh, the fishy dock laughs
the sea laughs. The Island laughs.
The Absurd laughs.
Dearest dealer,
I with my royal straight flush,
love you so for your wild card,
that untamable, eternal, gut-driven *ha-ha*
and lucky love.[13]

Christian life is living in relationship to a transcendent, loving reality. It is beyond our control, yet not oblivious of the desires of our heart. It calls wild cards with little or no notice, and although we are outraged, we love it all the more for that. Within the Christian tradition, we believe the final wild card is resurrection.

To be touched by divine love through other people is to love the divine back through those same people. But we are capable of focusing on the divine more directly, and we do this in prayer. But this prayer does not leave behind the earth; it pushes us more deeply into the heart of the world. We focus on God as the source of human solidarity, the power that transforms personal and social life, and the loving reality that sustains us but does not submit to us.

It is this last quality that we must explore further. What does it mean for people to love a divine reality which, however immanent and understandable, remains transcendent and unknowable? This is the struggle the synoptic Gospels portray the moment Jesus leaves the waters of sin with the word *Son* in his ears.

### The Temptations of Jesus

No sooner is Jesus baptized than he is "conducted by the Spirit into the desert for forty days, where he was tempted by the devil" (Lk. 4:1–2). The temptations of Jesus in the desert are often understood as possible false uses of messianic power. Jesus has been declared the beloved Son at the baptism, and that sonship entails a mission. The question is how he will carry out his assignment; what will be his strategies.

Satan has some suggestions. Jesus should use his power to provide a kingdom of bread which will feed all people. Jesus responds that there is more to life than bread. Satan's second proposal is to float down from the pinnacle of the Temple. This will establish his authority beyond doubt, and people will eagerly follow him from miracle to miracle.

When this strategy is rejected, Satan suggests they join forces for world domination. Political conquest is the way the mission should be enacted. Dostoyevsky's Grand Inquisitor is the classic proponent of this interpretation. He tells the silent Jesus that if he really loved people he would have fed them, relieved their doubts with miracles, and imposed global government. Instead he left them their freedom, a dubious gift at best.

This approach to the temptations has far-reaching implications and has been effectively used in understanding the social and political dimensions of Christian faith. But another approach sees the three temptations as christological rather than soteriological.[14] It is not Jesus' relationship to other people that is being tested, but his relationship to God.

The title under which Satan tempts him is not messiah, but Son of God. Also the fact that the Spirit led him into the desert recalls Israel's sojourn in the desert of sin after the Exodus liberation. That story concerns the rocky relationship between Yahweh and his people. In the desert, Israel was tested and found wanting. The apologetic interests of the early Church place Jesus in the same desert. He will be tested and found to be the true Son. In the context of our concerns, the temptations tell us more about what it means to return love to God.

Significant portions of the Bible portray the relationship between Yahweh and his people as a stormy love affair. What makes for the storm is that at various times both partners feel unappreciated and misunderstood. The declared love between them is not being lived out the way they had expected. They look for new pledges of love that are both spoken and enacted.

In Chapter Four we traced the insidious way the sinful heart puts God to the test in search of a pledge of love. The result is succinctly stated in Romans:

> It is precisely in this that God proves his love for us:
> that while we were still sinners, Christ died for us.
>
> Romans 5:8

This divine sharing in the human condition revitalizes the love relationship:

> For I am certain that neither death nor life, neither angels nor principalities, neither the present nor the future nor powers, neither height nor depth nor any other creature, will be able to separate us from the love of God that comes to us in Christ Jesus, our Lord.
>
> Romans 8:38

Looking at the cross of Christ, the human heart can say, "Now I know."

But sin not only tests God before people. In our reformulated understanding of testing narratives, it also tests people before God. The temptations of Jesus represent the trials love for God will undergo. They are episodes that detail Jesus' steadfast love, love that endures all the doubts and terrors that beset it.

The traditional Christian statement of faith in Christ is that he is truly God and truly man. When we were exploring divine love for people, we stressed the divine dimension of Jesus Christ and his life as revelatory of God's intentions. The death of the Son of God is the assurance of divine love. We are now exploring how people love God, so we will stress the human dimension and his life as revelatory of a full human response:

> [Christ is] not only the offer of divine love to man made visible but, at the same time, as prototype (or primordial model), he is the supreme realization of the response of human love to this divine offer.[15]

The first temptation takes place in the desert and so recalls Israel's testing in the desert of sin (Ex. 16, 17). Yahweh had led Israel out of Egypt. In Yahweh's eyes they should love him for this act alone. But in the desert they begin to grumble:

> Would that we had died at the Lord's hand in the land of Egypt, as we sat by our fleshpots and ate our fill of bread! But you had to lead us into this desert to make the whole community die of famine!
> Exodus 16:3

So Yahweh hears their grumbling and gives them manna in the morning and quail at evening.

But already there is the beginning of a problem. As later rabbis commented, Yahweh gave the manna with a light countenance but the quail with a heavy countenance. Yahweh's command that comes with this gift of food is that they may not gather the manna on the Sabbath. Some break this command, but they find no manna on the ground. The countenance of Yahweh grows darker.

Then at Massah the grumbling grows louder. "Give us water to drink." They demand another miracle and make it the condition for knowing "Is the Lord in our midst or not?" Yahweh hears them again and tells Moses, "Strike the rock, and the water will flow from it for the people to drink." But there is little doubt that the character of Yahweh in the story whose feelings are reflected in Moses is beginning to wonder if the people he loves love him in return.

The trouble between Yahweh and his people is often stated as lack of trust. The Israelites doubted whether God would take care of them. But this is only the surface of the difficulty. Yahweh has given them freedom from slavery. But they want more. Every time any need arises, they petition God to fill it. And Yahweh, in his love for them, does fill it. Bread, meat, and water miraculously arrive.

But it is beginning to dawn on Yahweh that his love may be one-sided. They are taking Yahweh for granted and turning him into a "go for."From God's point of view, he is being taken advantage of. He is not loved but only used for what he can provide, and the moment he stops providing, their praise turns to grumbling. No crisis is integrated into the past loving history of the relationship. Each crisis threatens the relationship itself. This is a sure sign that God is not loved, but only manipulated for his gifts. After each gift is greedily accepted, the people respond, "Thank you. But what have you done for us lately?"

This is the atmosphere of the first go-around between Jesus and Satan. Jesus is hungry and Satan suggests that a divine miracle is the ideal way to fulfill that need. "If you are the Son of God, command these stones to turn into bread." Jesus replies, "Not on bread alone is man to live, but on every word that comes from the mouth of God."

At the baptism, a word has already come from the mouth of God, and the word was "Beloved Son." There is no need to test that word at every turn. Satan is playing upon the possibility in Jesus of a petulant and greedy heart. "If you really love me, then . . . " He does not want any stability in the relationship between Jesus and God. He wants each new happening to be "the be-all and end-all" of the relationship. When Israel hungered, they forgot that Yahweh rescued them from Egypt. Satan wants Jesus' hunger to so dominate him that he will forget the loving word of the water and demand a new miracle—not a voice from the sky but bread from stone. And oh yes, what Satan leaves unsaid, tomorrow there will be a need for another miracle.

This temptation strikes at the heart of all faith. There is no problem in loving God when the sun shines. It is the rain that brings doubt. In the Book of Job, Satan chides God with the remark, "Is it for nothing that Job is God-fearing?" And he recounts Job's many blessings. His smug observation is that if you take away the blessings, Job's love of God will soon turn to cursing.

What is fascinating in this temptation is the idealism of the human lover and the realism of the divine lover. From the human point of view, pain, suffering, and death should not happen and are taken as signs of an indifferent God. From the divine point of view, pain, suffering, and death are going to happen, why take them as signs of the lack of love? The key to God's point of view in the narratives is that he has declared his love "no matter what." The foundation of human trust in God in times of want and crisis are the previous experiences of divine fidelity.

An illuminating approach to this Satan-Jesus dialogue is to see Satan as concentrating on satisfaction-assurance and Jesus as countering with reality-assurance. These terms are coined by Donald Evans.[16] Satisfaction-assurance means that all our physical and emotional needs are being met. Reality-assurance is the assurance that life is worth living because it has already "received the meaning and the reality which are necessary for human fulfillment."[17]

These twin assurances are related yet distinct. When there is food, clothing, friendship, and shelter to satisfy us, we are to take these "goods" as symbols of an ultimate assurance. But when these are lacking, we do not take the lack as symbols of an ultimate rejection. In these situations, we fall back on our deeper sense of reality-assurance. This is what Jesus does. He will not take the lack of bread as a symbol of his lack of worth, the fact that God does not love him. His worth has already been established. He will integrate his hunger into the word of the water—"Beloved Son."

The second temptation takes place on the parapet of the Temple. The Temple is the place of special divine protection, and this temptation has to do with twisting divine love into special privilege. Satan proposes that Jesus' sonship is a prerogative to be exploited. The proper response to divine love is to parade the fact that you are loved. Jesus' insistence is that you do not love the fact that you are loved, but you love the Love that loves you.

This means that you will pursue that Love even when your own life is slipping away. This is the thrust of the quote from Salinger which opened the chapter. The man with the slit throat sees the jug safely over the hill. This commitment is to Love wherever it is manifesting itself. The fact that his own life

JOHN SHEA

is diminishing is a secondary concern next to the beauty that
he is appreciating and helping to bring about. This concentration on divine love even when your own life is failing is, need-
less to say, extraordinary. That is why Zooey's remark is so
appropriate: "I'd like to see him do it, the bastard."

In Zooey's colloquialism, Jesus was the "bastard who did
it." In the Gospel of Luke, the temptation narrative ends with
"The devil left him . . . to await another opportunity."
Satan's finest opportunity is when life is ebbing in Jesus. On
the cross, Satan waits to see if Jesus can love God and God's
work when God is not shielding him.

The words of Jesus on the cross in Luke are "Father, forgive them for they know not what they do." Jesus is the Son,
and that does not mean protection from harm but concern,
above all, with the salvific presence of God. Loving God is just
that—loving God. It is not loving the fact that you are loved.
James Mackey has an insightful passage about what loving
God in the face of death means:

> Like the rest of us, the man Jesus came from noth-
> ing and he had nothing except what was given to
> him. His very life and everything which came to
> him in life was gift. Out of the bounty freely given
> he freely gave. Life itself, and everything that
> became part of that life, he held as a grace, as one
> holds a precious gift, gently, as one holds a soft,
> delicate thread which, as it is drawn back will, if
> one does not pull at it and break it, draw one to its
> very source. With this lived conviction, this faith
> that is made real only in act, he inspired some and
> as deeply offended the deepest convictions of oth-
> ers. When force was brought to bear on him,
> inevitably, in order to make him divide and grasp

242

like the rest, then, in final witness to the faith by which he lived and by which alone life is served, he refused to do so. He held the thread as gently as ever, as it was drawn back, and in doing so he deprived death of its sting, robbed it of its only victory. Death's victory over us is to enslave us in fear, to make us grasp more eagerly and tear more savagely at the things we think can give us the life we want, and, as we do so, feel more utterly the futility, and fear more persistently the hopelessness of it all. Jesus denied death that victory.

In denying death that victory, Jesus recorded the only victory over death, but also the one real victory over death, which is given to mortals to achieve. The Prince of Life was victorious over death in the act of dying. The one whose conviction of grace had wagered for life in life, whose living faith had overcome in life the agents of death, the grasping, tearing divisions of human kind, now consummated the victory of life over death by still treating life as grace at the one moment in which the conviction that life is gift is subjected to the ultimate test, the final trial, the moment when the gift is withdrawn. His death was the supreme act of faith in God the Father, the giver of the grace of life, and so it was the supreme act of hope.[18]

Loving God is not exemption from harm but the faithful pursuit of love in the face of death.

Loving God is a difficult idea for many to appreciate today. It seems so abstract, especially when it is compared to loving the person next to me. But loving God means valuing Love more than life and death. It means appreciating the ultimate worthwhileness of life without needing to survive, and usually to survive in style, at every moment. Most statements about loving God in our culture are indirect homages. One of the finest comes from Henri Nouwen. He is reflecting on his fiftieth birthday:

> Within a few years (five, ten, twenty, or thirty) I will no longer be on this earth. The thought of this does not frighten me but fills me with a quiet peace. I am a small part of life, a human being in the midst of thousands of other human beings. It is good to be young, to grow old, and to die. It is good to live with others, and to die with others. God became flesh to share with us in this simple living and dying and thus made it good. I can feel today that it is good to be and especially to be one of many. What counts are not the special and unique. accomplishments in life that make me different from others, but the basic experiences of sadness and joy, pain and healing, which make me part of humanity. The time is indeed growing short for me, but that knowledge sets me free to prevent mourning from depressing me and joy from exciting me. Mourning and joy can now both deepen my quiet desire for the day when I realize that the many kisses and embraces I received today were simple incarnations of the eternal embrace of the Lord himself.[19]

What is interesting in reading this beautiful yet indirect passage on the love of God is that our minds immediately move to "refuting situations." This felt-perception may be possible at the birthday party, but what about a death bed or, worse, a torture chamber. We always envision a test case to see if this "state of soul" is permanent or only an illusory peace. We may be a long way from the cultural testing patterns of ancient Israel, but there is still an instinct that says the truth is known only in fire.

The third temptation in the Gospel of Matthew is for Jesus to change allegiance. Satan takes him to a mountaintop where he can see the kingdoms of the world and offers him everything if only he will bow down and worship him. This temptation is properly placed. Jesus has just opted for an invisible Love. He has stated that he will love God when the mediations of love are lacking (the bread) and when he is not protected from the powers of diminishment and death.

This appears to be a groundless love. Satan is offering him something concrete. He seems to be saying, "You love a God who won't prove it. Love me, and I'll prove it. Take the earth over this heaven you are guessing at." Jesus' response seems to be "I cannot love you because you are not Love." The ultimate truth of Jesus' response to his experience of God as Abba is that he cannot love anything that does not manifest Love.

This is the most telling reason why love of God cannot be collapsed into love of neighbor. The brutal fact is that the neighbor will not be loved authentically unless God is co-loved in the act of loving the neighbor. Unless there is a vision of sustaining and transforming love and a commitment to it above all else, it is too easy to give in.

Satan is right. The long haul of trying to love in the absence of mediations and protection moves inevitably to the strategy of quick, short gains at the expense of others. "No one can serve two masters," said Jesus. But a person can move back and forth, serving God when convenient and serving mammon when convenient. It is often stressed that Christian faith does not hold that Jesus was not tempted. It holds that he did not sin. There are many renditions of what this means. Perhaps it is just simply that he could not bring himself to love what was not Love.

Our core conviction is that the surrender to divine love means the liberation of human love. This liberated love moves in two complementary directions, toward God and toward neighbor. In the movement toward God, human love encompasses the mediators and goes through them to the permeating divine love. It cultivates this divine love in prayer.

This prayer relationship is a mapping of the ways of divine love as it binds people together and solicits human cooperation in its sustaining and transforming activity. But it also situates the one who prays in a living relationship to a transcendent graciousness. This means, among other things, living in a Love we cannot control and whose ways remain a mystery to us.

Anything beyond our control and which is not constantly solicitous of us on our own terms we tend to dismiss. The temptations of Jesus spell out the inevitable problems. We must love the Love that loves us even when mediation and protection are missing and the desire to grasp and tear and divide and conquer are overwhelming. It is with this divine love in our hearts that we co-love our neighbor.

**Toward Neighbor**
The front of the unemployment office is all brick. The street never sees what happens inside. Next to this building is a bakery with a plate-glass window. Every day everybody who passes can see the baker "doing whatever it is that bakers do. " Lately the baker has taken to doing "unbakerlike" things. He is making sandwiches at lunch time and giving them to people waiting in the unemployment lines. He will not take any money.

This is news. So the television mini-cam people arrived to get the scoop. They interviewed the baker who stood outside his shop like a giant jelly roll.

"Why are you doing this?"

"When I was twenty, I went hungry for a week. Finally, a man I'll never forget took me in." The baker stopped. He said no more. He just smiled as if everything was now accounted for.

Whatever happened to the baker when he was twenty, from a Christian point of view he got the message. He not only remembers and loves the one who fed him, he feeds others, The response to love received is love passed on. We would need more conversation to see if in the human love he received, he discerned a larger love and if in his care for others, he was communicating to them a larger care. But as is usually the case in contemporary life, divine love is incognito. It is intuited and relied on but seldom made explicit.

In Christian code, the baker probably did not see Christ in the man who fed him, and he probably does not see Christ in the hungry he feeds. There is no doubt the judgment of Christ will provoke surprise in most people, "When did I see you hungry . . . " (Mt. 28). But also this passage seems to suggest that explicitation is secondary. What is important is to be there when being there is what is needed.

But we are trying to make connections, to uncover the depth of love received and loved passed on. Our not-so-modest suggestion (which would have to be checked out) is that the baker loved the man who fed him in God and is loving the ones he feeds in God. If he did not love God through his love for the one who fed him, he would not be in the lunch business. He would remember the person who fed him as an example of kindness and himself as one "lucky son-of-a-bitch" to have bumped into him when he did. But there would be no impulse to feed others.

The reason the baker feeds others is because, as the second half of the double commandment says, he sees them as himself. The underlying power that allows us to see the other as ourself is the power that connects the two of us—the power of God. To love God is to experience a baffling solidarity with other people.

Christians have construed this relationship between the love of God and the love of neighbor in many different ways. One of the most destructive renditions of the relationship is to see them as competing interests. When the question is phrased "Whom do you love more, God or your neighbor?" we are already on the wrong track.

But this is a track many have taken. Total love of God demands the loss of earth. If you love God, you forsake the world, and if your love of "worldly things" is too great, God is certainly not being adequately attended to. The most cited scriptural backing for this tension is in Matthew:

> Whoever loves father or mother, son or daughter,
> more than me is not worthy of me.
>
> Matthew 10:37

This is a jealous God and a jealous Christ who want the undivided attention of their worshippers. Love of God is not the transformation of love for others, but its substitute.

People who hold strongly to this heavy contrast position can find themselves in a somewhat ludicrous and illogical problem. They say they love God more than anything else. In fact, their intense love of God has made them indifferent to the concerns of earth. This life and its loves are passing. Set your heart on eternal treasure.

But the God they love loves the concerns of earth. The entire Christian revelation revolves around God's unrelenting activity in time and history. Loving God certainly means loving what God loves. This is the polemical edge of 1 John:

> If anyone says, "My love is fixed on God," yet hates his brother, he is a liar. One who has no love for the brother he has seen cannot love the God he has not seen.
>
> 1 John 4:20–21

The competition scheme not only leads to odious comparisons; it also subtly suggests an essential rift between God and his creation.

A second misunderstanding deals with the motivation for loving the neighbor. The logic runs this way: We are children of God who love what God loves. God loves everybody; God's love is universal. Therefore, we love everybody because God does. This syllogistic procedure has its problems. First, the neighbor in his or her uniqueness is lost. Our universalist motivation obscures the particularity of the person loved. We love them for an outside reason, a reason external to their individuality. The one who is loved says inside herself or himself: "This person loves me because God loves me, not because of anything I am in myself." But what we all want is a love that embraces us in all our irreducible otherness. W. H. Auden spelled it out.

> For the error bred in the bone
> Of each woman and man
> Craves what it cannot have
> Not universal love
> But to be loved alone.[20]

Loving from a divine universalist motivation overlooks the warts, and everybody knows there can be no love that misses the warts.

Second, external divine motivation often plays into the faulty understanding of how God loves. In Mary Gordon's *Final Payments,* Isabel More reflects:

> I would love Margaret now as God loved his crea-
> tures: impartially, impervious to their individual
> natures and thus incapable of being really hurt by
> them . . . I could not love with God's intensity.
> But I would choose His mode: the impartial, the
> invulnerable, removed from loss.[21]

This understanding distances the lover from the one loved. There is very little compassionate sharing of the life of the one loved. What there is is risk-free help. There is aid from the outside but no involvement from the inside. To say this is how divine love works is an effective denial of the Incarnation. To parody this style of loving in the human world is to become the saddest of all sights, the joyless giver.

This motivation scheme has an even more externalist rendition. It is not that God loves the neighbor and so then do we, but that God has commanded it and we must obey. The interconnection of love of God and neighbor begins and ends on the level of obligation. No deeper understanding is sought.

The argument is airtight. Love of neighbor does not entail affectionate feelings. If that were the case, the category of neighbor would be constricted to friends. Loving is not liking. Why then do we love our neighbor? God has commanded love of neighbor and attached rewards and punishments to the command. Loving the neighbor is not a matter of the heart but a matter of the  will, and the will is under the sovereign dictates of God, what Kierkegaard called "the shalt of eternity."

If the command is obeyed, the reward is heaven; if it is disobeyed, the punishment is hell. Therefore, if you love God and hear God's commands, love your neighbor. This understanding turns the neighbor into a stepping-stone. Heaven is the goal; helping people I do not like is the means.

Love of God is neither in competition with love of neighbor nor is it the external motivation for loving others. How should the bonding between them be understood? Gunther Bornkamm starts us in the right direction:

> Surrender to God now no longer means a retreat of the soul into a paradise of spirituality and the dissolution of selfhood in adoration and mediation, but a waiting and preparedness for the call of God, who calls to us in the person of our neighbour. In this sense the love of our neighbour is the test of our love of God. [22]

Loving God makes us attentive to dimensions of reality which we might otherwise overlook. We see and hear differently.[23] The rejected heart saw all things devalued. The envious heart saw all things in competition. The forgiven heart sees all things immersed in the love of God.

Loving God enables the neighbor to be seen. At the most radical level, the problem is that the neighbor is invisible. We have explored the parable of the Good Samaritan twice, in Chapter Two and Chapter Four. A third foray into this remarkable story will prove helpful. In the tale, three people notice the man in the ditch. The priest and the Levite look at him and pass by. The Samaritan sees him and is moved with compassion. But do they all see the same reality?

This story is set within the framework of the double commandment. In particular, it explores the second commandment, "Love your neighbor as yourself," because it is an answer to the question "Who is my neighbor?" In this context, what the priest and Levite see is "not me." What the Samaritan sees is "me." He is moved with compassion because he is in the ditch.

There are many interpretations of loving your neighbor as yourself. One is the golden rule: Do unto others as you would want them to do unto you. This takes our natural self-love and extends it into a universal principle. Kierkegaard has insightfully spelled out this dynamic:

> If we are to love our neighbour AS OURSELVES, then this commandment opens, as with a master-key, the lock of our self-love and snatches it away from us. Should the commandment to love our neighbour be formulated in another way than by the expression AS THYSELF, which can be handled so easily and yet has the tension of all eternity, the commandment could not master our self-love so effectively. The meaning of AS THYSELF cannot be twisted and turned; judging man with the insight of eternity, it penetrates the innermost part of his soul, where his egoism resides. It does not allow our egoism to make the least excuse, nor to evade it in any way. What a wonderful thing! One might have made longer penetration speeches about the way man should love his neighbour, but again and again our egoism would have managed to produce excuses and evasions, because the matter would not have been completely exhausted, a certain aspect would have passed over, a point would not have been described precisely enough or would not have been sufficiently binding in its expression. This AS THYSELF however—truly, no wrestler could clasp his opponent more firmly

or inextricably than this commandment clasps
our egoism.[24]

As clever and persuasive as this rendition is, there is a
not-so-subtle glorification of egoism. The one loving is not
freed from self-preoccupation but trapped within it, and then
forced by an internal logic to move outside himself or herself.
More importantly, there is no overt connection with loving
God. There is no indication that the self this person is seeing
in the neighbor is the self that is loved by God and loves God
in return.

How do people who have experienced God's love for them
and love God in return love themselves? They love themselves
as loved by God. If they had cultivated a rejected heart, they
secretly hated themselves. They were nobodies, uncared for
by the origin and destiny of their lives. They acted out their
insignificance by becoming socially insignificant.

If they cultivated an envious heart, they secretly questioned their loveability. They bolstered it every chance they
had because they were so unsure of it. They acted out this
inner panic by acquiring for themselves the "things" that
would make them valuable and depriving others of those
same "things."

The only way that these two hearts could love themselves
was if someone loved them, independent of their self-depre-
cation in the first case and their self-aggrandizement in the
second case. They both had to come to the awareness that
they were the unique recipient of a free, unconditional love.

This is the self the Samaritan sees in the ditch. He loves
him as he loves himself, as the unique recipient of divine love.
He is not a rich man or a poor man or a Jew or a Gentile or a
man or a woman or a master or a slave. All these are categories which may be needed for the well-ordering of society,

but they have been superseded by divine love. Co-loving the neighbor with the love of God means uncovering their uniqueness and responding to them as an actual other. The forgiven heart is a perceptive heart.

> The more deeply we penetrate into a man through an understanding cognition guided by personal love, the more unsubstitutable, irreplaceable, nonexchangeable, individual, and unique does he become for us. So much the more do the various "wrappings" that are there fall from his individual personal center. These "wrappings" refer to the more or less social "self" of the man, the general bondage to similar drives, needs of life, and passion, as well as to the idols of language that hide from us the individual nuances of experience insofar as they allow us to apply the same words and signs to them.[25]

The love of God in our heart has opened our eyes to the unique worth of each person.

It is each person too. A consistent comment on the parable of the Good Samaritan is that the categories of neighbor and enemy are abolished. The neighbor is simply the next person met, especially if he or she is in need. Kierkegaard summed it up succinctly:

> If there are only two men, the other man is the neighbor; if there are millions, each one of these is the neighbor.[26]

The terrible effect of seeing all people in God is that our enemies are taken from us. Enemies supply energy. When we wake each morning in mode of anger and attack, we know we are alive. We may lose the battles we are mentally envisioning, but the task is clear: dragons abound, dragonslayer.

But when the enemy becomes the sinner, a strange perceptual shift occurs. The enemy's aggression flows from his or her shaken center and reflects his or her frantic flight from God. When we see this in the enemy, we know all about it. We have been there. It is different each time we see it, but it is similar enough for the message to get through. The enemy is "ourself,' and we must love this enemy in his or her sin as we were loved in our sin. This is not mental gymnastics or psychological reductionism. It is simply what the heart that loves God sees.

What we see is what we love. The love of God sees each person embracing and resisting divine and human love. The person who co-loves her neighbor with the love of God inserts herself into this dynamic. This love does not confer value on the person from outside. It spies the real value which is struggling to emerge. Love is not blind, but a process of penetrating sight. It knows the heart and helps it toward salvation.

> Persons who hate themselves often come to discover and love their ideal essence through responsive co-loving with the one who loves them. Zacchaeus came to love what Jesus loved in him. When we love, we make it possible for the beloved to be transformed and ultimately to achieve that salvation which is the destiny toward which God's creative love is beckoning. The Christian God is not merely a Grecian all-knowing God who contemplates eternal essences in himself; he is an all-loving God who redeems his creation. When we co-love with God's love, we effectively co-create with God the beloved's salvation.[27]

Co-creating with God the beloved's salvation is what it means to be a neighbor to the next person met.

### The Liberation of Power

Religious imperatives are maddeningly vague. They become concrete only on the road from Jerusalem to Jericho. Each new situation provides the raw material for creative acts of loving.

But love does not just happen. It takes ingenuity and, properly understood, skullduggery. Creative loving means knowing the price of salvation and finding a way to pay it. Jesus suggested that it is foolish to announce plans for a twelve-story building when you have materials for only five stories, and if you are planning to wage a war against a king with ten thousand men while you only have five thousand men, you had better sue for peace. Loving the neighbor is costly. The exact cost will shift from situation to situation, but it will most likely entail an expenditure of power.

An overlooked phrase of the double commandment is that we are to love God with all our might. One interpretation of this phrase is that it means whatever constitutes our power. It could include money, property, position, charisma, time, knowledge—whatever gives us leverage in life.

In other words, we are to put all we are in the service of divine love. Power is a relative reality.[28] It has many different understandings and an infinitely diverse amount of embodiments—from presidents to legislators to paper carriers. But everyone has power. We all generate influence in the diverse situations of our lives. Even a first-grader has a kindergarten kid to push around. Loving God with all our might and our neighbor as ourselves means a specific use of power—power as service to the next person met.

A limited, but interesting, way to explore power as service is to trace the disagreements Jesus had with his disciples, especially with Peter. In almost all the conflicts Jesus had with his disciples (and he had many), the issue of power and authority was present.

> Once inside the house, Jesus began to ask them, "What were you discussing on the way home?" At this they fell silent, for on the way they had been arguing about who was the most important.
>
> Mark 9:33–34

Peter is the special foil for Jesus' views on a loving use of power. In Matthew 16:13–20, Peter recognizes that the source of Jesus' power is his appropriation of true Sonship. Jesus is the Son of the Living God. He is rewarded for this insight, which is credited not to himself but to God's gift, with the keys to the Kingdom. Peter and, by implication, the others now have the power which accrues to the accepting of divine love. The type of power that divine love generates will prove to be more a demand than a privilege. Further episodes reveal the radical nature of this power.

In the very next incident in the Gospel of Matthew (16:21–23) the conflict between Jesus and Peter about the use of power begins. Jesus predicts that he will go up to Jerusalem where he will be put to death and rise on the third day. Peter will have none of it: "Heaven preserve you, Lord. This must not happen to you. " For this sincere display of concern, Peter is called Satan and told to get back into the following of Jesus, to allow Jesus to show the way.

Peter knows that Jesus is the Son of Power, and he knows how power works. Power is for the purpose of exempting yourself from the fate which the powerless have to undergo. The sons of kings never die in the wars their fathers start. The daughters of legislators are never ground up in the tax laws their mothers enact. Those in power use it to secure themselves against the factors which would diminish them.

In this context, it is certainly folly for the Son of Ultimate Power to submit to the conditions of powerlessness. But Jesus is redefining the understanding and use of power. Power embraces the conditions of life in a new way; it does not exempt itself. The power that flows from divine love is not armor but increased vulnerability, an openness to life which will overcome its destructiveness by undergoing it.

A second episode which contains a conflict about power is Matthew 18:21–22. Peter, knowing that Jesus is forgiveness-prone, offers a generous estimate of how many times our brothers and sisters should be forgiven. "As often as seven times?" In this interchange, his rebuke is milder but just as undercutting. "Not seven, I tell you, but seventy times seven."

There is more here than just the contrast between a definite number and an infinite capacity. Peter has the keys and what good are keys unless you can lock some people in and others out. Power only knows itself as power when it excludes. Until it excommunicates, it is never sure that it is communicating. Peter is subtly asking when he can exercise his power and exclude. Jesus' rejoinder is questioning his assumption. Power is not for the purposes of exclusion; it is for the mission of inclusion. The power that flows from loving God with all your might brings people together; it does not tear them apart.

A third episode, and the most famous conflict between Jesus and Peter, is recorded in the thirteenth chapter of the Gospel of John. Jesus is washing the feet of the disciples. Peter refuses this service. Jesus says that if Peter does not allow himself to be washed he will have nothing in common with him. The impetuous Peter then requests an entire bath.

The disconcerting factor in the story is initially that the master has become the servant. The lesson is not lost on

Peter. If Jesus who is the master acts like this, what does it say about Peter's use of his authority and power. Peter's reluctance would seem to stem from the fact that this feet-washing is a prophecy for his own life.

But the issue of power in the story goes beyond the mere fact of reversal. It is what Jesus has chosen to serve that is the core of Peter's balking. The master serves concrete human needs. Dirty feet are the objects of his ministrations. But the rhetoric of service which abounds in the  Christian Church is often more noble than this. Service is given to the Kingdom, the idealized social order, the vision of the future. And when this is what is served, a crushed body is tolerated, a mangled spirit is surely an acceptable price. Divine love not only demands that power serve but demands that it serve concrete human need.

Two short episodes in Luke (9:49–50 and 9:51–56) further specify the use of power. John tells Jesus that the disciples met a man who was casting out devils in his name and they told him to stop. The reason that they urged the man to stop was that "he was not one of us."

John expects to be commended by Jesus. Instead he is rebuked: "You must not stop him. Anyone who is not against you is for you." Power often wants to stop goodness if it cannot get anything out of it. It wants to control the good. If it cannot be attributed to our group, then it must be stopped. The bolstering of the group takes precedence over salvific action. The fact that now there lives a person free of demons is insignificant. The matter of importance is that we have not worked this wonder. This tendency to usurp the good and to deny it where it cannot be usurped is a distortion of the overflowing power of divine love.

The disciples went on ahead to make preparations in a Samaritan village. The Samaritans would not receive them.

James and John suggested to Jesus that he call down fire from heaven and burn them up. Jesus suggested that they find another village. The tendency of power is to use it for revenge. If we have been rejected, reject back—only harder. Lack of hospitality is met by cremation. The way of power is retribution. The disciples know this, but Jesus knows something different. Power is invitation to new life, and when it is rejected, it seeks other opportunities. The preoccupation of power is not violence, but creative invitation.

The consequence of experiencing God as love and ourselves as daughters and sons of Love is the freedom to use our power to serve the neighbor. Since we have ultimately grounded ourselves in God and not in our own efforts, our powers are redirected. They are creatively released for Kingdom activity.

This means that we do not use power to exempt ourselves from the conditions of life but to embrace those conditions in an effort to transform them; that we do not use power to exclude but to include; that we do not dedicate our talents to the service of abstract ideals but to real human needs; that we use our authority to allow the good to flourish and not to co-opt it; that we use whatever position we have to create opportunities and not to avenge ourselves on others. Once human power has been regrounded in divine love, it has a radically different agenda. Loving God with all our might means placing our power at the service of our neighbor.

## A Story of Loving the Neighbor

When we think of loving the neighbor as ourselves, we immediately feel that the challenge is to love the stranger. It is taken for granted that we will love family and friends. But the truth is that the next person we meet is easier to love than the ones we meet every day. In his fascinating book *The Silence of Jesus,*

James Breech suggests that it is those who eat with us who become the test of love:

> Many people would be willing to sacrifice their lives, if necessary, out of "love" for another. But such acts of immediate heroism which occur as it were on a stage with everyone watching, and which terminate the ordeal of living in the presence of the concrete other, are not to be confused with love of neighbour, which means hard work and tenacity, and which involves learning to affirm the actual other who sits across from one at the table, whether his or her table manners are graceful or ungraceful, his or her conversation engaging or boring, his or her habits mannerly or ill-mannered. The prayer that Jesus taught his table companions to say before sitting down to eat and drink together shows that Jesus understood the fundamental dynamics of such occasions, that it was during that time, as perhaps at no other, that they were most in need of that power which would sustain them in their readiness to be present in fellowship.[29]

If this is true, it is fitting to close our exploration of the experience named Spirit, the interwoven reality of divine and human love, with a story about the love of neighbor. Not the neighbor in the ditch but the neighbor at the table.

"Why bother?" is what Margaret Mary Mulligan told her husband, Michael Joseph Mulligan, in June of 1948 when, upon his retirement from Sears after thirty years, he proposed they take their granddaughter, who had just graduated from grammar school, and go back to Ireland to see his oldest brother. Margaret, as was her custom, repeated her opinion:

"Why bother?"

But when he told his granddaughter, she was delighted and asked, "Gramp, are you and Gram going to go back to live in Ireland."

"Why should I?" he answered without taking the pipe out of his mouth. "I starved there."

And indeed he had. He was the second son of four sons and three daughters. His older brother was obviously in line for the farm. That was the way it was. There was not much for him and the others to do but move along. And the sooner the better. For what food there was would go farther with one less. So, as he likes to tell it, he threw his shoes over his shoulder to save the wear and tear, walked barefoot over the mountain, and got on the boat for America. That was May 1908.

First, there was a series of jobs in New York—stock boy, wagon driver, street repairman, a humiliating stint as a servant—"Hey, Paddy, get the dog." Then he took a chance. He moved to Chicago, and with some luck and a good word from a cousin's cousin, he landed a steady job at Sears. He met Margaret and settled down. Three children came along but so did the Great Depression. The little prosperity they had was wiped out.

But with careful planning—scrimping here and saving there—he got back on his feet. Just as he was standing up, he looked around to find out he was old. When it was his wife Margaret's turn to speak at the retirement party, she said, "Ah, Mike, where did it all go? Where did it all go?"

Through the years, Michael Thomas Mulligan kept in touch with his older brother. Every year at Christmas he wrote a letter telling the news he could remember. He was not much of a letter writer, and so his yearly epistles often began " Not much new here." But he always sent a check. After the first of the year, a return letter would arrive. More often than not it began "Not much new here either." The check was never mentioned.

But in June 1948, the day after Margaret had said, "Why bother?" he wrote a letter out of season. "Margaret, I, and our granddaughter are coming to Ireland for a visit. Would you be home on July 11 in the evening?" A return letter arrived on the last day of June, one day before the train to New York and three days before the sailing to Ireland. It read: "I would. We will be expecting you for dinner."

On July 11, Michael Thomas Mulligan, the second son of four sons and three daughters, rented the newest model Packard he could find, put on this three-piece, broad-lapelled, broad-striped suit, placed his large gold watch in the pocket of his vest and ran the gold chain prominently to the vest pocket, looked approvingly at his wife Margaret in her best hat and dress, and told his granddaughter, "No pedal pushers. I want you to wear a dress." He was on his way to see his older brother.

The stone and thatch cottage was much like he remembered it. Only it seemed farther from the main road and by the time they got there the car was covered with mud. It might as well have been a '32 Ford. Gerald John Mulligan and his wife stood at the door. "Jerry," said the younger brother with his hand extended. "Mike," said the older brother taking it. Their eyes never met. Inside the table was already set.

The dinner was plain and good. The talk was general— about the brothers and sisters, America, children, Ireland, the war. The granddaughter escaped to the room where she was to sleep as soon as she could. She propped herself up with a pillow and began reading a Nancy Drew mystery. Not much later the wives, sensing they should, said good night. The two brothers sat alone. After some time the older brother broke the silence.

JOHN SHEA

"Are you now a rich yank?"

"I am not," said the younger brother. "Are you now a pros-
perous land owner?"

"I am not," said the older brother.

The older brother stood up, moved to the cabinet, got a
large loaf of fresh bread and a knife, and sat down. The
younger brother stood up and went to the back bedroom.
Margaret lay on one bed and his granddaughter, peering into
a book, lay on the other. "Is it all right with him?" Margaret
asked. "Get some rest," her husband said. He opened the suit-
case and rummaged his arm under the neatly folded clothes.
His hand brought out a quart bottle of Kentucky Bourbon. "Is
it all right with him?" she said again. "Get some rest," he said.
But he smiled, and for the first time since they arrived in
Ireland, she thought she might.

In the kitchen sat the two brothers and between them the
bread the older brother had wrested from the stubborn land
and the bottle the younger brother had brought back from the
far country.

The first up in the morning was the granddaughter. She
tiptoed out of the room without waking her grandmother. The
kitchen table was filled with crumbs. In the middle of the
crumbs was a knife and an empty bottle. The door to the cottage was open. She took it as an invitation and went outside.

The new day had just begun. The sun was climbing into
the clear sky. It shimmered off the ocean in the distance and
lit the land all the way up to the cottage. In the middle of the
field stood the two brothers, pipes in their mouths, inspecting
the earth the way a mother checks a newborn baby. "They
must have been up all night," the granddaughter thought
to herself.

Then the brothers turned, saw her, and waved. And side
by side, stride by stride, step by step, they came toward her,

and although she herself had never yet stayed up all night to beat back the darkness with her love, she knew that when her time came she would be able to do it. And when they came within earshot, she shouted out to them, "O Wow! You made it all the way to morning!"

ENDNOTES

## Chapter One

1. Robert Penn Warren, *Being There* (New York: Random House, 1980), dedication page.

2. Romano Guardini, "The Church: Encounter with Christ," in *The Church* (New York: P. J. Kenedy & Sons, 1963), p. 28.

3. Quoted in Yves Congar, *The Meaning of Tradition* (New York: Hawthorn Books, 1964), p. 16.

4. Robert Browning, "A Death in the Desert" in *The Poems and Plays of Robert Browning* (New York: The Modern Library, 1934), p. 297.

5. Walter Kasper, *Jesus the Christ* (New York: Paulist Press, 1976), p. 28.

6. John Coventry, *Christian Truth* (New York: Paulist Press, 1975), p. 65.

7. Cf. David Tracy, *The Analogical Imagination* (New York: Crossroad, 1981), pp. 236–241.

8. Willi Marxsen, *The Beginnings of Christology: A Study in its Problems* (Philadelphia: Fortress Press, 1969), p. 20–21.

9. Cf. Edward Schillebeeckx, *Interim Report on the Books Jesus & Christ* (New York: Crossroad, 1981), p. 12.

10. Willi Marxsen, *The New Testament as the Church's Book* (Philadelphia: Fortress Press, 1972), p 92.

11. Edward Schillebeeckx, *God and Man* (New York: Sheed and Ward, 1969), p. 164.

12. John Bowker, *The Religious Imagination and the Sense of God* (Oxford: Clarendon Press, 1978), p. 126.

13. Boniface Willems, *The Reality of Redemption* (New York: Herder and Herder, 1970), p. 61.

14. David Stanley, "Contemplation of the Gospels, Ignatius Loyola, and the Contemporary Christian," in *Theological Studies,* Vol. 29, No. 3, p. 425.

15. Cf. Ernst Kasemann, *The Testament of Jesus: A Study of the Gospel of John in the Light of Chapter Seventeen* (London: SCM Press, 1968).

16. Ray Brown, *The Gospel According to John* (New York: Doubleday & Company, Inc., 1966), p. 1139.

17. James D. G. Dunn, *Jesus and the Spirit* (Philadelphia: Westminster Press, 1975), p. 351.

18. G. W. H. Lampe, God as Spirit (Oxford: 1977), p. 144.

19. Edmund J. Dobbin, "Towards a Theology of the Holy Spirit, I." in *The Heythrop Journal,* Vol. XVII (Jan. 1976), p. 7.

20. Dunn, *op. cit.,* p. 351.

21. Often experience and consciousness are distinguished. We may be experiencing something but not be aware of it. The most obvious example is blood. We are constantly experiencing the nourishing effects of our blood, but we seldom explicitly focus on it and bring it to the level of awareness. We will not be consistently employing this distinction. When we use the word *experience,* it will refer to conscious experience.

22. D. E. H. Whiteley, *The Theology of St. Paul* (Oxford: Basil Blackwell, 1964), p. 197.

23. There is much discussion about the connection of metaphor and reality. Sometimes they are contrasted as this statement from the "Faith and Order Report" at Lund: "The Pauline image of the Church as the body of Christ is no mere metaphor, but expresses a living reality." This report is cited by G. C. Berkouwer who comments that this contrast between metaphor and reality is an "unenlightening dilemma . . . because there cannot be a contradiction between figurative language and reality: figurative language undoubtedly intends to refer to reality. A metaphor is not a vague, unreal expression, but intends,

in the service of revelation, to open one's eyes to a deep, fascinating reality. And so, the question is not 'real or not real?' but is directed to the nature of the reality that is pointed out." *Studies in Dogmatics: The Church* (Grand Rapids, Michigan: William B. Eerdmans, 1976), p. 81.

24. Edward Schillebeeckx, *Christ: The Experience of Jesus as Lord* (New York: Crossroad, 1980), p. 19.

25. Our investigation does not take into account the reports of saints and mystics that they were visited by the Risen Lord. These reports are fascinating and open to many diverse interpretations. But they seem to be the privilege of the few. We are exploring the more accessible mode of the presence of Christ—through the people animated by his Spirit. We are also not considering, in any detail, the relationship between the Risen Lord and the Spirit. For our purpose it is enough to say that the Risen Lord sends the Spirit and that the presence of the Spirit mediated the presence of the Risen Lord. For a fuller treatment consult Peter C. Hodgson, *New Birth of Freedom* (Philadelphia: Fortress Press, 1976), pp. 324–332.

26. Quoted in Gerald O'Collins, *Fundamental Theology* (New York: Paulist Press, 1981), p. 209.

27. Cf. James D. G. Dunn, *Unity and Diversity in the New Testament* (Philadelphia: Westminster Press, 1977), pp. 192–193.

28. Ibid., p. 194.

29. Congar, *op. cit.,* p. 148.

30. Northrop Frye, *The Great Code* (New York: Harcourt Brace Jovanovich, Publishers, 1981), p. 128.

31. Quoted in Robert Funk, *Language, Hermeneutic, and Word of God* (New York: Harper & Row, 1966), introductory quote.

32. John Hick, "Mystical Experience as Cognition," in *Mystics and Scholars,* Coward and Penelhum, eds. (Ontario, Canada: Wilfrid Laurier Press).

33. Spirit and Memory are more than critical correctives. They are also mutual partners in bringing about the experience named Spirit. We will investigate this partnership in Chapter Three.

34. Jurgen Moltmann, *The Trinity and the Kingdom* (San Francisco: Harper & Row, 1981), p. 94.

**Chapter Two**

1. David Tracy, *The Analogical Imagination* (New York: Crossroad, 1981), p. 249.

2. Quoted in Yves M. J. Congar, O.P., *Tradition and Traditions* (New York: Macmillan Company, 1966), p. 364.

3. Cf. Nathan Mitchell, O.S.B., *Cult and Controversy: The Worship of the Eucharist Outside Mass* (New York: Pueblo Publishing Company, 1982).

4. Teilhard de Chardin, *Hymn to the Universe* (New York: Harper & Row, 1961), p. 48.

5. Cf. Larry D. Shinn, *Two Sacred Worlds* (Nashville: Abingdon, 1977), chapter three.

6. John Macquarrie, *Principles of Christian Theology* (New York: Charles Scribner's Sons, 1966), pp. 92–93.

7. Paul Tillich, *Systematic Theology,* Vol. 1 (Chicago: University of Chicago Press, 1951), pp. 126–28.

8. Cf. Charles Davis, *Body as Spirit* (New York: Seabury Press, 1976), chapter one.

9. For a clear theory of how this happens, which is indebted to the philosophy of Sussanne K. Lange,r cf. Ronald J. Allen, "Feeling and Form in Biblical Interpretation," *Encounter,* Vol. 43, No. 1, Winter 1982.

10. Edward Schillebeeckx, *Jesus* (New York: Seabury Press, 1979), p. 549.

11. For an example of this type of acculturation of belief confer Charles Meyer, *Religious Belief in a Scientific Age* (Chicago: Thomas More Press, 1983).

12. Cf. John Shea, *Stories of God* (Allen TX: Thomas More Publishing, 1996), chapter one.

13. Cf. Friedrich Nietzche, *Beyond Good and Evil: A Philosophy for the Future,* translated by Walter Kaufman (New York: Random House, 1966).

14. For a good explanation of pervasive attitudes confer Donald Evans, *Struggle and Fulfillment* (Cleveland: Collins, 1976).

15. Cf. Ray Hart, *Unfinished Man and the Imagination* (New York: Herder and Herder, 1966), pp. 143–151.

16. Quoted in Congar, *op. cit.,* p. 364.

17. Quoted in James D. G. Dunn, *Jesus and the Spirit* (Philadelphia: Westminster Press, 1975), p. 456.

## Chapter Three

1 John V. Taylor, *The Go-Between God* (Philadelphia: Fortress Press, 1972), p. 7.

2. Johann Baptist Metz, *Faith in History and Society* (New York: The Seabury Press, 1980), p. 210.

3. In Chapter One, we suggested that Spirit and Memory must be held in tension as the Christian people journey through space and time. They act as critical correctives to the dangerous tendencies in each other. This chapter explores their partnership, the way they work together to facilitate the experience named Spirit.

4. Paul Pruyser, *A Dynamic Psychology of Religion* (New York: Harper & Row, 1968), p. 12.

5. A helpful contrast of these two sets of triggers can be found in James Joyce's *A Portrait of the Artist as a Young Man* (New York: B. W. Huebsch, 1916). The long and terrifying retreat cannot move Stephen's soul. The traditional facilitators of religious experience are bankrupt. But at the stream at Clontarf he sees the young girl and exclaims,"'Heavenly God!' . . . He turned away from her suddenly and set off the strand. His cheeks were aflame; his body was aglow; his limbs were trembling. On and on and on he strode, far out over the sands, singing wildly to the sea, crying to greet the advent of life that had cried to him" (pp. 199–200).

6. R. Stark, "A Taxonomy of Religious Experience," *Journal for the Scientific Study of Religion,* 1965, 5, pp. 98–116.

7. Cf. John Shea, *Stories of Faith* (Allen TX: Thomas More Publishing, 1996), chapter one and chapter two.

8. Quoted in Edward Robinson, *The Original Vision* (Manchester College, Oxford: The Religious Experience Research Unit, 1977), p. 148.

9. D. Hammarskjold, *Markings* (London: 1966), p. 163.

10. Walter Gulick, "Archetypal Experienccs," *Soundings,* Fall 1981, p. 262.

11. Yves Congar, The Meaning of Tradition (New York: Hawthorn Books, 1964), p. 75.

12. Cf. Ian Barbour, *Myths, Models, and Paradigms* (New York: Harper & Row, 1974), chapter four.

13. Ernest Hemingwayr, *The Old Man and the Sea* (New York: Scribner's Sons, 1952), p. 107.

14. Cf. George W. Stroup, *The Promise of Narrative Theology* (Atlanta: John Knox Press, 1981), Part II, Christian Identity.

15. In Ian T. Ramsey, ed., Christian Ethics and Contemporary Philosophy (S.C.M. Press, 1966), p. 86.

16. Cf. C. Daniel Batson, J. Christiaan Beker, and W. Malcolm Clark, Commitment Without Ideology (Philadelphia: United Church Press, 1973), chapter three.

17. This story was related at a faith and storytelling seminar.

18. Quoted in Robinson, op. cit., pp. 69–70.

19. Quoted in Metz, op. cit., p. 207.

20. Cf. John Shea, "Religious–Imaginative Encounters with Scriptural Stories," in Art/Literature/Religion: Life on the Borders (Chico, California: Scholars Press, 1983), pp. 173–180.

21. Edward Schillebeeckx, Jesus (New York: Seabury Press, 1979), p. 266.

22. Norman Perrin, Jesus and the Language of the Kingdom (Philadelphia: Fortress Press, 1976). Part II, The Interpretation of Kingdom of God in the Message of Jesus.

23. James D. G. Dunn, Jesus and the Spirit: A Study of the Religious and Charismatic Experience of Jesus and the First Christians as Reflected in the New Testament (Philadelphia: Westminster Press, 1975), p. 40.

24. Cf. G. B. Caird, The Language and Imagery of the Bible (Philadelphia: Westminster Press, 1980), chapter ten.

25. Ibid., p. 145.

## Chapter Four

1. Sebastian Moore, The Fire and the Rose Are One (New York: Seabury Press, 1980), p. 14.

2. Nikos Kazantzakis, The Greek Passion (New York: Simon and Schuster, 1953), p. 429.

3. James D. G . Dunn, *Jesus and the Spirit* (Philadelphia: Westminster Press, 1975), p. 65.

4. James Mackey, *Jesus: The Man and the Myth* (New York: Paulist Press, 1979), pp. 143–144.

5. Dunn, *op. cit.,* pp. 47–48.

6. Cf. Norman Perrin, *Rediscovering the Teachings of Jesus* (New York: Harper & Row, 1967), chapter five.

7. Colin Brown, ed., *The New International Dictionary of New Testament Theology,* Vol. 2 (Exeter: The Pater Noster Press, 1971), p. 182.

8. Cf. Birger Gerhardsson, *The Testing of God's Son* (Lund: Coniectanea Biblica, 1966).

9. Cf. James Breech, *The Silence of Jesus* (Philadelphia: Fortress Press, 1983), pp. 46–49.

10. Cf. Robert Tannehill, *The Sword of His Mouth* (Philadelphia: Fortress Press, 1975), pp. 11–36

11. Sebastian Moore, *The Crucified Jesus Is No Stranger* (New York: Seabury Press, 1977); *The Fire and the Rose Are One* (New York: Seabury Press, 1980); *The Inner Loneliness* (New York: Crossroad, 1982). All three of these books are profound meditations on human sinfulness and divine redemption.

12. Moore, *The Fire and the Rose,* p. 11.

13. Ibid., p. 13.

14. Ibid., p. 37.

15. Cf. John Shea, *Stories of Faith* (Allen, TX: Thomas More Publishing, 1996), chapter two.

16. Flannery O'Connor, *Everything That Rises Must Converge* (New York: Farrar, Straus and Giroux, 1965), p. 190.

17. Jarnes Mackey, *op. cit.,* p. 170.

18. Cf. Ben Meyer, *The Aims of Jesus* (SCM Press,LTD) and John Riches, *Jesus and the Transformation of Judaism* (London: Darton, Longman & Todd, 1980).

19. This is not an attempt at a sociological analysis or a suggestion that the complexity of sin can be reduced to these two options. It merely points to two "wrong centerings" as types of responses the panicked inner self is prone to.

20. Meyer, *op. cit.,* p. 161.

21. Mackey, *op. cit.,* pp. 143–144.

22. Paul Ricoeur, "Biblical Hermeneutics," *Semeia* 1975.

23. Dorothy Sollee has some interesting reflections on testing in *Suffering* (Philadelphia: Fortress Press, 1973), chapter four.

24. Gerhardsson, *op. cit.,* p. 31.

## Chapter Five

1. J. D. Salinger, *Franny and Zooey* (Boston: Little, Brown, and Company, 1961), p. 153. Quoted in James Breech *The Silence of Jesus* (Philadelphia: Fortress Press, 1983).

2. Idries Shah, *The Way of the Sufi* (New York: E. P. Dutton, 1968), p. 63.

3. William James, "The Divided Self and Conversion," in *Conversion,* ed., Walter E. Conn (New York: Alba House, 1978), p. 128.

4. Ibid.

5. Donald Evans, *Struggle and Fulfillment* (New York: Collins, 1979), p. 53.

6. Cf. Kenneth E. Bailey, *Through Peasant Eyes* (Grand Rapids, Michigan: William B. Eerdmans, 1980).

7. John Cobb, *The Structure of Christian Existence* (Philadelphia: Westminster Press, 1968), p. 135.

8. Cf. Victor Paul Furnish, *The Love Command in the New Testament* (New York: Abingdon Press, 1972), chapter four.

9. Don E. Saliers, *The Soul in Paraphrase* (New York: Crossroad, 1980), p. 71.

10. Cf. Jon Sobrino, *Christology at the Crossroads* (Maryknoll, New York– Orbis Books, 1978).

11. Norman Perrin, *Rediscovering the Teachings of Jesus* (New York: Harper & Row, 1967), p. 94.

12. Nikos Kazantzakis, *Report to Greco* (New York: Simon and Schuster, 1976).

13. Anne Sexton, *The Awful Rowing Toward God* (Boston: Houghton Mifflin Company, 1975), pp. 85–86.

14. Cf. Birger Gerhardsson, *The Testing of God's Son* (CWK Gleerup Lund Sweden, 1966); John A. T. Robinson, *Twelve New Testament Studies* (Naperville, Ill.: Alec R. Allenson, Inc., 1962), pp. 53–60.

15. Edward Schillebeeckx, *Christ: The Sacrament of the Encounter with God* (New York: Sheed & Ward, 1963), p. 18.

16. Donald Evans, Struggle and Fulfillment (New York: Collins, 1979).

17. Ibid., p. 23.

18. James Mackey, *Jesus: The Man and the Myth* (NewYork: Paulist Press, 1979), pp. 192–193.

19. Henri Nouwen, *Gracias!* (San Francisco: Harper & Row, 1983), p. 120.

20. Quoted in Mary Gordon, *Final Payments* (New York: Ballantine Books, 1978), p. 232.

21. Ibid., p. 260.

22. Gunther Bornkamm, *Jesus of Nazareth* (New York: Harper & Row, 1960), p. 111.

23. Cf. C. Daniel Batson and W. Larry Ventis, *The Religious Experience* (New York: Oxford University Press, 1982), chapter three.

24. Quoted in Bornkamm, *op. cit.*, p. 113.

25. Max Scheler, *The Nature of Sympathy* (Hamden, Conn.: Shoe String Press, 1973), p. 121.

26. Quoted in Furnish, *op. cit.*, p. 210.

27. Edward V. Vacek, "Scheler's Phenomenology of Love" in *The Journal of Religion,* Vol. 62 (April 1982), p. 167.

28. Confer the diverse and fascinating attempts to reflect on power theologically in "The Proceedings of the Thirty–Seventh Annual Convention of the Catholic Theological Society of America," Luke Salm, ed.

29. Breech, *op. cit.*, p. 61.